Building Machine Learning Powered Applications

Powered Applications

Going from Idea to Product

T0219377

Emmanuel Ameisen

Beijing · Boston · Farnham · Sebastopol · Tokyo

Building Machine Learning Powered Applications

by Emmanuel Ameisen

Published by O'Reilly Media, Inc., 1005 Gravenstein Highway North, Sebastopol, CA 95472.

O'Reilly books may be purchased for educational, business, or sales promotional use. Online editions are also available for most titles (*http://oreilly.com*). For more information, contact our corporate/institutional sales department: 800-998-9938 or *corporate@oreilly.com*.

Acquisitions Editor: Jonathan Hassell	**Indexer:** Judith McConville
Development Editor: Melissa Potter	**Interior Designer:** David Futato
Production Editor: Deborah Baker	**Cover Designer:** Karen Montgomery
Copyeditor: Kim Wimpsett	**Illustrator:** Rebecca Demarest
Proofreader: Christina Edwards	

February 2020:   First Edition

Revision History for the First Edition

2020-01-17:   First Release
2020-02-14:   Second Release

See *http://oreilly.com/catalog/errata.csp?isbn=9781492045113* for release details.

978-1-492-04511-3

[LSI]

Table of Contents

Part II. Build a Working Pipeline

Part III.   Iterate on Models

Part IV. Deploy and Monitor

Preface

The Goal of Using Machine Learning Powered Applications

Over the past decade, machine learning (ML) has increasingly been used to power a variety of products such as automated support systems, translation services, recommendation engines, fraud detection models, and many, many more.

Surprisingly, there aren't many resources available to teach engineers and scientists how to build such products. Many books and classes will teach how to train ML models or how to build software projects, but few blend both worlds to teach how to build practical applications that are powered by ML.

Deploying ML as part of an application requires a blend of creativity, strong engineering practices, and an analytical mindset. ML products are notoriously challenging to build because they require much more than simply training a model on a dataset. Choosing the right ML approach for a given feature, analyzing model errors and data quality issues, and validating model results to guarantee product quality are all challenging problems that are at the core of the ML building process.

This book goes through every step of this process and aims to help you accomplish each of them by sharing a mix of methods, code examples, and advice from me and other experienced practitioners. We'll cover the practical skills required to design, build, and deploy ML–powered applications. The goal of this book is to help you succeed at every part of the ML process.

Use ML to Build Practical Applications

If you regularly read ML papers and corporate engineering blogs, you may feel overwhelmed by the combination of linear algebra equations and engineering terms. The hybrid nature of the field leads many engineers and scientists who could contribute their diverse expertise to feel intimidated by the field of ML. Similarly, entrepreneurs and product leaders often struggle to tie together their ideas for a business with what is possible with ML today (and what may be possible tomorrow).

This book covers the lessons I have learned working on data teams at multiple companies and helping hundreds of data scientists, software engineers, and product managers build applied ML projects through my work leading the artificial intelligence program at Insight Data Science.

The goal of this book is to share a step-by-step practical guide to building ML–powered applications. It is practical and focuses on concrete tips and methods to help you prototype, iterate, and deploy models. Because it spans a wide range of topics, we will go into only as much detail as is needed at each step. Whenever possible, I will provide resources to help you dive deeper into the topics covered if you so desire.

Important concepts are illustrated with practical examples, including a case study that will go from idea to deployed model by the end of the book. Most examples will be accompanied by illustrations, and many will contain code. All of the code used in this book can be found in the book's companion GitHub repository (*https://oreil.ly/ml-powered-applications*).

Because this book focuses on describing the process of ML, each chapter builds upon concepts defined in earlier ones. For this reason, I recommend reading it in order so that you can understand how each successive step fits into the entire process. If you are looking to explore a subset of the process of ML, you might be better served with a more specialized book. If that is the case, I've shared a few recommendations.

Additional Resources

- If you'd like to know ML well enough to write your own algorithms from scratch, I recommend *Data Science from Scratch*, by Joel Grus. If the theory of deep learning is what you are after, the textbook *Deep Learning* (MIT Press), by Ian Goodfellow, Yoshua Bengio, and Aaron Courville, is a comprehensive resource.

- If you are wondering how to train models efficiently and accurately on specific datasets, Kaggle (*https://www.kaggle.com/*) and fast.ai (*https://fast.ai*) are great places to look.

- If you'd like to learn how to build scalable applications that need to process a lot of data, I recommend looking at *Designing Data-Intensive Applications* (O'Reilly), by Martin Kleppmann.

If you have coding experience and some basic ML knowledge and want to build ML–driven products, this book will guide you through the entire process from product idea to shipped prototype. If you already work as a data scientist or ML engineer, this book will add new techniques to your ML development toolkit. If you do not know how to code but collaborate with data scientists, this book can help you understand the process of ML, as long as you are willing to skip some of the in-depth code examples.

Let's start by diving deeper into the meaning of practical ML.

Practical ML

For the purpose of this introduction, think of ML as the process of leveraging patterns in data to automatically tune algorithms. This is a general definition, so you will not be surprised to hear that many applications, tools, and services are starting to integrate ML at the core of the way they function.

Some of these tasks are user-facing, such as search engines, recommendations on social platforms, translation services, or systems that automatically detect familiar faces in photographs, follow instructions from voice commands, or attempt to provide useful suggestions to finish a sentence in an email.

Some work in less visible ways, silently filtering spam emails and fraudulent accounts, serving ads, predicting future usage patterns to efficiently allocate resources, or experimenting with personalizing website experiences for each user.

Many products currently leverage ML, and even more could do so. Practical ML refers to the task of identifying practical problems that could benefit from ML and delivering a successful solution to these problems. Going from a high-level product goal to ML–powered results is a challenging task that this book tries to help you to accomplish.

Some ML courses will teach students about ML methods by providing a dataset and having them train a model on them, but training an algorithm on a dataset is a small part of the ML process. Compelling ML–powered products rely on more than an aggregate accuracy score and are the results of a long process. This book will start from ideation and continue all the way through to production, illustrating every step on an example application. We will share tools, best practices, and common pitfalls learned from working with applied teams that are deploying these kinds of systems every day.

What This Book Covers

To cover the topic of building applications powered by ML, the focus of this book is concrete and practical. In particular, this book aims to illustrate the whole process of building ML–powered applications.

To do so, I will first describe methods to tackle each step in the process. Then, I will illustrate these methods using an example project as a case study. The book also contains many practical examples of ML in industry and features interviews with professionals who have built and maintained production ML models.

The entire process of ML

To successfully serve an ML product to users, you need to do more than simply train a model. You need to thoughtfully *translate* your product need to an ML problem, *gather* adequate data, efficiently *iterate* in between models, *validate* your results, and *deploy* them in a robust manner.

Building a model often represents only a tenth of the total workload of an ML project. Mastering the entire ML pipeline is crucial to successfully build projects, succeed at ML interviews, and be a top contributor on ML teams.

A technical, practical case study

While we won't be re-implementing algorithms from scratch in C, we will stay practical and technical by using libraries and tools providing higher-level abstractions. We will go through this book building an example ML application together, from the initial idea to the deployed product.

I will illustrate key concepts with code snippets when applicable, as well as figures describing our application. The best way to learn ML is by practicing it, so I encourage you to go through the book reproducing the examples and adapting them to build your own ML–powered application.

Real business applications

Throughout this book, I will include conversations and advice from ML leaders who have worked on data teams at tech companies such as StitchFix, Jawbone, and FigureEight. These discussions will cover practical advice garnered after building ML applications with millions of users and will correct some popular misconceptions about what makes data scientists and data science teams successful.

Prerequisites

This book assumes some familiarity with programming. I will mainly be using Python for technical examples and assume that the reader is familiar with the syntax. If you'd like to refresh your Python knowledge, I recommend *The Hitchhiker's Guide to Python* (O'Reilly), by Kenneth Reitz and Tanya Schlusser.

In addition, while I will define most ML concepts referred to in the book, I will not cover the inner workings of all ML algorithms used. Most of these algorithms are standard ML methods that are covered in introductory-level ML resources, such as the ones mentioned in "Additional Resources" on page x.

Our Case Study: ML–Assisted Writing

To concretely illustrate this idea, we will build an ML application together as we go through this book.

As a case study, I chose an application that can accurately illustrate the complexity of iterating and deploying ML models. I also wanted to cover a product that could produce value. This is why we will be implementing a *machine learning–powered writing assistant*.

Our goal is to build a system that will help users write better. In particular, we will aim to help people write better questions. This may seem like a very vague objective, and I will define it more clearly as we scope out the project, but it is a good example for a few key reasons.

Text data is everywhere
> Text data is abundantly available for most use cases you can think of and is core to many practical ML applications. Whether we are trying to better understand the reviews of our product, accurately categorize incoming support requests, or tailor our promotional messages to potential audiences, we will consume and produce text data.

Writing assistants are useful
> From Gmail's text prediction feature to Grammarly's smart spellchecker, ML–powered editors have proven that they can deliver value to users in a variety of ways. This makes it particularly interesting for us to explore how to build them from scratch.

ML–assisted writing is self-standing
> Many ML applications can function only when tightly integrated into a broader ecosystem, such as ETA prediction for ride-hailing companies, search and recommendation systems for online retailers, and ad bidding models. A text editor, however, even though it could benefit from being integrated into a document editing ecosystem, can prove valuable on its own and be exposed through a simple website.

Throughout the book, this project will allow us to highlight the challenges and associated solutions we suggest to build ML–powered applications.

The ML Process

The road from an idea to a deployed ML application is long and winding. After seeing many companies and individuals build such projects, I've identified four key successive stages, which will each be covered in a section of this book.

1. *Identifying the right ML approach:* The field of ML is broad and often proposes a multitude of ways to tackle a given product goal. The best approach for a given problem will depend on many factors such as success criteria, data availability, and task complexity. The goals of this stage are to set the right success criteria and to identify an adequate initial dataset and model choice.

2. *Building an initial prototype:* Start by building an end-to-end prototype before working on a model. This prototype should aim to tackle the product goal with no ML involved and will allow you to determine how to best apply ML. Once a prototype is built, you should have an idea of whether you need ML, and you should be able to start gathering a dataset to train a model.

3. *Iterating on models:* Now that you have a dataset, you can train a model and evaluate its shortcomings. The goal of this stage is to repeatedly alternate between error analysis and implementation. Increasing the speed at which this iteration loop happens is the best way to increase ML development speed.

4. *Deployment and monitoring:* Once a model shows good performance, you should pick an adequate deployment option. Once deployed, models often fail in unexpected ways. The last two chapters of this book will cover methods to mitigate and monitor model errors.

There is a lot of ground to cover, so let's dive right in and start with Chapter 1!

Conventions Used in This Book

The following typographical conventions are used in this book:

Italic
> Indicates new terms, URLs, email addresses, filenames, and file extensions.

`Constant width`
> Used for program listings, as well as within paragraphs to refer to program elements such as variable or function names, databases, data types, environment variables, statements, and keywords.

`Constant width bold`
> Shows commands or other text that should be typed literally by the user.

`Constant width italic`
> Shows text that should be replaced with user-supplied values or by values determined by context.

 This element signifies a tip or suggestion.

This element signifies a general note.

 This element indicates a warning or caution.

Using Code Examples

Supplemental code examples for this book are available for download at *https://oreil.ly/ml-powered-applications*.

If you have a technical question or a problem using the code examples, please send email to *bookquestions@oreilly.com*.

This book is here to help you get your job done. In general, if example code is offered with this book, you may use it in your programs and documentation. You do not need to contact us for permission unless you're reproducing a significant portion of the code. For example, writing a program that uses several chunks of code from this book does not require permission. Selling or distributing examples from O'Reilly books does require permission. Answering a question by citing this book and quoting example code does not require permission. Incorporating a significant amount of example code from this book into your product's documentation does require permission.

We appreciate, but generally do not require, attribution. An attribution usually includes the title, author, publisher, and ISBN. For example: *Building Machine Learning Powered Applications* by Emmanuel Ameisen (O'Reilly). Copyright 2020 Emmanuel Ameisen, 978-1-492-04511-3."

If you feel your use of code examples falls outside fair use or the permission given here, feel free to contact us at *permissions@oreilly.com*.

O'Reilly Online Learning

 For more than 40 years, *O'Reilly Media* has provided technology and business training, knowledge, and insight to help companies succeed.

Our unique network of experts and innovators share their knowledge and expertise through books, articles, conferences, and our online learning platform. O'Reilly's online learning platform gives you on-demand access to live training courses, in-depth learning paths, interactive coding environments, and a vast collection of text and video from O'Reilly and 200+ other publishers. For more information, please visit *http://oreilly.com*.

How to Contact Us

Please address comments and questions concerning this book to the publisher:

O'Reilly Media, Inc.
1005 Gravenstein Highway North
Sebastopol, CA 95472
800-998-9938 (in the United States or Canada)
707-829-0515 (international or local)
707-829-0104 (fax)

You can access the web page for this book, where we list errata, examples, and any additional information, at *https://oreil.ly/Building_ML_Powered_Applications*.

Email *bookquestions@oreilly.com* to comment or ask technical questions about this book.

For more information about our books, courses, conferences, and news, see our website at *http://www.oreilly.com*.

Find us on Facebook: *http://facebook.com/oreilly*

Follow us on Twitter: *http://twitter.com/oreillymedia*

Watch us on YouTube: *http://www.youtube.com/oreillymedia*

Acknowledgments

The project of writing this book started as a consequence of my work mentoring Fellows and overseeing ML projects at Insight Data Science. For giving me the opportunity to lead this program and for encouraging me to write about the lessons learned doing so, I'd like to thank Jake Klamka and Jeremy Karnowski, respectively. I'd also like to thank the hundreds of Fellows I've worked with at Insight for allowing me to help them push the limits of what an ML project can look like.

Writing a book is a daunting task, and the O'Reilly staff helped make it more manageable every step of the way. In particular, I would like to thank my editor, Melissa Potter, who tirelessly provided guidance, suggestions, and moral support throughout the journey that is writing a book. Thank you to Mike Loukides for somehow convincing me that writing a book was a reasonable endeavor.

Thank you to the tech reviewers who combed through early drafts of this book, pointing out errors and offering suggestions for improvement. Thank you Alex Gude, Jon Krohn, Kristen McIntyre, and Douwe Osinga for taking the time out of your busy schedules to help make this book the best version of itself that it could be. To data practitioners whom I asked about the challenges of practical ML they felt needed the most attention, thank you for your time and insights, and I hope you'll find that this book covers them adequately.

Finally, for their unwavering support during the series of busy weekends and late nights that came with writing this book, I'd like to thank my unwavering partner Mari, my sarcastic sidekick Eliott, my wise and patient family, and my friends who refrained from reporting me as missing. You made this book a reality.

## PART I

Find the Correct ML Approach

Most individuals or companies have a good grasp of which problems they are interested in solving—for example, predicting which customers will leave an online platform or building a drone that will follow a user as they ski down a mountain. Similarly, most people can quickly learn how to train a model to classify customers or detect objects to reasonable accuracy given a dataset.

What is much rarer, however, is the ability to take a problem, estimate how best to solve it, build a plan to tackle it with ML, and confidently execute on said plan. This is often a skill that has to be learned through experience, after multiple overly ambitious projects and missed deadlines.

For a given product, there are many potential ML solutions. In Figure I-1, you can see a mock-up of a potential writing assistant tool on the left, which includes a suggestion and an opportunity for the user to provide feedback. On the right of the image is a diagram of a potential ML approach to provide such recommendations.

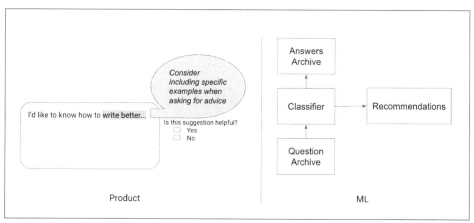

Figure I-1. From product to ML

This section starts by covering these different potential approaches, as well as methods to choose one over the others. It then dives into methods to reconcile a model's performance metrics with product requirements.

To do this, we will tackle two successive topics:

Chapter 1

By the end of this chapter, you will be able to take an idea for an application, estimate whether it is possible to solve, determine whether you would need ML to do so, and figure out which kind of model would make the most sense to start with.

Chapter 2

In this chapter, we will cover how to accurately evaluate your model's performance within the context of your application's goals and how to use this measure to make regular progress.

## CHAPTER 1

From Product Goal to ML Framing

ML allows machines to learn from data and behave in a probabilistic way to solve problems by optimizing for a given objective. This stands in opposition to traditional programming, in which a programmer writes step-by-step instructions describing *how* to solve a problem. This makes ML particularly useful to *build systems for which we are unable to define a heuristic solution.*

Figure 1-1 describes two ways to write a system to detect cats. On the left, a program consists of a procedure that has been manually written out. On the right, an ML approach leverages a dataset of photos of cats and dogs labeled with the corresponding animal to allow a model to learn the mapping from image to category. In the ML approach, there is no specification of how the result should be achieved, only a set of example inputs and outputs.

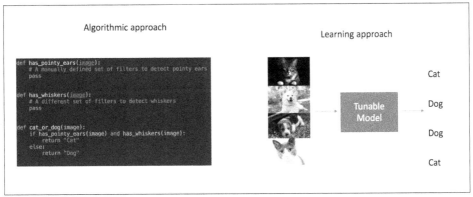

Figure 1-1. From defining procedures to showing examples

ML is powerful and can unlock entirely new products, but since it is based on pattern recognition, it introduces a level of uncertainty. It is important to identify which parts of a product would benefit from ML and how to frame a learning goal in a way that minimizes the risks of users having a poor experience.

For example, it is close to impossible (and extremely time-consuming to attempt) for humans to write step-by-step instructions to automatically detect which animal is in an image based on pixel values. By feeding thousands of images of different animals to a convolutional neural network (CNN), however, we can build a model that performs this classification more accurately than a human. This makes it an attractive task to tackle with ML.

On the other side, an application that calculates your taxes automatically should rely on guidelines provided by the government. As you may have heard, having errors on your tax return is generally frowned upon. This makes the use of ML for automatically generating tax returns a dubious proposition.

You never want to use ML when you can solve your problem with a manageable set of deterministic rules. By manageable, I mean a set of rules that you could confidently write and that would not be too complex to maintain.

So while ML opens up a world of different applications, it is important to think about which tasks *can* and *should* be solved by ML. When building products, you should start from a concrete business problem, determine whether it requires ML, and then work on finding the ML approach that will allow you to iterate as rapidly as possible.

We will cover this process in this chapter, starting with methods to estimate what tasks are able to be solved by ML, which ML approaches are appropriate for which product goals, and how to approach data requirements. I will illustrate these methods with the ML Editor case study that we mentioned in "Our Case Study: ML–Assisted Writing" on page xii, and an interview with Monica Rogati.

Estimate What Is Possible

Since ML models can tackle tasks without humans needing to give them step-by-step instructions, that means they are able to perform some tasks better than human experts (such as detecting tumors from radiology images or playing Go) and some that are entirely inaccessible to humans (such as recommending articles out of a pool of millions or changing the voice of a speaker to sound like someone else).

The ability of ML to learn directly from data makes it useful in a broad range of applications but makes it harder for humans to accurately distinguish which problems are solvable by ML. For each successful result published in a research paper or a corporate blog, there are hundreds of reasonable-sounding ideas that have entirely failed.

While there is currently no surefire way to predict ML success, there are guidelines that can help you reduce the risk associated with tackling an ML project. Most importantly, you should always start with a product goal to then decide how best to solve it.

At this stage, be open to any approach whether it requires ML or not. When considering ML approaches, make sure to evaluate those approaches based on how appropriate they are for the product, not simply on how interesting the methods are in a vacuum.

The best way to do this is by following two successive steps: (1) framing your product goal in an ML paradigm, and (2) evaluating the feasibility of that ML task. Depending on your evaluation, you can readjust your framing until we are satisfied. Let's explore what these steps really mean.

1. *Framing a product goal in an ML paradigm*: When we build a product, we start by thinking of what service we want to deliver to users. As we mentioned in the introduction, we'll illustrate concepts in this book using the case study of an editor that helps users write better questions. The goal of this product is clear: we want users to receive actionable and useful advice on the content they write. ML problems, however, are framed in an entirely different way. An ML problem concerns itself with *learning a function from data*. An example is learning to take in a sentence in one language and output it in another. For one product goal, there are usually many different ML formulations, with varying levels of implementation difficulty.

2. *Evaluating ML feasibility*: All ML problems are not created equal! As our understanding of ML has evolved, problems such as building a model to correctly classify photos of cats and dogs have become solvable in a matter of hours, while others, such as creating a system capable of carrying out a conversation, remain open research problems. To efficiently build ML applications, it is important to consider multiple potential ML framings and start with the ones we judge as the simplest. One of the best ways to evaluate the difficulty of an ML problem is by looking at both the kind of data it requires and at the existing models that could leverage said data.

To suggest different framings and evaluate their feasibility, we should examine two core aspects of an ML problem: data and models.

We will start with models.

Models

There are many commonly used models in ML, and we will abstain from giving an overview of all of them here. Feel free to refer to the books listed in "Additional Resources" on page x for a more thorough overview. In addition to common models, many model variations, novel architectures, and optimization strategies are published on a weekly basis. In May 2019 alone, more than 13,000 papers were submitted to ArXiv (*https://arxiv.org*), a popular electronic archive of research where papers about new models are frequently submitted.

It is useful, however, to share an overview of different categories of models and how they can be applied to different problems. To this end, I propose here a simple taxonomy of models based on how they approach a problem. You can use it as a guide for selecting an approach to tackle a particular ML problem. Because models and data are closely coupled in ML, you will notice some overlap between this section and "Data types" on page 13.

ML algorithms can be categorized based on whether they require labels. Here, a label refers to the presence in the data of an ideal output that a model should produce for a given example. Supervised algorithms leverage datasets that contain labels for inputs, and they aim to learn a mapping from inputs to labels. Unsupervised algorithms, on the other hand, do not require labels. Finally, weakly supervised algorithms leverage labels that aren't exactly the desired output but that resemble it in some way.

Many product goals can be tackled by both supervised and unsupervised algorithms. A fraud detection system can be built by training a model to detect transactions that differ from the average one, requiring no labels. Such a system could also be built by manually labeling transactions as fraudulent or legitimate, and training a model to learn from said labels.

For most applications, supervised approaches are easier to validate since we have access to labels to assess the quality of a model's prediction. This also makes it easier to train models since we have access to desired outputs. While creating a labeled dataset can sometimes be time-consuming initially, it makes it much easier to build and validate models. For this reason, this book will mostly cover supervised approaches.

With that being said, determining which kind of inputs your model will take in and which outputs it will produce will help you narrow down potential approaches significantly. Based on these types, any of the following categories of ML approaches could be a good fit:

- Classification and regression
- Knowledge extraction
- Catalog organization
- Generative models

I'll expand on these further in the following section. As we explore these different modeling approaches, I recommend thinking about which kind of data you have available to you or could gather. Oftentimes, data availability ends up being the limiting factor in model selection.

Classification and regression

Some projects are focused on effectively classifying data points between two or more categories or attributing them a value on a continuous scale (referred to as *regression* instead of *classification*). Regression and classification are technically different, but oftentimes methods to tackle them have significant overlap, so we lump them together here.

One of the reasons classification and regression are similar is because most classification models output a probability score for a model to belong to a category. The classification aspect then boils down to deciding how to attribute an object to a category based on said scores. At a high level, a classification model can thus be seen as a regression on probability values.

Commonly, we classify or score individual examples, such as spam filters that classify each email as valid or junk, fraud detection systems that classify users as fraudulent or legitimate, or computer vision radiology models that classify bones as fractured or healthy.

In Figure 1-2, you can see an example of classifying a sentence according to its sentiment, and the topic it covers.

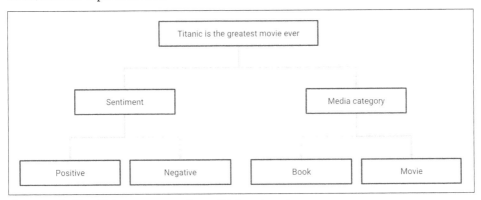

Figure 1-2. Classifying a sentence in multiple categories

In regression projects, instead of attributing a class to each example, we give them a value. Predicting the sale price of a home based on attributes such as how many rooms it has and where it is located is an example of a regression problem.

In some cases, we have access to a series of past data points (instead of one) to predict an event in the future. This type of data is often called a *time series*, and making predictions from a series of data points is referred to as *forecasting*. Time-series data could represent a patient's medical history or a series of attendance measurements from national parks. These projects often benefit from models and features that can leverage this added temporal dimension.

In other cases, we attempt to detect unusual events from a dataset. This is called *anomaly detection*. When a classification problem is trying to detect events that represent a small minority of the data and thus are hard to detect accurately, a different set of methods is often required. Picking a needle out of a haystack is a good analogy here.

Good classification and regression work most often requires significant feature selection and feature engineering work. Feature selection consists of identifying a subset of features that have the most predictive value. Feature generation is the task of identifying and generating good predictors of a target by modifying and combining existing features of a dataset. We will cover both of these topics in more depth in Part III.

Recently, deep learning has shown a promising ability to automatically generate useful features from images, text, and audio. In the future, it may play a larger part in simplifying feature generation and selection, but for now, they remain integral parts of the ML workflow.

Finally, we can often build on top of the classification or score described earlier to provide useful advice. This requires building an interpretable classification model and using its feature to generate actionable advice. More on this later!

Not all problems aim to attribute a set of categories or values to an example. In some cases, we'd like to operate at a more granular level and extract information from parts of an input, such as knowing where an object is in a picture, for example.

Knowledge extraction from unstructured data

Structured data is data that is stored in a tabular format. Database tables and Excel sheets are good examples of structured data. *Unstructured data* refers to datasets that are not in a tabular format. This includes text (from articles, reviews, Wikipedia, and so on), music, videos, and songs.

In Figure 1-3, you can see an example of structured data on the left and unstructured data on the right. Knowledge extraction models focus on taking a source of unstructured data and extracting structure out of it using ML.

In the case of text, knowledge extraction can be used to add structure to reviews, for example. A model can be trained to extract aspects such as cleanliness, service quality, and price from reviews. Users could then easily access reviews that mention topics they are interested in.

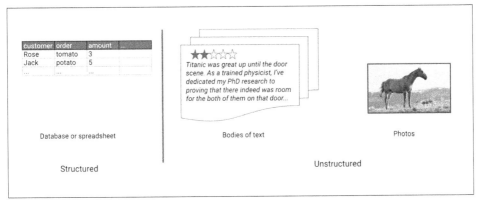

Figure 1-3. Example types of structured and unstructured data

In the medical domain, a knowledge extraction model could be built to take raw text from medical papers as input, and extract information such as the disease that is discussed in the paper, as well as the associated diagnosis and its performance. In Figure 1-4, a model takes a sentence as an input and extracts which words refer to a type of media and which words refer to the title of a media. Using such a model on comments in a fan forum, for example, would allow us to generate summaries of which movies frequently get discussed.

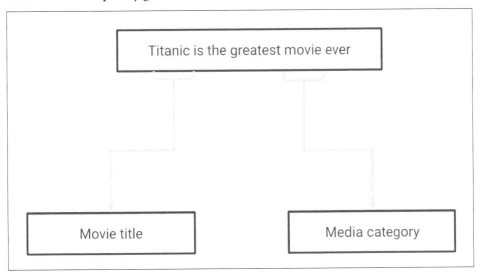

Figure 1-4. Extracting media type and title from a sentence

For images, knowledge extraction tasks often consist of finding areas of interest in an image and categorizing them. Two common approaches are depicted in Figure 1-5: object detection is a coarser approach that consists of drawing rectangles (referred to as *bounding boxes*) around areas of interest, while segmentation precisely attributes each pixel of an image to a given category.

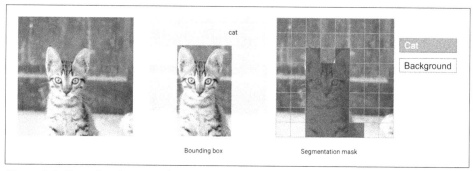

Figure 1-5. Bounding boxes and segmentation masks

Sometimes, this extracted information can be used as an input to another model. An example is using a pose detection model to extract key points from a video of a yogi, and feeding those key points to a second model that classifies the pose as correct or not based on labeled data. Figure 1-6 shows an example of a series of two models that could do just this. The first model extracts structured information (the coordinates of joints) from unstructured data (a photo), and the second one takes these coordinates and classifies them as a yoga pose.

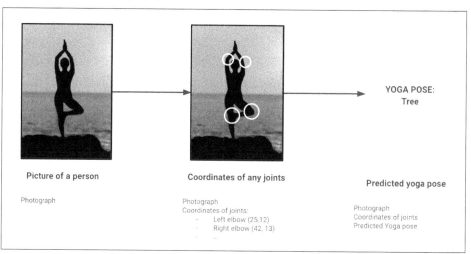

Figure 1-6. Yoga pose detection

The models we've seen so far focus on generating outputs conditioned on a given input. In some cases such as search engines or recommendation systems, the product goal is about surfacing relevant items. This is what we will cover in the following category.

Catalog organization

Catalog organization models most often produce a set of results to present to users. These results can be conditioned on an input string typed into a search bar, an uploaded image, or a phrase spoken to a home assistant. In many cases such as streaming services, this set of results can also be proactively presented to the user as content they may like without them making a request at all.

Figure 1-7 shows an example of such a system that volunteers potential candidate movies to watch based on a movie the user just viewed, but without having the user perform any form of search.

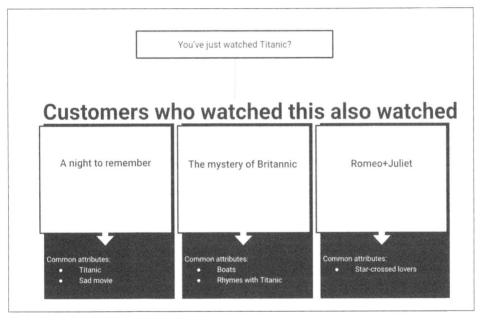

Figure 1-7. Movie recommendations

These models thus either *recommend* items that are related to an item the user already expressed interest in (similar Medium articles or Amazon products) or provide a useful way to *search* through a catalog (allowing users to search for items by typing text or submitting their own photos).

These recommendations are most often based on learning from previous user patterns, in which case they are called *collaborative* recommendation systems. Sometimes, they are based on particular attributes of items, in which case they are called *content-based* recommendation systems. Some systems leverage both collaborative and content-based approaches.

Finally, ML can also be used for creative purposes. Models can learn to generate aesthetically pleasing images, audio, and even amusing text. Such models are referred to as generative models.

Generative models

Generative models focus on generating data, potentially dependent on user input. Because these models focus on generating data rather than classifying it in categories, scoring it, extracting information from it, or organizing it, they usually have a wide range of outputs. This means that generative models are uniquely fit for tasks such as translation, where outputs are immensely varied.

On the other side, generative models are often used to train and have outputs that are less constrained, making them a riskier choice for production. For that reason, unless they are necessary to attain your goal, I recommend starting with other models first. For readers who would like to dive deeper into generative models, however, I recommend the book *Generative Deep Learning*, by David Foster.

Practical examples include translation, which maps sentences in one language to another; summarization; subtitle generation, which maps videos and audio tracks to transcripts; and neural style transfer (see Gatys et al., "A Neural Algorithm of Artistic Style") (*https://oreil.ly/XVwMs*), which maps images to stylized renditions.

Figure 1-8 shows an example of a generative model transforming a photograph on the left by giving it a style similar to a painting shown in the vignette on the right side.

Figure 1-8. Style transfer example from Gatys et al., "A Neural Algorithm of Artistic Style" (https://oreil.ly/XVwMs)

As you can tell by now, each type of model requires a different type of data to be trained on. Commonly, a choice of a model will strongly depend on the data you are able to obtain—data availability often drives model selection.

Let's cover a few common data scenarios and associated models.

Data

Supervised ML models leverage patterns in data to learn useful mappings between inputs and outputs. If a dataset contains features that are predictive of the target output, it should be possible for an appropriate model to learn from it. Most often, however, we do not initially have the right data to train a model to solve a product use case from end-to-end.

For example, say we are training a *speech recognition* system that will listen for requests from customers, understand their intent, and perform actions depending on said intent. When we start working on this project, we may define a set of intents we would want to understand, such as "playing a movie on the television."

To train an ML model to accomplish this task, we would need to have a dataset containing audio clips of users of diverse backgrounds asking in their own terms for the system to play a movie. Having a representative set of inputs is crucial, as any model will only be able to learn from the data that we present to it. If a dataset contains examples from only a subset of the population, a product will be useful to only that subset. With that in mind, because of the specialized domain we have selected, it is extremely unlikely that a dataset of such examples already exists.

For most applications we would want to tackle, we will need to search for, curate, and collect additional data. The data acquisition process can vary widely in scope and complexity depending on the specifics of a project, and estimating the challenge ahead of time is crucial in order to succeed.

To start, let's define a few different situations you can find yourself in when searching for a dataset. This initial situation should be a key factor in deciding how to proceed.

Data types

Once we've defined a problem as *mapping inputs to outputs*, we can search for data sources that follow this mapping.

For fraud detection, these could be examples of fraudulent and innocent users, along with features of their account that we could use to predict their behavior. For translation, this would be a corpus of sentence pairs in the source and target domains. For content organization and search, this could be a history of past searches and clicks.

We will rarely be able to find the exact mapping we are looking for. For this reason, it is useful to consider a few different cases. Think of this as a hierarchy of needs for data.

Data availability

There are roughly three levels of data availability, from best-case scenario to most challenging. Unfortunately, as with most other tasks, you can generally assume that the most useful type of data will be the hardest to find. Let's go through them.

Labeled data exists

This is the leftmost category in Figure 1-9. When working on a supervised model, finding a *labeled dataset* is every practitioner's dream. Labeled here means that many data points contain the target value that the model is trying to predict. This makes training and judging model quality much easier, as labels provide ground truth answers. Finding a labeled dataset that fits your needs and is freely available on the web is rare in practice. It is common, however, to mistake the dataset that you find for the dataset that you need.

Weakly labeled data exists

This is the middle category in Figure 1-9. Some datasets contain labels that are not exactly a modeling target, but somewhat correlated with it. Playback and skip history for a music streaming service are examples of a weakly labeled dataset for predicting whether a user dislikes a song. While a listener may have not marked a song as disliked, if they skipped it as it was playing, it is an indication that they may have not been fond of it. Weak labels are less precise by definition but often easier to find than perfect labels.

Unlabeled data exists

This category is on the right side of Figure 1-9. In some cases, while we do not have a labeled dataset mapping desired inputs to outputs, we at least have access to a dataset containing relevant examples. For the text translation example, we might have access to large collections of text in both languages, but with no direct mapping between them. This means we need to label the dataset, find a model that can learn from unlabeled data, or do a little bit of both.

We need to acquire data

In some cases, we are one step away from unlabeled data, as we need to first acquire it. In many cases, we do not have a dataset for what we need and thus will need to find a way to acquire such data. This is often seen as an insurmountable task, but many methods now exist to rapidly gather and label data. This will be the focus of Chapter 4.

For our case study, an ideal dataset would be a set of user-typed questions, along with a set of better worded questions. A *weakly labeled* dataset would be a dataset of many questions with some weak labels indicative of their quality such as "likes" or "upvotes." This would help a model learn what makes for good and bad questions but would not provide side-by-side examples for the same question. You can see both of these examples in Figure 1-9.

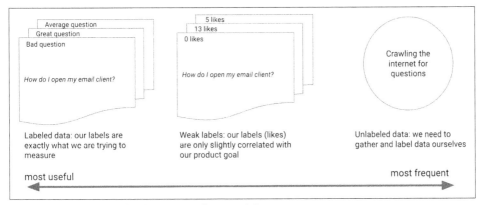

Figure 1-9. Data availability versus data usefulness

In general in ML, a weakly labeled dataset refers to a dataset that contains information that will help a model learn, but not the exact ground truth. In practice, most datasets that we can gather are weakly labeled.

Having an imperfect dataset is entirely fine and shouldn't stop you. The ML process is iterative in nature, so starting with a dataset and getting some initial results is the best way forward, regardless of the data quality.

Datasets are iterative

In many cases, since you will not be able to immediately find a dataset containing a direct mapping from inputs to your desired output, I suggest progressively iterating on the way you formulate the problem, making it easier to find an adequate dataset to start with. Each dataset you explore and use will provide you with valuable information that you can use to curate the next version of your dataset and generate useful features for your models.

Let's now dive into the case study and see how we can use what we've learned to identify different models and datasets we could use, and choose the most appropriate.

Framing the ML Editor

Let's see how we could iterate through a product use case to find the right ML framing. We'll get through this process by outlining a method to progress from a product goal (helping users write better questions) to an ML paradigm.

We would like to build an editor that accepts questions by users and improves them to be better written, but what does "better" mean in this case? Let's start by defining the writing assistant's product goal a little more clearly.

Many people use forums, social networks, and websites such as Stack Overflow (*https://stackoverflow.com/*) to find answers to their questions. However, the way that people ask questions has a dramatic impact on whether they receive a useful answer. This is unfortunate both for the user looking to get their question answered and for future users that may have the same problem and could have found an existing answer useful. To that end, our goal will be to *build an assistant that can help users write better questions*.

We have a product goal and now need to decide which modeling approach to use. To make this decision, we will go through the iteration loop of model selection and data validation mentioned earlier.

Trying to Do It All with ML: An End-to-End Framework

In this context, *end-to-end* means using a single model to go from input to output with no intermediary steps. Since most product goals are very specific, attempting to solve an entire use case by learning it from end-to-end often requires custom-built cutting-edge ML models. This may be the right solution for teams that have the resources to develop and maintain such models, but it is often worth it to start with more well-understood models first.

In our case, we could attempt to gather a dataset of poorly formulated questions, as well as their professionally edited versions. We could then use a generative model to go straight from one text to the other.

Figure 1-10 depicts what this would look like in practice. It shows a simple diagram with user input on the left, the desired output on the right, and a model in between.

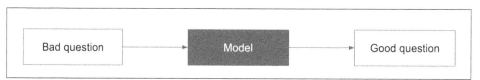

Figure 1-10. End-to-end approach

As you'll see, this approach comes with significant challenges:

Data

To acquire such a dataset, we would need to find pairs of questions with the same intent but of different wording quality. This is quite a rare dataset to find as is. Building it ourselves would be costly as well, as we would need to be assisted by professional editors to generate this data.

Model

Models going from one sequence of text to another, seen in the generative models category discussed earlier, have progressed tremendously in recent years.

Sequence-to-sequence models (as described in the paper by I. Sutskever et al., "Sequence to Sequence Learning with Neural Networks" (*https://arxiv.org/abs/1409.3215*)) were originally proposed in 2014 for translation tasks and are closing the gap between machine and human translation. The success of these models, however, has mostly been on sentence-level tasks, and they have not been frequently used to process text longer than a paragraph. This is because so far, they have not been able to capture long-term context from one paragraph to another. Additionally, because they usually have a large number of parameters, they are some of the slowest models to train. If a model is trained only once, this is not necessarily an issue. If it needs to be retrained hourly or daily, training time can become an important factor.

Latency

Sequence-to-sequence models are often *autoregressive models*, meaning they require the model's output of the previous word to start working on the next. This allows them to leverage information from neighboring words but causes them to be slower to train and slower to run inference on than the simpler models. Such models can take a few seconds to produce an answer at inference time, as opposed to subsecond latency for simpler models. While it is possible to optimize such a model to run quickly enough, it will require additional engineering work.

Ease of implementation

Training complex end-to-end models is a very delicate and error-prone process, as they have many moving parts. This means that we need to consider the trade-off between a model's potential performance and the complexity it adds to a pipeline. This complexity will slow us down when building a pipeline, but it also introduces a maintenance burden. If we anticipate that other teammates may need to iterate on and improve on your model, it may be worthwhile to choose a set of simpler, more well-understood models.

This end-to-end approach could work, but it will require a lot of upfront data gathering and engineering effort, with no success guarantee, so it would be worthwhile to explore other alternatives, as we will cover next.

The Simplest Approach: Being the Algorithm

As you'll see in the interview at the end of this section, it is often a great idea for data scientists to *be the algorithm* before they implement it. In other words, to understand how to best automate a problem, start by attempting to solve it manually. So, if we were editing questions ourselves to improve readability and the odds of getting an answer, how would we go about it?

A first approach would be to not use data at all but leverage prior art to define what makes a question or a body of text well written. For general writing tips, we could reach out to a professional editor or research newspapers' style guides to learn more.

In addition, we should dive into a dataset to look at individual examples and trends and let those inform our modeling strategy. We will skip this for now as we will cover how to do this in more depth in Chapter 4.

To start, we could look at existing research (*https://oreil.ly/jspYn*) to identify a few attributes we might use to help people write more clearly. These features could include factors such as:

Prose simplicity
> We often give new writers the advice to use simpler words and sentence structures. We could thus establish a set of criteria on the appropriate sentence and word length, and recommend changes as needed.

Tone
> We could measure the use of adverbs, superlatives, and punctuation to measure the polarity of the text. Depending on the context, more opinionated questions may receive fewer answers.

Structural features
> Finally, we could try to extract the presence of important structural attributes such as the use of greetings or question marks.

Once we have identified and generated useful features, we can build a simple solution that uses them to provide recommendations. There is no ML involved here, but this phase is crucial for two reasons: it provides a baseline that is very quick to implement and will serve as a yardstick to measure models against.

To validate our intuition about how to detect good writing, we can gather a dataset of "good" and "bad" text and see if we can tell the good from the bad using these features.

Middle Ground: Learning from Our Experience

Now that we have a baseline set of features, we can attempt to use them to *learn a model of style from a body of data*. To do this we can gather a dataset, extract the features we described earlier from it, and train a classifier on it to separate good and bad examples.

Once we have a model that can classify written text, we can inspect it to identify which features are highly predictive and use those as recommendations. We will see how to do this in practice in Chapter 7.

Figure 1-11 describes this approach. On the left side, a model is trained to classify a question as good or bad. On the right side, the trained model is given a question and scores candidate reformulations of this question that will lead to it receiving a better score. The reformulation with the highest score is recommended to the user.

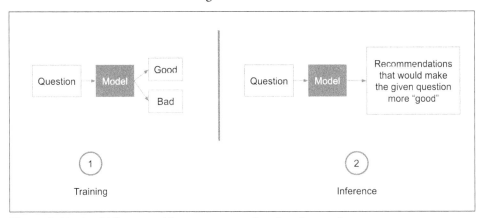

Figure 1-11. A middle ground between manual and end-to-end

Let's examine the challenges we outlined in "Trying to Do It All with ML: An End-to-End Framework" on page 16 and see whether the classifier approach makes them any easier:

Dataset

We could obtain a dataset of good and bad examples by gathering questions from an online forum along with some measure of their quality, such as the number of views or upvotes. As opposed to the end-to-end approach, this does not require us to have access to revisions of the same questions. We simply need a set of good and bad examples we can hope to learn aggregate features from, which is an easier dataset to find.

Model

We need to consider two things here: how predictive a model is (can it efficiently separate good and bad articles?) and how easily features can be extracted from it (can we see which attributes were used to classify an example?). There are many potential models that we could use here, along with different features we could extract from text to make it more explainable.

Latency

Most text classifiers are quite quick. We could start with a simple model such as a random forest, which can return results in less than a tenth of a second on regular hardware, and move on to more complex architectures if needed.

Ease of implementation

Compared to text generation, text classification is relatively well understood, meaning building such a model should be relatively quick. Many examples of working text classification pipelines exist online, and many such models have already been deployed to production.

If we start with a human heuristic and then build this simple model, we will quickly be able to have an initial baseline, and the first step toward a solution. Moreover, the initial model will be a great way to inform what to build next (more on this in Part III).

For more on the importance of starting with simple baselines, I sat down with Monica Rogati, who shares some of the lessons she has learned helping data teams deliver products.

Monica Rogati: How to Choose and Prioritize ML Projects

After getting her Ph.D. in computer science, Monica Rogati started her career at LinkedIn where she worked on core products such as integrating ML into the People You May Know algorithm and built the first version of job-to-candidate matching. She then became VP of data at Jawbone where she built and led the entire data team. Monica is now an adviser to dozens of companies whose number of employees ranges from 5 to 8,000. She has kindly agreed to share some of the advice she often gives to teams when it comes to designing and executing on ML products.

Q: *How do you scope out an ML product?*

A: You have to remember that you are trying to use the best tools to solve a problem, and only use ML if it makes sense.

Let's say you wanted to predict what a user of an application will do and show it to them as a suggestion. You should start by combining discussions on modeling and product. Among other things, this includes designing the product around handling ML failures gracefully.

You could start by taking into account the confidence our model has in its prediction. We could then formulate our suggestions differently based on the confidence score. If the confidence is above 90%, we present the suggestion prominently; if it is over 50%, we still display it but with less emphasis, and we do not display anything if the confidence is below this score.

Q: *How do you decide what to focus on in an ML project?*

A: You have to find the *impact bottleneck*, meaning the piece of your pipeline that could provide the most value if you improve on it. When working with companies, I often find that they may not be working on the right problem or not be at the right growth stage for this.

There are often problems around the model. The best way to find this out is to replace the model with something simple and debug the whole pipeline. Frequently, the issues will not be with the accuracy of your model. Frequently, your product is dead even if your model is successful.

Q: *Why do you usually recommend starting with a simple model?*

A: The goal of our plan should be to derisk our model somehow. The best way to do this is to start with a "strawman baseline" to evaluate worst-case performance. For our earlier example, this could be simply suggesting whichever action the user previously took.

If we did this, how often would our prediction be correct, and how annoying would our model be to the user if we were wrong? Assuming that our model was not much better than this baseline, would our product still be valuable?

This applies well to examples in natural language understanding and generation such as chatbots, translation, Q&A, and summarization. Oftentimes in summarization, for example, simply extracting the top keywords and categories covered by an article is enough to serve most users' needs.

Q: *Once you have your whole pipeline, how do you identify the impact bottleneck?*

A: You should start with imagining that the impact bottleneck is solved, and ask yourself whether it was worth the effort you estimated it would take. I encourage data scientists to compose a tweet and companies to write a press release before they even start on a project. That helps them avoid working on something just because they thought it was cool and puts the impact of the results into context based on the effort.

The ideal case is that you can pitch the results regardless of the outcome: if you do not get the best outcome, is this still impactful? Have you learned something or validated some assumptions? A way to help with this is to build infrastructure to help lower the required effort for deployment.

At LinkedIn, we had access to a very useful design element, a little window with a few rows of text and hyperlinks, that we could customize with our data. This made it easier to launch experiments for projects such as job recommendations, as the design was already approved. Because the resource investment was low, the impact did not have to be as large, which allowed for a faster iteration cycle. The barrier then becomes about nonengineering concerns, such as ethics, fairness, and branding.

Q: *How do you decide which modeling techniques to use?*

A: The first line of defense is looking at the data yourself. Let's say we want to build a model to recommend groups to LinkedIn users. A naive way would be to recommend the most popular group containing their company's name in the group title. After looking at a few examples, we found out one of the popular groups for the company Oracle was "Oracle sucks!" which would be a terrible group to recommend to Oracle employees.

It is always valuable to spend the manual effort to look at inputs and outputs of your model. Scroll past a bunch of examples to see if anything looks weird. The head of my department at IBM had this mantra of doing something manually for an hour before putting in any work.

Looking at your data helps you think of good heuristics, models, and ways to reframe the product. If you rank examples in your dataset by frequency, you might even be able to quickly identify and label 80% of your use cases.

At Jawbone, for example, people entered "phrases" to log the content of their meals. By the time we labeled the top 100 by hand, we had covered 80% of phrases and had strong ideas of what the main problems we would have to handle, such as varieties of text encoding and languages.

The last line of defense is to have a diverse workforce that looks at the results. This will allow you to catch instances where a model is exhibiting discriminative behavior, such as tagging your friends as a gorilla, or is insensitive by surfacing painful past experiences with its smart "this time last year" retrospective.

Conclusion

As we've seen, building an ML-powered application starts with judging feasibility and picking an approach. Most often, picking a supervised approach is the simplest way to get started. Among those, classification, knowledge extraction, catalog organization, or generative models are the most common paradigms in practice.

As you are picking an approach, you should identify how easily you'll be able to access strongly or weakly labeled data, or any data at all. You should then compare potential models and datasets by defining a product goal and choosing the modeling approach that best allows you to accomplish this goal.

We illustrated these steps for the ML Editor, opting to start with simple heuristics and a classification-based approach. And finally, we covered how leaders such as Monica Rogati have been applying these practices to successfully ship ML models to users.

Now that we have chosen an initial approach, it is time to define success metrics and create an action plan to make regular progress. This will involve setting minimal performance requirements, doing a deep dive into available modeling and data resources, and building a simple prototype.

We will cover all of those in Chapter 2.

## CHAPTER 2

Create a Plan

In the previous chapter, we covered how to estimate if ML is necessary, find where it could be most appropriately used, and convert a product goal to the most appropriate ML framing. In this chapter, we will cover the use of metrics to track ML and product progress and compare different ML implementations. Then, we will identify methods to build a baseline and plan modeling iterations.

I have had the unfortunate opportunity to see many ML projects be doomed from the start due to a misalignment between product metrics and model metrics. More projects fail by producing good models that aren't helpful for a product rather than due to modeling difficulties. This is why I wanted to dedicate a chapter to metrics and planning.

We will cover tips to leverage existing resources and the constraints of your problem to build an actionable plan, which will dramatically simplify any ML project.

Let's start with defining performance metrics in more detail.

Measuring Success

When it comes to ML, the first model we build should be the simplest model that could address a product's needs, because generating and analyzing results is the fastest way to make progress in ML. In the previous chapter, we covered three potential approaches of increasing complexity for the ML Editor. Here they are as a reminder:

Baseline; designing heuristics based on domain knowledge
> We could start with simply defining rules ourselves, based on prior knowledge of what makes for well-written content. We will test these rules by seeing if they help differentiate between well-written text and poorly written text.

Simple model; classifying text as good or bad, and using the classifier to generate recommendations

> We could then train a simple model to differentiate between good and bad questions. Provided that the model performs well, we can then inspect it to see which features it found to be highly predictive of a good question, and use those features as recommendations.

Complex model; training an end-to-end model that goes from bad text to good text

> This is the most complex approach, both in terms of model and data, but if we had the resources to gather the training data and build and maintain a complex model, we could solve the product requirements directly.

All of these approaches are different and may evolve as we learn more from prototypes along the way, but when working on ML, you should define a common set of metrics to compare the success of modeling pipelines.

You Don't Always Need ML

You may have noticed that the baseline approach does not rely on ML at all. As we discussed in Chapter 1, some features do not require ML. It is important to also realize that even features that could benefit from ML can often simply use a heuristic for their first version. Once the heuristic is being used, you may even realize that you do not need ML at all.

Building a heuristic is also often the fastest way to build a feature. Once the feature is built and used, you'll have a clearer view of your user's needs. This will allow you to evaluate whether you need ML, and select a modeling approach.

In most cases, starting without ML is the fastest way to build an ML product.

To that end, we will cover four categories of performance that have a large impact on the usefulness of any ML product: business metrics, model metrics, freshness, and speed. Clearly defining these metrics will allow us to accurately measure the performance of each iteration.

Business Performance

We've talked about the importance of starting with a clear product or feature goal. Once this goal is clear, a metric should be defined to judge its success. This metric should be separate from any model metrics and only be a reflection of the product's success. Product metrics may be as simple as the number of users a feature attracts or more nuanced such as the click-through rate (CTR) of the recommendations we provide.

Product metrics are ultimately the only ones that matter, as they represent the goals of your product or feature. All other metrics should be used as tools to improve product metrics. Product metrics, however, do not need to be unique. While most projects tend to focus on improving one product metric, their impact is often measured in terms of multiple metrics, including *guardrail metrics*, metrics that shouldn't decline below a given point. For example, an ML project can aim to increase a given metric such as CTR, while also holding other metrics steady, such as the average user session length, for example.

For the ML Editor, we will pick a metric that measures the usefulness of a recommendation. For example, we could use the proportion of times that users follow suggestions. In order to compute such a metric, the interface of the ML editor should capture whether a user approves of a suggestion, by overlaying it above the input and making it clickable, for example.

We've seen that each product lends itself to many potential ML approaches. To measure the effectiveness of an ML approach, you should track model performance.

Model Performance

For most online products, the ultimate product metric that determines the success of a model is the proportion of visitors who use the output of a model out of all the visitors who could benefit from it. In the case of a recommendation system, for example, performance is often judged by measuring how many people click on recommended products (see Chapter 8 for potential pitfalls of this approach).

When a product is still being built and not deployed yet, it is not possible to measure usage metrics. To still measure progress, it is important to define a separate success metric called an *offline metric* or a *model metric*. A good offline metric should be possible to evaluate without exposing a model to users, and be as correlated as possible with product metrics and goals.

Different modeling approaches use different model metrics, and changing approaches can make it much easier to reach a level of modeling performance that is sufficient to accomplish product goals.

For example, let's say you are trying to offer helpful suggestions to users as they type a search query on an online retail website. You'll measure the success of this feature by measuring CTR, how often users click on the suggestions you make.

To generate the suggestions, you could build a model that attempts to guess the words a user will type and present the predicted completed sentence to them as they write. You could measure the performance of this model by computing its word-level accuracy, calculating how often it predicts the correct next set of words. Such a model would need to reach extremely high accuracy to help increase the product's CTR, because a prediction error of one word would be enough to render a suggestion useless. This approach is sketched out on the left side of Figure 2-1.

Another approach would be to train a model that classifies user input into categories in your catalog and suggests the three most likely predicted categories. You'd measure the performance of your model using accuracy over all categories rather than accuracy over every English word. Since the number of categories in a catalog is much smaller than the English vocabulary, this would be a much easier modeling metric to optimize. In addition, the model only needs to predict one category correctly to generate a click. It is much easier for this model to increase the product's CTR. You can see a mock-up of how this approach would work in practice on the right side of Figure 2-1.

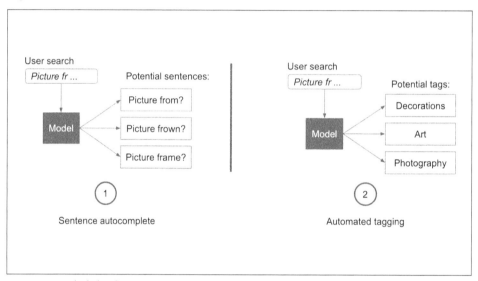

Figure 2-1. Slightly altering a product can make modeling tasks much easier

As you can see, small changes to the interaction between the model and product can make it possible to use a more straightforward modeling approach and deliver results more reliably. Here are a few other examples of updating an application to make a modeling task easier:

- *Changing an interface so that a model's results can be omitted if they are below a confidence threshold.* When building a model to autocomplete a sentence typed by the user, for example, the model may perform well only on a subset of sentences. We can implement logic to only show a suggestion to users if the model's confidence score exceeds 90%.

- *Presenting a few other predictions or heuristics in addition to a model's top prediction.* For example, most websites display more than one recommendation suggested by a model. Displaying five candidate items instead of just one makes it more likely that suggestions will be useful to users, even if the model is the same.

- *Communicating to users that a model is still in an experimental phase and giving them opportunities to provide feedback.* When automatically detecting a language that is not in the user's native tongue and translating it for them, websites often add a button for a user to let them know whether the translation was accurate and useful.

Even when a modeling approach is appropriate for a problem, it can sometimes be worthwhile to generate additional model metrics that correlate better with product performance.

I once worked with a data scientist who built a model to generate HTML from hand-drawn sketches of simple websites (see his post, "Automated Front-End Development Using Deep Learning" (*https://oreil.ly/SdYQj*)). The model's optimization metric compares each predicted HTML token to the correct one using cross-entropy loss. The goal of the product, however, is for the generated HTML to produce a website that looks like the input sketch, regardless of the order of tokens.

Cross-entropy does not account for alignment: if a model generates a correct HTML sequence except for one extra token at the start, all of the tokens will be shifted by one compared to the target. Such an output would lead to a very high loss value, despite producing an almost ideal result. This means that when trying to evaluate the usefulness of the model, we should look beyond its optimization metric. In this example, using a BLEU Score (*https://oreil.ly/8s9JE*) provides a better measurement of the similarity between the generated HTML and the ideal output.

Finally, a product should be designed with reasonable assumptions of model performance in mind. If a product relies on a model being perfect to be useful, it is very likely to produce inaccurate or even dangerous results.

For example, if you are building a model that lets you take a picture of a pill and tells patients its type and dosage, what is the worst accuracy a model could have and still be useful? If this accuracy requirement is hard to attain with current methods, could you redesign your product to make sure users are well served by it and not put at risk by prediction errors it could make?

In our case, the product we want to build will provide writing advice. Most ML models have certain input they excel at and certain inputs they will struggle with. From a product standpoint, if we are not able to help—we need to make sure we are not going to hurt—we would like to limit the amount of time that we output a result that is worse than the input. How could we express this in model metrics?

Let's say we build a classification model that attempts to predict whether a question is good as measured by the number of upvotes it received. The classifier's precision would be defined as the proportion of questions that are truly good out of the ones it predicts as good. Its recall on the other side is the proportion of questions that it predicts as good out of all the good questions in the dataset.

If we want to always have advice that is relevant, we would want to prioritize the model's *precision* because when a high-precision model classifies a question as good (and thus makes a recommendation), there is a high chance that this question is actually good. High precision means that when we do make a recommendation, it will tend to be correct. For more about why high-precision models are more useful for writing recommendations, feel free to refer to "Chris Harland: Shipping Experiments" on page 180.

We measure such metrics by looking through the outputs of a model on a representative validation set. We will dive into what this means in "Evaluate Your Model: Look Beyond Accuracy" on page 109, but for now, think of a validation set as a set of data that is held out from training and used to estimate how your model performs on unseen data.

Initial model performance is important, but so is the ability of a model to stay useful in the face of changing user behavior. A model trained on a given dataset will perform well on similar data, but how do we know whether we need to update a dataset?

Freshness and Distribution Shift

Supervised models draw their predictive power from learning correlations between input features and prediction targets. This means that most models need to have been exposed to training data that is similar to a given input to perform well on it. A model that was trained to predict the age of a user from a photo using only photos of men will not perform well on photos of women. But even if a model is trained on an adequate dataset, many problems have a distribution of data that changes as time goes on. When the distribution of the data *shifts*, the model often needs to change as well in order to maintain the same level of performance.

Let's imagine that after noticing the impact of rain on traffic in San Francisco, you built a model to predict traffic conditions based on the amount of rain in the past week. If you built your model in October using data from the past 3 months, your model was likely trained on data with daily precipitation lower than an inch. See Figure 2-2 for an example of how such a distribution might look. As winter approaches, the average precipitation will become closer to 3 inches, which is higher than anything the model was exposed to during training, as you can see in Figure 2-2. If the model isn't trained on more recent data, it will struggle to keep performing well.

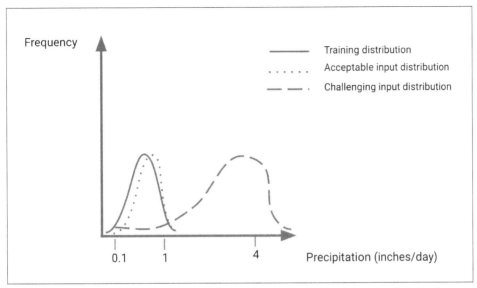

Figure 2-2. Changing distributions

In general, a model can perform well on data it hasn't seen before as long as it is similar enough to the data it was exposed to during training.

Not all problems have the same freshness requirements. Translation services for ancient languages can expect the data they operate to remain relatively constant, while search engines need to be built with the assumption that they will need to evolve as fast as users change their search habits.

Depending on your business problem, you should consider how hard it will be to keep models *fresh*. How often will you need to retrain models, and how much will it cost you each time we do so?

For the ML editor, we imagine that the cadence at which the definition of "well-formulated English prose" changes is relatively low, perhaps in the order of a year. Freshness requirements would change if we targeted specific domains, however. For example, the right way to ask a question about mathematics will change much more slowly than the best phrasing of questions concerning music trends. Since we estimate that models will need to be retrained every year, we will require fresh data to train on yearly.

Our baseline and simple model can both learn from unpaired data, which makes the data gathering process simpler (we'd simply need to find new questions from the last year). The complex model requires paired data, meaning we will have to find examples of the same sentences, said in a "good" and "bad" way, every year. This means satisfying the freshness requirement we've defined will be much harder for a model requiring paired data, since it is more time-consuming to acquire an updated dataset.

For most applications, popularity can help alleviate data gathering requirements. If our question phrasing service goes viral, we could add a button for users to rate the quality of outputs. We could then gather past inputs from users along with the model's predictions and associated user ratings and use them as a training set.

For an application to be popular, however, it should be useful. Oftentimes, this requires responding to user requests in a timely manner. The speed at which a model can deliver predictions is thus an important factor to take into account.

Speed

Ideally, a model should deliver a prediction quickly. This allows users to interact with it more easily and makes it easier to serve a model to many concurrent users. So how fast does a model need to be? For some use cases, such as translating a short sentence, users will expect an answer immediately. For others, such as a medical diagnosis, patients would be happy to wait 24 hours if it meant that they would get the most accurate results.

In our case, we will consider two potential ways we could deliver suggestions: through a submission box where the user writes, clicks Submit, and gets a result or by dynamically updating each time the user enters a new letter. While we may want to favor the latter because we would be able to make the tool much more interactive, it would require models to perform much faster.

We could conceivably imagine a user waiting a couple seconds for a result once they click a submission button, but for a model to run as a user is editing text, it would need to run significantly under a second. The most powerful models take longer to process data, so as we iterate through models, we will keep this requirement in mind. Any model we use should be able to process an example through its whole pipeline in under two seconds.

Model inference runtimes increase as models get more complex. The difference is significant even in a domain where each individual data point can be relatively small data such as NLP (as opposed to tasks on live videos, for example). On the text data used for the case study in this book, for example, an LSTM is about three times slower than a random forest (around 22 ms for an LSTM, while the random forest takes only 7 ms). On an individual datapoint, this difference are small, but they can quickly add up when needing to run inference on tens of thousands of examples at a time.

For complex applications where an inference call will be associated with multiple network calls or database queries, model execution time can become short compared to the rest of the application logic. In those cases, the speed of said models becomes less of an issue.

Depending on your problem, there are other categories you could consider, such as hardware constraints, development time, and maintainability. It is important to develop an understanding of your needs before choosing a model so that you make sure to pick said model in an informed way.

Once you identify requirements and associated metrics, it's time to start making a plan. This requires estimating the challenges that lie ahead. In the next section, I'll cover ways to leverage prior work and explore a dataset to decide what to build next.

Estimate Scope and Challenges

As we've seen, ML performance is often reported in terms of model metrics. While these metrics are useful, they should be used to improve the product metrics we defined, which represent the actual task we are trying to solve. As we iterate on a pipeline, we should keep in mind product metrics and aim to improve them.

The tools we have covered so far will help us determine whether a project is worth tackling at all, and measure how well we are currently doing. A logical next step is to sketch out a plan of attack to estimate the scope and duration of a project and anticipate potential roadblocks.

In ML, success generally requires understanding the context of the task well, acquiring a good dataset, and building an appropriate model.

We will cover each of these categories in the following section.

Leverage Domain Expertise

The simplest model we can start with is a heuristic: a good rule of thumb based on knowledge of the problem and the data. The best way to devise heuristics is to see what experts are currently doing. Most practical applications are not entirely novel. How do people currently solve the problem you are trying to solve?

The second best way to devise heuristics is to look at your data. Based on your dataset, how would you solve this task if you were doing it manually?

To identify good heuristics, I recommend either learning from experts in the field or getting familiar with the data. I'll describe both in a little more detail next.

Learning from experts

For many domains we might want to automate, learning from experts in the domain can save us dozens of hours of work. If we are attempting to build a predictive maintenance system for factory equipment, for example, we should start by reaching out to a factory manager to understand which assumptions we can reasonably make. This could include understanding how often maintenance is currently performed, which symptoms usually indicate that a machine will require maintenance soon, and the legal requirements concerning maintenance.

There are, of course, examples where finding domain experts is likely to be difficult—such as proprietary data for a novel use case like predicting usage of a unique website feature. In these cases, however, we can often find professionals who have had to tackle similar problems and learn from their experiences.

This will allow us to learn about useful features we can leverage, find pitfalls we should avoid, and most importantly prevent us from reinventing the wheel that many data scientists get a bad rep for.

Examining the data

As both Monica Rogati in "Monica Rogati: How to Choose and Prioritize ML Projects" on page 20 and Robert Munro in "Robert Munro: How Do You Find, Label, and Leverage Data?" on page 89 mention, it's key to look at the data before we start modeling.

Exploratory data analysis (EDA) is the process of visualizing and exploring a dataset, often to get an intuition to a given business problem. EDA is a crucial part of building any data product. In addition to EDA, it is crucial to individually label examples in the way you hope a model would. Doing so helps validate assumptions and confirms that you chose models that can appropriately leverage your dataset.

The EDA process will allow you to get an understanding of the trends in your data, and labeling it yourself will force you to build a set of heuristics to solve your problem. After having done both previous steps, you should have a clearer idea of which kind of models will serve you best, as well as any additional data gathering and labeling strategies we may require.

The next logical step is to see how others have tackled similar modeling problems.

Stand on the Shoulders of Giants

Have people solved similar problems? If so, the best way to get started is to understand and reproduce existing results. Look for public implementations either with similar models or similar datasets, or both.

Ideally, this would involve finding open source code and an available dataset, but these aren't always easy to come by, especially for very specific products. Nevertheless, the fastest way to get started on an ML project is to reproduce existing results and then build on top of them.

In a domain with as many moving pieces as ML, it is crucial to stand on the shoulders of giants.

If you're planning to use open source code or datasets in your work, please make sure that you are allowed to do so. Most repositories and datasets will include a license that defines acceptable usages. In addition, credit any source you end up using, ideally with a reference to their original work.

It can often be a good idea to build a convincing proof of concept before committing significant resources to a project. Before using time and money to label data, for example, we need to convince ourselves that we can build a model that will learn from said data.

So, how do we find an efficient way to start? Like most topics we will cover in this book, this includes two main parts: data and code.

Open data

You might not always be able to find a dataset that matches your desires, but you can often find a dataset that is similar enough in nature to be helpful. What does a similar dataset mean in this context? Thinking about ML models as mapping an input to an output is helpful here. With this in mind, a similar dataset simply means a dataset with similar input and output types (but not necessarily domains).

Frequently, models using similar inputs and outputs can be applied to entirely different contexts. On the left side of Figure 2-3 are two models that both predict a text sequence from an image input. One is used to describe photos, while the other generates HTML code for a website from a screenshot of said website. Similarly, the right side of Figure 2-3 shows a model that predicts a type of food from a text description in English, and another that predicts a music genre from a sheet music transcription.

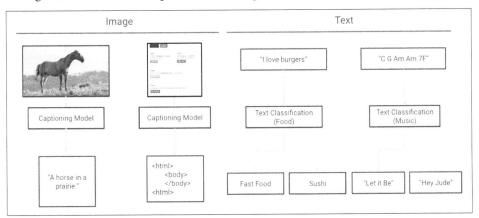

Figure 2-3. Different models with similar inputs and outputs

For example, let's say we are trying to build a model to predict viewership of news articles but are struggling to find a dataset of news articles and associated view counts. We could start with the openly accessible dataset of Wikipedia page traffic statistics (*https://oreil.ly/PdwgN*) and train a predictive model on it. If we are happy with its performance, it is reasonable to believe that given a dataset of views for a news article, our model could perform reasonably well. Finding a similar dataset can help prove the validity of an approach and makes it more reasonable to spend resources to acquire data.

This method also works when working on proprietary data. Oftentimes, the dataset you need for a prediction task may not be easy to access. In some cases, the data you would need is not being currently collected. In such cases, building a model that performs well on a similar dataset can often be the best way to convince stakeholders to build a novel data collection pipeline or facilitate access to an existing one.

When it comes to publicly accessible data, new data sources and collections appear regularly. The following are a few that I've found useful:

- The Internet archive (*https://oreil.ly/tIjl9*) maintains a set of datasets including website data, videos, and books.

- The subreddit r/datasets (*http://reddit.com/r/datasets*) is dedicated to sharing datasets.

- Kaggle's Datasets page (*https://www.kaggle.com/datasets*) offers a large selection in a variety of domains.

- The UCI Machine Learning Repository (*https://oreil.ly/BXLA5*) is a vast resource of ML datasets.

- Google's dataset search (*https://oreil.ly/Gpv8S*) covers a large searchable index of accessible datasets.

- Common Crawl (*https://commoncrawl.org*) crawls and archives data from across the web and makes results publicly available.

- Wikipedia also has a great evolving list of ML research datasets (*https://oreil.ly/kXGiz*).

For most use cases, one of these sources will provide you with a dataset sufficiently similar to the one you would need.

Training a model on this *tangential dataset* will allow you to prototype and validate your results rapidly. In some cases, you can even train a model on a tangential dataset and transfer some of its performance to your final dataset (more on this in Chapter 4).

Once you have an idea of which dataset you'll start with, it is time to turn your attention to models. While it can be tempting to simply start building your own pipeline from scratch, it can often be worthwhile to at least observe what others have done.

Open source code

Searching for existing code can achieve two high-level goals. It lets us see which challenges others have faced when doing similar modeling and surfaces potential issues with the given dataset. For this reason, I recommend looking for both pipelines tackling your product goal and code working with the dataset you have chosen. If you find an example, the first step would be to reproduce its results yourself.

I have seen many data scientists attempt to leverage ML code they found online only to find that they are unable to train the given models to a similar level of accuracy claimed by the authors. Because new approaches are not always accompanied with well-documented and functioning code, ML results are often hard to reproduce and thus should always be verified.

Similar to your search for data, a good way to find similar codebases is to abstract your problem to its input and output types and find codebases tackling problems with similar types.

For example, when attempting to generate HTML code from screenshots of a website, Tony Beltramelli, the author of the paper, "pix2code: Generating Code from a Graphical User Interface Screenshot" (*https://oreil.ly/rTQyD*), realized that his problem boiled down to translating an image into a sequence. He leveraged existing architectures and best practices from a field that was more mature and also generated sequences from images, meaning image captioning! This allowed him to get excellent results on an entirely new task and leverage years of work in an adjacent application.

Once you've looked at data and at code, you're ready to move forward. Ideally, this process has given you a few pointers to start your work and acquire a more nuanced perspective on your problem. Let's sum up the situations you can find yourself in after looking for prior work.

Bring both together

As we just discussed, leveraging existing open code and datasets can help make implementation faster. In the worst case, if none of the existing models performs well on an open dataset, you now at least know that this project will require significant modeling and/or data collection work.

If you have found an existing model that solves a similar task and managed to train it on the dataset it was originally trained on, all that is left is to adapt it to your domain. To do so, I recommend going through the following successive steps:

1. Find a similar open source model, ideally paired with a dataset it was trained on, and attempt to reproduce the training results yourself.

2. Once you have reproduced the results, find a dataset that is closer to your use case, and attempt to train the previous model on that dataset.

3. Once you have integrated the dataset to the training code, it is time to judge how your model is doing using the metrics you defined and start iterating.

We'll explore the pitfalls of each of these steps and how to overcome them starting in Part II. For now, let's go back to the case study and review the process we just described.

ML Editor Planning

Let's examine common writing advice and search for candidate datasets and models for the ML editor.

Initial Plan for an Editor

We should start by implementing heuristics based on common writing guidelines. We'll gather these rules by searching existing guides for writing and editing, like those described in "The Simplest Approach: Being the Algorithm" on page 17.

Our perfect dataset would consist of questions and their associated quality. First, we should quickly find a similar dataset that is easier to acquire. Based on observed performance on this dataset, we will then expand and deepen our search if needed.

Social media posts and online forums are good examples of text associated with a quality metric. Since most of these metrics exist to favor useful content, they often include quality metrics such as "likes" or "upvotes."

Stack Exchange (*https://stackexchange.com/*), a network of Q&A communities, is a popular site for questions and answers. There's also an entire anonymized data dump of Stack Exchange on the Internet Archive (*https://oreil.ly/NR6iQ*), one of the data sources we mentioned earlier. This is a great dataset to start with.

We can build an initial model by using Stack Exchange questions and trying to predict a question's upvotes score from its content. We will also use this opportunity to look through the dataset and label it, trying to find patterns.

The model we want to build attempts to classify text quality accurately, to then provide writing recommendations. Many open source models exist for text classification; check out this popular Python ML library scikit-learn tutorial (*https://oreil.ly/y6Qdp*) on the topic.

Once we have a working classifier, we will cover how to leverage it to make recommendations in Chapter 7.

Now that we have a potential initial dataset, let's transition to models and decide what we should start with.

Always Start with a Simple Model

An important takeaway of this chapter is that the purpose of building an initial model and dataset is to produce informative results that will guide further modeling and data gathering work toward a more useful product.

By starting with a simple model and extracting trends of what makes a Stack Overflow question successful, we can quickly measure performance and iterate on it.

The opposite approach of trying to build a perfect model from scratch does not work in practice. This is because ML is an iterative process where the fastest way to make progress is to see how a model fails. The faster your model fails, the more progress you will make. We will dive into this iterative process in much more detail in Part III.

We should keep caveats of each approach in mind, however. For example, the engagement that a question receives depends on many more factors than just the quality of its formulation. The context of the post, the community it was posted in, the popularity of the poster, the time at which it was posted, and many other details that the initial model will ignore also matter very much. To take such factors into account, we will restrict our dataset to a subset of communities. Our first model will ignore all metadata related to a post, but we will consider incorporating it if it seems necessary.

As such, our model uses what is often referred to as a *weak label*, one that is only slightly correlated with the desired output. As we analyze how the model performs, we will determine whether this label contains enough information for it to be useful.

We have a starting point, and we can now decide how we will progress. Making regular progress in ML can often seem hard due to the unpredictable aspect of modeling. It is hard to know ahead of time to which extent a given modeling approach will succeed. Because of this, I'd like to share a few tips to make steady progress.

To Make Regular Progress: Start Simple

It is worth repeating that much of the challenge in ML is similar to one of the biggest challenges in software—resisting the urge to build pieces that are not needed yet. Many ML projects fail because they rely on an initial data acquisition and model building plan and do not regularly evaluate and update this plan. Because of the stochastic nature of ML, it is extremely hard to predict how far a given dataset or model will get us.

For that reason, it is *vital* to start with the simplest model that could address your requirements, build an end-to-end prototype including this model, and judge its performance not simply in terms of optimization metrics but in terms of your product goal.

Start with a Simple Pipeline

In the vast majority of cases, looking at the performance of a simple model on an initial dataset is the best way to decide what task should be tackled next. The goal is then to repeat this approach for each of the following steps, making small incremental improvements that are easy to track, rather than attempting to build the perfect model in one go.

To do this, we will need to build a pipeline that can take data in and return results. For most ML problems, there are actually two separate pipelines to consider.

Training

For your model to be able to make accurate predictions, you first need to train it.

A training pipeline ingests all of the labeled data you would like to train on (for some tasks, datasets can be so large that they cannot fit on a single machine) and passes it to a model. It then trains said model on the dataset until it reaches satisfactory performance. Most often, a training pipeline is used to train multiple models and compare their performance on a held-out validation set.

Inference

This is your pipeline in production. It serves the results of a trained model to your user.

At a high level, an inference pipeline starts by accepting input data and preprocessing it. The preprocessing phase usually consists of multiple steps. Most commonly, these steps will include cleaning and validating the input, generating features a model needs, and formatting the data to a numerical representation appropriate for an ML model. Pipelines in more complex systems also often need to fetch additional information the model needs such as user features stored in a database, for example. The pipeline then runs the example through the model, applies any postprocessing logic, and returns a result.

Figure 2-4 shows a flowchart of a typical inference and training pipeline. Ideally, the cleaning and preprocessing steps should be the same for both training and inference pipelines to ensure that a trained model receives data with the same format and characteristics at inference time.

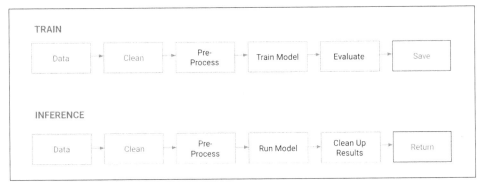

Figure 2-4. Training and inference pipelines are complementary

Pipelines for different models will be built with different concerns in mind, but generally, the high-level infrastructure remains relatively stable. This is why it is valuable to start by building both your training and inference pipeline end-to-end to quickly evaluate the impact bottleneck Monica Rogati mentioned in "Monica Rogati: How to Choose and Prioritize ML Projects" on page 20.

Most pipelines have a similar high-level structure, but because of differences in the structure of datasets, the functions themselves often have nothing in common. Let's illustrate this by looking at the pipeline for the editor.

Pipeline for the ML Editor

For the editor, we will be building both training and inference pipelines using Python, which is a common language of choice in ML. The goal in this first prototype is to build an end-to-end pipeline without being too concerned with its perfection.

As it should be done in any work that takes time, we can, and *will*, revisit parts of it to improve them. For training, we will write a pretty standard pipeline, one broadly applicable to many ML problems and which has a few functions, mainly ones that:

- Load records of data.
- Clean data by removing incomplete records and input missing values when necessary.
- Preprocess and format data in a way that can be understood by a model.
- Remove a set of data that will not be trained on but used to validate model results (a validation set).
- Train a model on a given subset of data and return a trained model and summary statistics.

For inference, we will leverage some functions from the training pipeline, as well as writing a few custom ones. Ideally, we would need functions that:

- Load a trained model and keep it in memory (to provide faster results)
- Will preprocess (same as training)
- Gather any relevant outside information
- Will pass one example through a model (an inference function)
- Will postprocess, to clean up results before serving them to users

It is often easiest to visualize a pipeline as a flowchart, such as the one depicted for Figure 2-5.

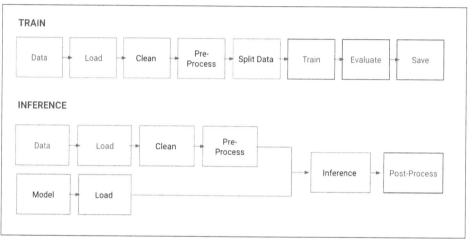

Figure 2-5. Pipelines for the editor

In addition, we will write various analysis and exploration functions to help us diagnose problems, such as:

- A function that visualizes examples the model performs the best and worst on
- Functions to explore data
- A function to explore model results

Many pipelines contain steps that validate inputs to the model and check its final outputs. Such checks help with debugging, as you'll see in Chapter 10, and help guarantee a standard of quality for an application by catching any poor results before displaying them to a user.

Remember that when using ML, the outputs of models on unseen data can often be unpredictable and will not always be satisfactory. For this reason, it is important to acknowledge that models will not always work and to architect systems around this potential for mistakes.

Conclusion

We have now seen how to define core metrics that allow us to compare entirely different models and understand the trade-offs between each of them. We covered resources and methods to use to speed up the building process of your first few pipelines. We then outlined an overview of what we'll need to build for each pipeline to get a first set of results.

We now have an idea framed as an ML problem, a way to measure progress, and an initial plan. It is time to dive into the implementation.

In Part II, we will dive into how to build a first pipeline and explore and visualize an initial dataset.

Build a Working Pipeline

Since researching, training, and evaluating models is a time-consuming process, going in the wrong direction can be very costly in ML. This is why this book focuses on reducing risk and identifying the highest priority to work on.

While Part I focused on planning in order to maximize our speed and chances of success, this chapter will dive into implementation. As Figure II-1 shows, in ML like in much of software engineering, you should get to a minimum viable product (MVP) as soon as possible. This section will cover just that: the quickest way to get a pipeline in place and evaluating it.

Improving said model will be the focus of Part III of this book.

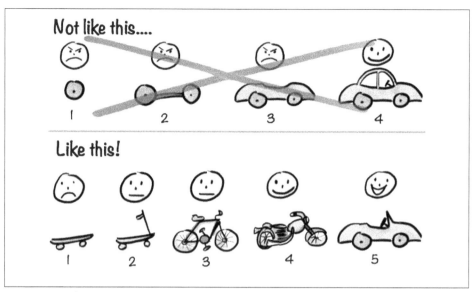

Figure II-1. The right way to build your first pipeline (reproduced with permission from Henrik Kniberg)

We will build our initial model in two steps:

Chapter 3

In this chapter, we will build the structure and scaffolding of our application. This will involve building a pipeline to take user input and return suggestions, and a separate pipeline to train our models before we use them.

Chapter 4

In this chapter, we will focus on gathering and inspecting an initial dataset. The goal here is to quickly identify patterns in our data and predict which of these patterns will be predictive and useful for our model.

## CHAPTER 3

Build Your First End-to-End Pipeline

In Part I, we started by covering how to go from product requirements to candidate modeling approaches. Then, we moved on to the planning stage and described how to find relevant resources and leverage them to make an initial plan of what to build. Finally, we discussed how building an initial prototype of a functioning system was the best way to make progress. This is what we will cover in this chapter.

This first iteration will be lackluster by design. Its goal is to allow us to have all the pieces of a pipeline in place so that we can prioritize which ones to improve next. Having a full prototype is the easiest way to identify the impact bottleneck that Monica Rogati described in "Monica Rogati: How to Choose and Prioritize ML Projects" on page 20.

Let's start by building the simplest pipeline that could produce predictions from an input.

The Simplest Scaffolding

In "Start with a Simple Pipeline" on page 38, we described how most ML models consist of two pipelines, training and inference. Training allows us to generate a high-quality model, and inference is about serving results to users. See "Start with a Simple Pipeline" on page 38 for more about the difference between training and inference.

For the first prototype of an application, we will focus on being able to deliver results to users. This means that out of the two pipelines we described in Chapter 2, we will start with the inference pipeline. This will allow us to quickly examine how users may interact with the output of a model, therefore gathering useful information to make training a model easier.

If we are only focusing on inference, we will ignore training for now. And since we are not training a model, we can instead write some simple rules. Writing such rules or heuristics is often a great way to get started. It is the quickest way to build a prototype and allows us to see a simplified version of the full application right away.

While this may seem superfluous if we are aiming to implement an ML solution anyway (as we will later in the book), it is a critical forcing function to make us confront our problem and devise an initial set of hypotheses about how best to solve it.

Building, validating, and updating hypotheses about the best way to model data are core parts of the iterative model building process, which starts before we even build our first model!

Here are a couple of examples of great heuristics from projects I have seen used by Fellows I mentored at Insight Data Science.

- *Code quality estimation:* When building a model aiming to predict whether a coder performed well on HackerRank (a competitive coding website) from a sample of code, Daniel started by counting the number of open and closed parentheses, brackets, and curly braces.

  In the majority of proper working code, the counts of opening and closing brackets match, so this rule proved to be quite a strong baseline. Furthermore, it gave him the intuition to focus his modeling on using an abstract syntax tree (*https:// oreil.ly/L0ZFk*) to capture even more structural information about code.

- *Tree counting:* When trying to count trees in a city from satellite imagery, after looking at some data, Mike started by devising a rule estimating tree density based on counting the proportion of green pixels in a given image.

  It turns out that this approach worked for trees that were spread apart but failed when it came to groves of trees. Again, this helped define the next modeling steps, which focused on building a pipeline that can handle densely grouped trees.

The vast majority of ML projects should start with a similar heuristic. The key is to remember to devise it based on expert knowledge and data exploration and to use it to confirm initial assumptions and speed up iteration.

Once you have a heuristic, it is time to create a pipeline that can gather input, preprocess it, apply your rules to it, and serve results. This could be as simple as a Python script you could call from the terminal or a web application that gathers a user's camera feed to then serve live results.

The point here is to do for your product the same thing we did for your ML approach, simplify it as much as possible, and build it so you have a simple functional version. This is often referred to as an MVP (minimum viable product) and is a battle-tested method for getting useful results as fast as possible.

Prototype of an ML Editor

For our ML editor, we will leverage common editing recommendations to craft a few rules about what makes for good or bad questions and display the results of those rules to users.

For a minimal version of our project that takes user input from the command line and returns suggestions, we only need to write four functions, shown here:

```
input_text = parse_arguments()
processed = clean_input(input_text)
tokenized_sentences = preprocess_input(processed)
suggestions = get_suggestions(tokenized_sentences)
```

Let's dive into each of them! We will keep the argument parser simple and start with taking a string of text from the user, with no options. You can find the source code for the example and all other code examples in this book's GitHub repository (*https:// oreil.ly/ml-powered-applications*).

Parse and Clean Data

First, we simply parse incoming data coming from the command line. This is relatively straightforward to write in Python.

```
def parse_arguments():
    """

    :return: The text to be edited
    """
    parser = argparse.ArgumentParser(
        description="Receive text to be edited"
    )
    parser.add_argument(
        'text',
        metavar='input text',
        type=str
    )
    args = parser.parse_args()
    return args.text
```

Whenever a model runs on user input, you should start by validating and verifying it! In our case, users will type in data, so we will make sure that their input contains characters we can parse. To clean our input, we will remove non-ASCII characters.

This shouldn't restrict our users' creativity too much and allow us to make reasonable assumptions about what is in the text.

```python
def clean_input(text):
    """

    :param text: User input text
    :return: Sanitized text, without non ascii characters
    """
    # To keep things simple at the start, let's only keep ASCII characters
    return str(text.encode().decode('ascii', errors='ignore'))
```

Now, we need to preprocess our input and provide recommendations. To get us started, we will lean on some of the existing research about classifying text we mentioned in "The Simplest Approach: Being the Algorithm" on page 17. This will involve counting words such as "told" and "said" and computing summary statistics of syllables, words, and sentences to estimate sentence complexity.

To compute word-level statistics, we need to be able to identify words from sentences. In the world of natural language processing, this is known as *tokenization*.

Tokenizing Text

Tokenization is not straightforward, and most simple methods you can think of, such as splitting our input into words based on spaces or periods, will fail on realistic text due to the diversity of ways words can be separated. Consider this sentence, provided as an example by Stanford's NLP class (*https://oreil.ly/vdrZW*), for example:

"Mr. O'Neill thinks that the boys' stories about Chile's capital aren't amusing."

Most simple methods will fail on this sentence due to the presence of periods and apostrophes that carry various meanings. Instead of building our own tokenizer, we will leverage nltk (*https://www.nltk.org/*), a popular open source library, which allows us to do this in two easy steps, as follows:

```python
def preprocess_input(text):
    """

    :param text: Sanitized text
    :return: Text ready to be fed to analysis, by having sentences and
    words tokenized
    """
    sentences = nltk.sent_tokenize(text)
    tokens = [nltk.word_tokenize(sentence) for sentence in sentences]
    return tokens
```

Once our output is preprocessed, we can use it to generate features that will help judge the quality of a question.

Generating Features

The last step is to write a few rules we could use to give advice to our users. For this simple prototype, we will start by computing the frequency of a few common verbs and connectors and then count adverb usage and determine the Flesch readability score (*https://oreil.ly/iKhmk*). We will then return a report of these metrics to our users:

```python
def get_suggestions(sentence_list):
    """
    Returns a string containing our suggestions
    :param sentence_list: a list of sentences, each being a list of words
    :return: suggestions to improve the input
    """
    told_said_usage = sum(
        (count_word_usage(tokens, ["told", "said"]) for tokens in sentence_list)
    )
    but_and_usage = sum(
        (count_word_usage(tokens, ["but", "and"]) for tokens in sentence_list)
    )
    wh_adverbs_usage = sum(
        (
            count_word_usage(
                tokens,
                [
                    "when",
                    "where",
                    "why",
                    "whence",
                    "whereby",
                    "wherein",
                    "whereupon",
                ],
            )
            for tokens in sentence_list
        )
    )
    result_str = ""
    adverb_usage = "Adverb usage: %s told/said, %s but/and, %s wh adverbs" % (
        told_said_usage,
        but_and_usage,
        wh_adverbs_usage,
    )
    result_str += adverb_usage
    average_word_length = compute_total_average_word_length(sentence_list)
    unique_words_fraction = compute_total_unique_words_fraction(sentence_list)

    word_stats = "Average word length %.2f, fraction of unique words %.2f" % (
        average_word_length,
        unique_words_fraction,
    )
    # Using HTML break to later display on a webapp
```

```
result_str += "<br/>"
result_str += word_stats

number_of_syllables = count_total_syllables(sentence_list)
number_of_words = count_total_words(sentence_list)
number_of_sentences = len(sentence_list)

syllable_counts = "%d syllables, %d words, %d sentences" % (
    number_of_syllables,
    number_of_words,
    number_of_sentences,
)
result_str += "<br/>"
result_str += syllable_counts

flesch_score = compute_flesch_reading_ease(
    number_of_syllables, number_of_words, number_of_sentences
)

flesch = "%d syllables, %.2f flesch score: %s" % (
    number_of_syllables,
    flesch_score,
    get_reading_level_from_flesch(flesch_score),
)

result_str += "<br/>"
result_str += flesch

return result_str
```

Voilà, we can now call our application from the command line and see its results live. It is not very useful yet, but we have a starting point we can test and iterate from, which we'll do next.

Test Your Workflow

Now that we've built this prototype, we can test our assumptions about the way we've framed our problem and how useful our proposed solution is. In this section, we will take a look both at the objective quality of our initial rules and examine whether we are presenting our output in a useful manner.

As Monica Rogati shared earlier, "Frequently, your product is dead even if your model is successful." If the method we have chosen excels at measuring question quality but our product does not provide any advice to users to improve their writing, our product will not be useful despite the quality of our method. Looking at our complete pipeline, let's evaluate both the usefulness of the current user experience and the results of our handcrafted model.

User Experience

Let's first examine how satisfying our product is to use, independently of the quality of our model. In other words, if we imagine that we will eventually get a model that performs well enough, is this the most useful way to present results to our users?

If we are building a tree census, for example, we may want to present our results as a summary of a long-running analysis of an entire city. We may want to include the number of reported trees, as well as broken-down statistics per neighborhood, and a measure of the error on a gold standard test set.

In other words, we would want to make sure that the results we present are useful (or will be if we improve our model). On the flip side, of course, we'd also like our model to perform well. That is the next aspect we'll evaluate.

Modeling Results

We mentioned the value of focusing on the right metric in "Measuring Success" on page 23. Having a working prototype early on will allow us to identify and iterate on our chosen metrics to make sure they represent product success.

As an example, if we were building a system to help users search for rental cars nearby, we may use a metric such as discounted cumulative gain (DCG). DCG measures ranking quality by outputting a score that is highest when the most relevant items are returned earlier than others (see the Wikipedia article on DCG (*https:// oreil.ly/b_8Xq*) for more information about ranking metrics). When initially building our tool, we may have assumed that we wanted at least one useful suggestion to appear in our first five results. We thus used DCG at 5 to score our model. However, when having users try the tool, we may notice that users only ever consider the first three results displayed. In that case, we should change our metric of success from DCG at 5 to 3.

The goal of considering both user experience and model performance is to make sure we are working on the most impactful aspect. If your user experience is poor, improving your model is not helpful. In fact, you may realize you would be better served with an entirely different model! Let's look at two examples.

Finding the impact bottleneck

The goal of looking both at modeling results and at the current presentation of the product is to identify which challenge to tackle next. Most of the time, this will mean iterating on the way we present results to our users (which could mean changing the way we train our models) or improving model performance by identifying key failure points.

While we will dive into error analysis more in Part III, we should identify failure modes and appropriate ways to resolve them. It is important to determine whether the most impactful task to work on is in the modeling or product domain, as they each require different remediations. Let's see an example of each:

On the product side

Let's say you have built a model that looks at images of research papers and predicts whether they will be accepted to top conferences (see Jia-Bin Huang's paper "Deep Paper Gestalt," (https://oreil.ly/RRfIN) which tackles this issue). However, you've noticed that returning only a probability of rejection to a user is not the most satisfying of outputs. In this case, improving your model would *not* be helpful. It would make sense to focus on extracting advice from the model so that we can help our users improve their papers and increase their chances of being accepted.

On the model side

You've built a credit scoring model and are noticing that with all other factors being equal, it assigns higher risks of defaulting to a certain ethnic group. This is likely due to a bias in the training data you have been using, so you should gather more representative data and build a new cleaning and augmentation pipeline to attempt to address this. In this case, regardless of the manner in which you present results, *the model needs to be fixed*. Examples like this are common and a reason why you should always dive deeper than an aggregate metric and look at the impact of your model on different slices of your data. This is what we will do in Chapter 5.

To illustrate this further, let's go through this exercise for our ML Editor.

ML Editor Prototype Evaluation

Let's see how our initial pipeline fares both in terms of user experience and model performance. Let's start by throwing in a few inputs to our application. We will start by testing a simple question, a convoluted question, and a full paragraph.

Since we are using a reading ease score, we would ideally like our workflow to return a high score for the simple sentence, a low score for the convoluted one, and suggestions for improving our paragraph. Let's actually run a few examples through our prototype.

Simple question:

```
$ python ml_editor.py  "Is this workflow any good?"
Adverb usage: 0 told/said, 0 but/and, 0 wh adverbs
Average word length 3.67, fraction of unique words 1.00
6 syllables, 5 words, 1 sentences
6 syllables, 100.26 flesch score: Very easy to read
```

Convoluted question:

```
$ python ml_editor.py  "Here is a needlessly obscure question, that"\
"does not provide clearly which information it would"\
"like to acquire, does it?"

Adverb usage: 0 told/said, 0 but/and, 0 wh adverbs
Average word length 4.86, fraction of unique words 0.90
30 syllables, 18 words, 1 sentences
30 syllables, 47.58 flesch score: Difficult to read
```

Entire paragraph (that you'll recognize from earlier):

```
$ python ml_editor.py "Ideally, we would like our workflow to return a positive"\
" score for the simple sentence, a negative score for the convoluted one, and "\
"suggestions for improving our paragraph. Is that the case already?"
Adverb usage: 0 told/said, 1 but/and, 0 wh adverbs
Average word length 4.03, fraction of unique words 0.76
52 syllables, 33 words, 2 sentences
52 syllables, 56.79 flesch score: Fairly difficult to read
```

Let's examine these results using both of the aspects we've just defined.

Model

It is unclear whether our results align well with what we would consider quality writing. The convoluted sentence and the entire paragraph receive a similar readability score. Now, I will be the first to admit that my prose can sometimes be difficult to read, but the earlier paragraph is more comprehensible than the convoluted sentence we tested before it.

The attributes we are extracting from the text are not necessarily the most correlated with "good writing." This is usually due to not having defined success clearly enough: given two questions, how can we say one is better than the other? When we build our dataset in the next chapter, we will define this more clearly.

As expected, we have some modeling work to do, but are we even presenting results in a useful manner?

User Experience

From the results shown earlier, two issues are immediately apparent. The information we return is both overwhelming and irrelevant. The goal of our product is to provide actionable recommendations to our users. The features and readability score are a quality metric but will not help a user decide how to improve their submission. We may want to boil down our recommendations to a single score, along with actionable recommendations to improve it.

For example, we could suggest general changes such as using fewer adverbs, or work at a more granular level by suggesting word- and sentence-level changes. Ideally, we could present results by highlighting or underlining the parts of the input that require users' attention. I've added a mock-up of how this could look in Figure 3-1.

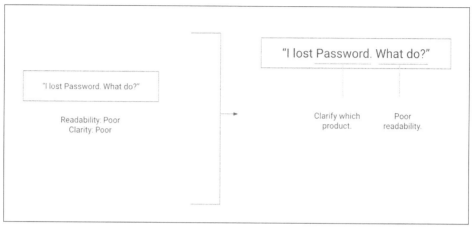

Figure 3-1. More actionable writing suggestions

Even if we were not able to directly highlight recommendations in the input string, our product could benefit from providing recommendations similar to the ones on the right side of Figure 3-1, which are more actionable than a list of scores.

Conclusion

We have built an initial inference prototype and used it to evaluate the quality of our heuristics and the workflow of our product. This allowed us to narrow down our performance criteria and iterate on the way we would like to present results to our users.

For the ML Editor, we've learned that we should both focus on providing a better user experience by providing actionable recommendations and improve our modeling approach by looking at data to more clearly define what makes for a good question.

In the first three chapters, we've used our product goals to define which initial approach to take, explored existing resources to make a plan for our approach, and built an initial prototype to validate our plan and assumptions.

Now, it is time to dive into what is often the most overlooked part of an ML project— exploring our dataset. In Chapter 4, we will see how to gather an initial dataset, assess its quality, and iteratively label subsets of it to help guide our feature generation and modeling decisions.

## CHAPTER 4

Acquire an Initial Dataset

Once you have a plan to solve your product needs and have built an initial prototype to validate that your proposed workflow and model are sound, it is time to take a deeper dive into your dataset. We will use what we find to inform our modeling decisions. Oftentimes, understanding your data well leads to the biggest performance improvements.

In this chapter, we will start by looking at ways to efficiently judge the quality of a dataset. Then, we will cover ways to vectorize your data and how to use said vectorized representation to label and inspect a dataset more efficiently. Finally, we'll cover how this inspection should guide feature generation strategies.

Let's start by discovering a dataset and judging its quality.

Iterate on Datasets

The fastest way to build an ML product is to rapidly build, evaluate, and iterate on models. Datasets themselves are a core part of that success of models. This is why data gathering, preparation, and labeling should be seen as an *iterative process*, just like modeling. Start with a simple dataset that you can gather immediately, and be open to improving it based on what you learn.

This iterative approach to data can seem confusing at first. In ML research, performance is often reported on standard datasets that the community uses as benchmarks and are thus immutable. In traditional software engineering, we write deterministic rules for our programs, so we treat data as something to receive, process, and store.

ML engineering combines engineering and ML in order to build products. Our dataset is thus just another tool to allow us to build products. In ML engineering, choosing an initial dataset, regularly updating it, and augmenting it is often the *majority of the work.* This difference in workflow between research and industry is illustrated in Figure 4-1.

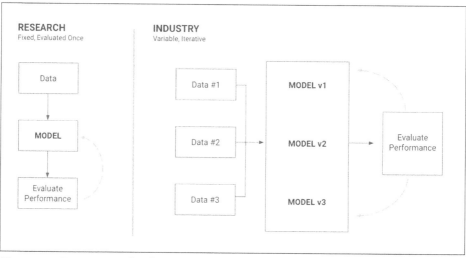

Figure 4-1. Datasets are fixed in research, but part of the product in industry

Treating data as part of your product that you can (and should) iterate on, change, and improve is often a big paradigm shift for newcomers to the industry. Once you get used to it, however, data will become your best source of inspiration to develop new models and the first place you look for answers when things go wrong.

Do Data Science

I've seen the process of curating a dataset be the main roadblock to building ML products more times than I can count. This is partly because of the relative lack of education on the topic (most online courses provide the dataset and focus on the models), which leads to many practitioners fearing this part of the work.

It is easy to think of working with data as a chore to tackle before playing with fun models, but models only serve as a way to extract trends and patterns from existing data. Making sure that the data we use exhibits patterns that are predictive enough for a model to leverage (and checking whether it contains clear bias) is thus a fundamental part of the work of a data scientist (in fact, you may have noticed the name of the role is not model scientist).

This chapter will focus on this process, from gathering an initial dataset to inspecting and validating its applicability for ML. Let's start with exploring a dataset efficiently to judge its quality.

Explore Your First Dataset

So how do we go about exploring an initial dataset? The first step of course is to gather a dataset. This is where I see practitioners get stuck the most often as they search for a perfect dataset. Remember, our goal is to get a simple dataset to extract preliminary results from. As with other things in ML, start simple, and build from there.

Be Efficient, Start Small

For most ML problems, more data can lead to a better model, but this does not mean that you should start with the largest possible dataset. When starting on a project, a small dataset allows you to easily inspect and understand your data and how to model it better. You should aim for an initial dataset that is easy to work with. Only once you've settled on a strategy does it make sense to scale it up to a larger size.

If you are working at a company with terabytes of data stored in a cluster, you can start by extracting a uniformly sampled subset that fits in memory on your local machine. If you would like to start working on a side project trying to identify the brands of cars that drive in front of your house, for example, start with a few dozens of images of cars on streets.

Once you have seen how your initial model performs and where it struggles, you will be able to iterate on your dataset in an informed manner!

You can find many existing datasets online on platforms such as Kaggle (*https://www.kaggle.com/*) or Reddit (*https://www.reddit.com/r/datasets*) or gather a few examples yourself, either by scraping the web, leveraging large open datasets such as found on the Common Crawl site (*https://commoncrawl.org*), or generating data! For more information, see "Open data" on page 33.

Gathering and analyzing data is not only necessary, it will speed you up, especially early on in a project's development. Looking at your dataset and learning about its features is the easiest way to come up with a good modeling and feature generation pipeline.

Most practitioners overestimate the impact of working on the model and underestimate the value of working on the data, so I recommend always making an effort to correct this trend and bias yourself toward looking at data.

When examining data, it is good to identify trends in an exploratory fashion, but you shouldn't stop there. If your aim is to build ML products, you should ask yourself what the best way to leverage these trends in an automated fashion is. How can these trends help you power an automated product?

Insights Versus Products

Once you have a dataset, it is time to dive into it and explore its content. As we do so, let's keep in mind the distinction between data exploration for analysis purposes and data exploration for product building purposes. While both aim to extract and understand trends in data, the former concerns itself with creating insights from trends (learning that most fraudulent logins to a website happen on Thursdays and are from the Seattle area, for example), while the latter is about using trends to build features (using the time of a login attempt and its IP address to build a service that prevents fraudulent accounts logins).

While the difference may seem subtle, it leads to an extra layer of complexity in the product building case. We need to have confidence that the patterns we see will apply to data we receive in the future and quantify the differences between the data we are training on and the data we expect to receive in production.

For fraud prediction, noticing a seasonality aspect to fraudulent logins is the first step. We should then use this observed seasonal trend to estimate how often we need to train our models on recently gathered data. We will dive into more examples as we explore our data more deeply later in this chapter.

Before noticing predictive trends, we should start by examining quality. If our chosen dataset does not meet quality standards, we should improve it before moving on to modeling.

A Data Quality Rubric

In this section, we will cover some aspects to examine when first working with a new dataset. Each dataset comes with its own biases and oddities, which require different tools to be understood, so writing a comprehensive rubric covering anything you may want to look for in a dataset is beyond the scope of this book. Yet, there are a few categories that are valuable to pay attention to when first approaching a dataset. Let's start with formatting.

Data format

Is the dataset already formatted in such a way that you have clear inputs and outputs, or does it require additional preprocessing and labeling?

When building a model that attempts to predict whether a user will click on an ad, for example, a common dataset will consist of a historical log of all clicks for a given time period. You would need to transform this dataset so that it contains multiple instances of an ad being presented to a user and whether the user clicked. You'd also want to include any features of the user or the ad that you think your model could leverage.

If you are given a dataset that has already been processed or aggregated for you, you should validate that you understand the way in which the data was processed. If one of the columns you were given contains an average conversion rate, for example, can you calculate this rate yourself and verify that it matches with the provided value?

In some cases, you will not have access to the required information to reproduce and validate preprocessing steps. In those cases, looking at the quality of the data will help you determine which features of it you trust and which ones would be best left ignored.

Data quality

Examining the quality of a dataset is crucial before you start modeling it. If you know that half of the values for a crucial feature are missing, you won't spend hours debugging a model to try to understand why it isn't performing well.

There are many ways in which data can be of poor quality. It can be missing, it can be imprecise, or it can even be corrupted. Getting an accurate picture of its quality will not only allow you to estimate which level of performance is reasonable, it will make it easier to select potential features and models to use.

If you are working with logs of user activity to predict usage of an online product, can you estimate how many logged events are missing? For the events you do have, how many contain only a subset of information about the user?

If you are working on natural language text, how would you rate the quality of the text? For example, are there many incomprehensible characters? Is the spelling very erroneous or inconsistent?

If you are working on images, are they clear enough that you could perform the task yourself? If it is hard for you to detect an object in an image, do you think your model will struggle to do so?

In general, which proportion of your data seems noisy or incorrect? How many inputs are hard for you to interpret or understand? If the data has labels, do you tend to agree with them, or do you often find yourself questioning their accuracy?

I've worked on a few projects aiming to extract information from satellite imagery, for example. In the best cases, these projects have access to a dataset of images with corresponding annotations denoting objects of interest such as fields or planes. In some cases, however, these annotations can be inaccurate or even missing. Such errors have a significant impact on any modeling approach, so it is vital to find out about them early. We can work with missing labels by either labeling an initial dataset ourselves or finding a weak label we can use, but we can do so only if we notice the quality *ahead of time.*

After verifying the format and quality of the data, one additional step can help proactively surface issues: examining data quantity and feature distribution.

Data quantity and distribution

Let's estimate whether we have enough data and whether feature values seem within a reasonable range.

How much data do we have? If we have a large dataset, we should select a subset to start our analysis on. On the other hand, if our dataset is too small or some classes are underrepresented, models we train would risk being just as biased as our data. The best way to avoid such bias is to increase the diversity of our data through data gathering and augmentation. The ways in which you measure the quality of your data depend on your dataset, but Table 4-1 covers a few questions to get you started.

Table 4-1. A data quality rubric

Quality	Format	Quantity and distribution
Are any relevant fields ever empty?	How many preprocessing steps does your data require?	How many examples do you have?
Are there potential errors of measurement?	Will you be able to preprocess it in the same way in production?	How many examples per class? Are any absent?

For a practical example, when building a model to automatically categorize customer support emails into different areas of expertise, a data scientist I was working with, Alex Wahl, was given nine distinct categories, with only one example per category. Such a dataset is too small for a model to learn from, so he focused most of his effort on a data generation strategy (*https://oreil.ly/KRn0B*). He used templates of common formulations for each of the nine categories to produce thousands more examples that a model could then learn from. Using this strategy, he managed to get a pipeline to a much higher level of accuracy than he would have had by trying to build a model complex enough to learn from only nine examples.

Let's apply this exploration process to the dataset we chose for our ML editor and estimate its quality!

ML editor data inspection

For our ML editor, we initially settled on using the anonymized Stack Exchange Data Dump (*https://oreil.ly/6jCGY*) as a dataset. Stack Exchange is a network of question-and-answer websites, each focused on a theme such as philosophy or gaming. The data dump contains many archives, one for each of the websites in the Stack Exchange network.

For our initial dataset, we'll choose a website that seems like it would contain broad enough questions to build useful heuristics from. At first glance, the Writing community (*https://writing.stackexchange.com/*) seems like a good fit.

Each website archive is provided as an XML file. We need to build a pipeline to ingest those files and transform them into text we can then extract features from. The following example shows the `Posts.xml` file for *datascience.stackexchange.com*:

```
<?xml version="1.0" encoding="utf-8"?>
<posts>
  <row Id="5" PostTypeId="1" CreationDate="2014-05-13T23:58:30.457"
Score="9" ViewCount="516" Body="&lt;p&gt; &quot;Hello World&quot; example? "
OwnerUserId="5" LastActivityDate="2014-05-14T00:36:31.077"
Title="How can I do simple machine learning without hard-coding behavior?"
Tags="&lt;machine-learning&gt;" AnswerCount="1" CommentCount="1" />
  <row Id="7" PostTypeId="1" AcceptedAnswerId="10" ... />
```

To be able to leverage this data, we will need to be able to load the XML file, decode the HTML tags in the text, and represent questions and associated data in a format that would be easier to analyze such as a pandas DataFrame. The following function does just this. As a reminder, the code for this function, and all other code throughout this book, can be found in this book's GitHub repository (*https://oreil.ly/ml-powered-applications*).

```python
import xml.etree.ElementTree as ElT


def parse_xml_to_csv(path, save_path=None):
    """
    Open .xml posts dump and convert the text to a csv, tokenizing it in the
        process
    :param path: path to the xml document containing posts
    :return: a dataframe of processed text
    """

    # Use python's standard library to parse XML file
    doc = ElT.parse(path)
    root = doc.getroot()

    # Each row is a question
    all_rows = [row.attrib for row in root.findall("row")]

    # Using tdqm to display progress since preprocessing takes time
    for item in tqdm(all_rows):
        # Decode text from HTML
        soup = BeautifulSoup(item["Body"], features="html.parser")
        item["body_text"] = soup.get_text()

    # Create dataframe from our list of dictionaries
    df = pd.DataFrame.from_dict(all_rows)
    if save_path:
```

```
        df.to_csv(save_path)
    return df
```

Even for a relatively small dataset containing only 30,000 questions this process takes more than a minute, so we serialize the processed file back to disk to only have to process it once. To do this, we can simply use panda's `to_csv` function, as shown on the final line of the snippet.

This is generally a recommended practice for any preprocessing required to train a model. Preprocessing code that runs right before the model optimization process can slow down experimentation significantly. As much as possible, always preprocess data ahead of time and serialize it to disk.

Once we have our data in this format, we can examine the aspects we described earlier. The entire exploration process we detail next can be found in the dataset exploration notebook in this book's GitHub repository (*https://oreil.ly/ml-powered-applications*).

To start, we use `df.info()` to display summary information about our DataFrame, as well as any empty values. Here is what it returns:

```
>>>> df.info()

AcceptedAnswerId        4124 non-null float64
AnswerCount             33650 non-null int64
Body                    33650 non-null object
ClosedDate              969 non-null object
CommentCount            33650 non-null int64
CommunityOwnedDate      186 non-null object
CreationDate            33650 non-null object
FavoriteCount           3307 non-null float64
Id                      33650 non-null int64
LastActivityDate        33650 non-null object
LastEditDate            10521 non-null object
LastEditorDisplayName   606 non-null object
LastEditorUserId        9975 non-null float64
OwnerDisplayName        1971 non-null object
OwnerUserId             32117 non-null float64
ParentId                25679 non-null float64
PostTypeId              33650 non-null int64
Score                   33650 non-null int64
Tags                    7971 non-null object
Title                   7971 non-null object
ViewCount               7971 non-null float64
body_text               33650 non-null object
full_text               33650 non-null object
text_len                33650 non-null int64
is_question             33650 non-null bool
```

We can see that we have a little over 31,000 posts, with only about 4,000 of them having an accepted answer. In addition, we can notice that some of the values for Body, which represents the contents of a post, are null, which seems suspicious. We would expect all posts to contain text. Looking at rows with a null Body quickly reveals they belong to a type of post that has no reference in the documentation provided with the dataset, so we remove them.

Let's quickly dive into the format and see if we understand it. Each post has a PostTypeId value of 1 for a question, or 2 for an answer. We would like to see which type of questions receive high scores, as we would like to use a question's score as a weak label for our true label, the quality of a question.

First, let's match questions with the associated answers. The following code selects all questions that have an accepted answer and joins them with the text for said answer. We can then look at the first few rows and validate that the answers do match up with the questions. This will also allow us to quickly look through the text and judge its quality.

```
questions_with_accepted_answers = df[
    df["is_question"] & ~(df["AcceptedAnswerId"].isna())
]
q_and_a = questions_with_accepted_answers.join(
    df[["Text"]], on="AcceptedAnswerId", how="left", rsuffix="_answer"
)

pd.options.display.max_colwidth = 500
q_and_a[["Text", "Text_answer"]][:5]
```

In Table 4-2, we can see that questions and answers do seem to match up and that the text seems mostly correct. We now trust that we can match questions with their associated answers.

Table 4-2. Questions with their associated answers

Id	body_text	body_text_answer
1	I've always wanted to start writing (in a totally amateur way), but whenever I want to start something I instantly get blocked having a lot of questions and doubts.\nAre there some resources on how to start becoming a writer?\nI'm thinking something with tips and easy exercises to get the ball rolling.\n	When I'm thinking about where I learned most how to write, I think that reading was the most important guide to me. This may sound silly, but by reading good written newspaper articles (facts, opinions, scientific articles, and most of all, criticisms of films and music), I learned how others did the job, what works and what doesn't. In my own writing, I try to mimic other people's styles that I liked. Moreover, I learn new things by reading, giving me a broader background that I need when re...
2	What kind of story is better suited for each point of view? Are there advantages or disadvantages inherent to them?\nFor example, writing in the first person you are always following a character, while in the third person you can "jump" between story lines.\n	With a story in first person, you are intending the reader to become much more attached to the main character. Since the reader sees what that character sees and feels what that character feels, the reader will have an emotional investment in that character. Third person does not have this close tie; a reader can become emotionally invested but it will not be as strong as it will be in first person.\nContrarily, you cannot have multiple point characters when you use first person without ex...

Id	body_text	body_text_answer
3	I finished my novel, and everyone I've talked to says I need an agent. How do I find one?\n	Try to find a list of agents who write in your genre, check out their websites! \nFind out if they are accepting new clients. If they aren't, then check out another agent. But if they are, try sending them a few chapters from your story, a brief, and a short cover letter asking them to represent you.\nIn the cover letter mention your previous publication credits. If sent via post, then I suggest you give them a means of reply, whether it be an email or a stamped, addressed envelope.\nAgents...

As one last sanity check, let's look at how many questions received no answer, how many received at least one, and how many had an answer that was accepted.

```
has_accepted_answer = df[df["is_question"] & ~(df["AcceptedAnswerId"].isna())]
no_accepted_answers = df[
    df["is_question"]
    & (df["AcceptedAnswerId"].isna())
    & (df["AnswerCount"] != 0)
]
no_answers = df[
    df["is_question"]
    & (df["AcceptedAnswerId"].isna())
    & (df["AnswerCount"] == 0)
]

print(
    "%s questions with no answers, %s with answers, %s with an accepted answer"
    % (len(no_answers), len(no_accepted_answers), len(has_accepted_answer))
)
```

```
3584 questions with no answers, 5933 with answers, 4964 with an accepted answer.
```

We have a relatively even split between answered and partially answered and unanswered questions. This seems reasonable, so we can feel confident enough to carry on with our exploration.

We understand the format of our data and have enough of it to get started. If you are working on a project and your current dataset is either too small or contains a majority of features that are too hard to interpret, you should gather some more data or try a different dataset entirely.

Our dataset is of sufficient quality to proceed. It is now time to explore it more in depth, with the goal of informing our modeling strategy.

Label to Find Data Trends

Identifying trends in our dataset is about more than just quality. This part of the work is about putting ourselves in the shoes of our model and trying to predict what kind of structure it will pick up on. We will do this by separating data into different clusters (I will explain clustering in "Clustering" on page 80) and trying to extract commonalities in each cluster.

The following is a step-by-step list to do this in practice. We'll start with generating summary statistics of our dataset and then see how to rapidly explore it by leveraging vectorization techniques. With the help of vectorization and clustering, we'll explore our dataset efficiently.

Summary Statistics

When you start looking at a dataset, it is generally a good idea to look at some summary statistics for each of the features you have. This helps you both get a general sense for the features in your dataset and identify any easy way to separate your classes.

Identifying differences in distributions between classes of data early is helpful in ML, because it will either make our modeling task easier or prevent us from overestimating the performance of a model that may just be leveraging one particularly informative feature.

For example, if you are trying to predict whether tweets are expressing a positive or negative opinion, you could start by counting the average number of words in each tweet. You could then plot a histogram of this feature to learn about its distribution.

A histogram would allow you to notice if all positive tweets were shorter than negative ones. This could lead you to add word length as a predictor to make your task easier or on the contrary gather additional data to make sure that your model can learn about the content of the tweets and not just their length.

Let's plot a few summary statistics for our ML editor to illustrate this point.

Summary statistics for ML editor

For our example, we can plot a histogram of the length of questions in our dataset, highlighting the different trends between high- and low-score questions. Here is how we do this using pandas:

```
import matplotlib.pyplot as plt
from matplotlib.patches import Rectangle

"""
df contains questions and their answer counts from writers.stackexchange.com
We draw two histograms:
one for questions with scores under the median score
one for questions with scores over
For both, we remove outliers to make our visualization simpler
"""

high_score = df["Score"] > df["Score"].median()
```

```
# We filter out really long questions
normal_length = df["text_len"] < 2000

ax = df[df["is_question"] & high_score & normal_length]["text_len"].hist(
    bins=60,
    density=True,
    histtype="step",
    color="orange",
    linewidth=3,
    grid=False,
    figsize=(16, 10),
)

df[df["is_question"] & ~high_score & normal_length]["text_len"].hist(
    bins=60,
    density=True,
    histtype="step",
    color="purple",
    linewidth=3,
    grid=False,
)

handles = [
    Rectangle((0, 0), 1, 1, color=c, ec="k") for c in ["orange", "purple"]
]
labels = ["High score", "Low score"]
plt.legend(handles, labels)
ax.set_xlabel("Sentence length (characters)")
ax.set_ylabel("Percentage of sentences")
```

We can see in Figure 4-2 that the distributions are mostly similar, with high-score questions tending to be slightly longer (this trend is especially noticeable around the 800-character mark). This is an indication that question length may be a useful feature for a model to predict a question's score.

We can plot other variables in a similar fashion to identify more potential features. Once we've identified a few features, let's look at our dataset a little more closely so that we can identify more granular trends.

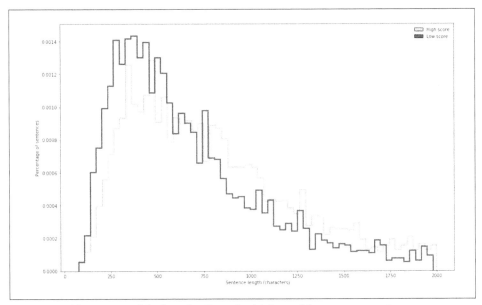

Figure 4-2. Histogram of the length of text for high- and low-score questions

Explore and Label Efficiently

You can only get so far looking at descriptive statistics such as averages and plots such as histograms. To develop an intuition for your data, you should spend some time looking at individual data points. However, going through points in a dataset at random is quite inefficient. In this section, I'll cover how to maximize your efficiency when visualizing individual data points.

Clustering is a useful method to use here. Clustering (*https://oreil.ly/16f7Z*) is the task of grouping a set of objects in such a way that objects in the same group (called a *cluster*) are more similar (in some sense) to each other than to those in other groups (clusters). We will use clustering both for exploring our data and for our model predictions later (see "Dimensionality reduction" on page 78).

Many clustering algorithms group data points by measuring the distance between points and assigning ones that are close to each other to the same cluster. Figure 4-3 shows an example of a clustering algorithm separating a dataset into three different clusters. Clustering is an unsupervised method, and there is often no single correct way to cluster a dataset. In this book, we will use clustering as a way to generate some structure to guide our exploration.

Because clustering relies on calculating the distance between data points, the way we choose to represent our data points numerically has a large impact on which clusters are generated. We will dive into this in the next section, "Vectorizing" on page 69.

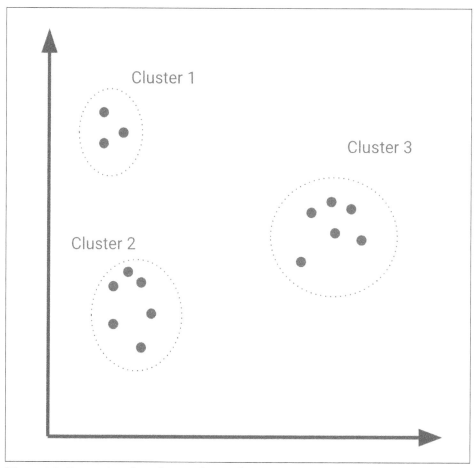

Figure 4-3. Generating three clusters from a dataset

The vast majority of datasets can be separated into clusters based on their features, labels, or a combination of both. Examining each cluster individually and the similarities and differences between clusters is a great way to identify structure in a dataset.

There are multiple things to look out for here:

- How many clusters do you identify in your dataset?
- Do each of these clusters seem different to you? In which way?
- Are any clusters much more dense than others? If so, your model is likely to struggle to perform on the sparser areas. Adding features and data can help alleviate this problem.

- Do all clusters represent data that seems as "hard" to model? If some clusters seem to represent more complex data points, make note of them so you can revisit them when we evaluate our model's performance.

As we mentioned, clustering algorithms work on vectors, so we can't simply pass a set of sentences to a clustering algorithm. To get our data ready to be clustered, we will first need to vectorize it.

Vectorizing

Vectorizing a dataset is the process of going from the raw data to a vector that represents it. Figure 4-4 shows an example of vectorized representations for text and tabular data.

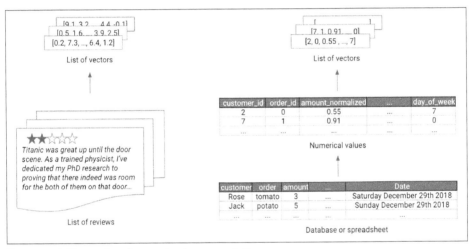

Figure 4-4. Examples of vectorized representations

There are many ways to vectorize data, so we will focus on a few simple methods that work for some of the most common data types, such as tabular data, text, and images.

Tabular data. For tabular data consisting of both categorical and continuous features, a possible vector representation is simply the concatenation of the vector representations of each feature.

Continuous features should be normalized to a common scale so that features with larger scale do not cause smaller features to be completely ignored by models. There are various way to normalize data, but starting by transforming each feature such that its mean is zero and variance one is often a good first step. This is often referred to as a *standard score* (*https://oreil.ly/QTEvI*).

Categorical features such as colors can be converted to a one-hot encoding: a list as long as the number of distinct values of the feature consisting of only zeros and a single one, whose index represents the current value (for example, in a dataset containing four distinct colors, we could encode red as [1, 0, 0, 0] and blue as [0, 0, 1, 0]). You may be curious as to why we wouldn't simply assign each potential value a number, such as 1 for red and 3 for blue. It is because such an encoding scheme would imply an ordering between values (blue is larger than red), which is often incorrect for categorical variables.

A property of one-hot encoding is that the distance between any two given feature values is always one. This often provides a good representation for a model, but in some cases such as days of the week, some values may be more similar than the others (Saturday and Sunday are both in the weekend, so ideally their vectors would be closer together than Wednesday and Sunday, for example). Neural networks have started proving themselves useful at learning such representations (see the paper "Entity Embeddings of Categorical Variables" (*https://arxiv.org/abs/1604.06737*), by C. Guo and F. Berkhahn). These representations have been shown to improve the performance of models using them instead of other encoding schemes.

Finally, more complex features such as dates should be transformed in a few numerical features capturing their salient characteristics.

Let's go through a practical example of vectorization for tabular data. You can find the code for the example in the tabular data vectorization notebook in this book's GitHub repository (*https://oreil.ly/ml-powered-applications*).

Let's say that instead of looking at the content of questions, we want to predict the score a question will get from its tags, number of comments, and creation date. In Table 4-3, you can see an example of what this dataset would look like for the *writers.stackexchange.com* dataset.

Table 4-3. Tabular inputs without any processing

Id	Tags	CommentCount	CreationDate	Score
1	\<resources>\<first-time-author>	7	2010-11-18T20:40:32.857	32
2	\<fiction>\<grammatical-person>\<third-person>	0	2010-11-18T20:42:31.513	20
3	\<publishing>\<novel>\<agent>	1	2010-11-18T20:43:28.903	34
5	\<plot>\<short-story>\<planning>\<brainstorming>	0	2010-11-18T20:43:59.693	28
7	\<fiction>\<genre>\<categories>	1	2010-11-18T20:45:44.067	21

Each question has multiple tags, as well as a date and a number of comments. Let's preprocess each of these. First, we normalize numerical fields:

```
def get_norm(df, col):
    return (df[col] - df[col].mean()) / df[col].std()

tabular_df["NormComment"]= get_norm(tabular_df, "CommentCount")
tabular_df["NormScore"]= get_norm(tabular_df, "Score")
```

Then, we extract relevant information from the date. We could, for example, choose the year, month, day, and hour of posting. Each of these is a numerical value our model can use.

```
# Convert our date to a pandas datetime
tabular_df["date"] = pd.to_datetime(tabular_df["CreationDate"])

# Extract meaningful features from the datetime object
tabular_df["year"] = tabular_df["date"].dt.year
tabular_df["month"] = tabular_df["date"].dt.month
tabular_df["day"] = tabular_df["date"].dt.day
tabular_df["hour"] = tabular_df["date"].dt.hour
```

Our tags are categorical features, with each question potentially being given any number of tags. As we saw earlier, the easiest way to represent categorical inputs is to one-hot encode them, transforming each tag into its own column, with each question having a value of 1 for a given tag feature only if that tag is associated to this question.

Because we have more than three hundred tags in our dataset, here we chose to only create a column for the five most popular ones that are used in more than five hundred questions. We could add every single tag, but because the majority of them appear only once, this would not be helpful to identify patterns.

```
# Select our tags, represented as strings, and transform them into arrays of tags
tags = tabular_df["Tags"]
clean_tags = tags.str.split("><").apply(
    lambda x: [a.strip("<").strip(">") for a in x])

# Use pandas' get_dummies to get dummy values
# select only tags that appear over 500 times
tag_columns = pd.get_dummies(clean_tags.apply(pd.Series).stack()).sum(level=0)
all_tags = tag_columns.astype(bool).sum(axis=0).sort_values(ascending=False)
top_tags = all_tags[all_tags > 500]
top_tag_columns = tag_columns[top_tags.index]

# Add our tags back into our initial DataFrame
final = pd.concat([tabular_df, top_tag_columns], axis=1)

# Keeping only the vectorized features
col_to_keep = ["year", "month", "day", "hour", "NormComment",
               "NormScore"] + list(top_tags.index)
final_features = final[col_to_keep]
```

In Table 4-4, you can see that our data is now fully vectorized, with each row consisting only of numeric values. We can feed this data to a clustering algorithm, or a supervised ML model.

Table 4-4. Vectorized tabular inputs

Id	Year	Month	Day	Hour	Norm-Comment	Norm-Score	Creative writing	Fiction	Style	Char-acters	Tech-nique	Novel	Pub-lishing
1	2010	11	18	20	0.165706	0.140501	0	0	0	0	0	0	0
2	2010	11	18	20	-0.103524	0.077674	0	1	0	0	0	0	0
3	2010	11	18	20	-0.065063	0.150972	0	0	0	0	0	1	1
5	2010	11	18	20	-0.103524	0.119558	0	0	0	0	0	0	0
7	2010	11	18	20	-0.065063	0.082909	0	1	0	0	0	0	0

Vectorization and Data Leakage

You would usually use the same techniques to vectorize data to visualize it and to feed it to a model. There is an important distinction, however. When you vectorize data to feed it to a model, you should vectorize your training data and save the parameters you used to obtain the training vectors. You should then use the same parameters for your validation and test sets.

When normalizing data, for example, you should compute summary statistics such as mean and standard deviation only on your training set (using the same values to normalize your validation data), and during inference in production.

Using both your validation and training data for normalization, or to decide which categories to keep in your one-hot encoding, would cause data leakage, as you would be leveraging information from outside your training set to create training features. This would artificially inflate your model's performance but make it perform worse in production. We will cover this in more detail in "Data leakage" on page 102.

Different types of data call for different vectorization methods. In particular, text data often requires more creative approaches.

Text data. The simplest way to vectorize text is to use a count vector, which is the word equivalent of one-hot encoding. Start by constructing a vocabulary consisting of the list of unique words in your dataset. Associate each word in our vocabulary to an index (from 0 to the size of our vocabulary). You can then represent each sentence or paragraph by a list as long as our vocabulary. For each sentence, the number at each index represents the count of occurrences of the associated word in the given sentence.

This method ignores the order of the words in a sentence and so is referred to as a *bag of words*. Figure 4-5 shows two sentences and their bag-of-words representations. Both sentences are transformed into vectors that contain information about the number of times a word occurs in a sentence, but not the order in which words are present in the sentence.

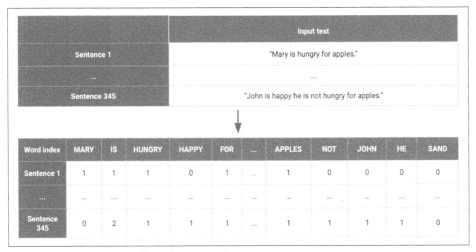

Figure 4-5. Getting bag-of-words vectors from sentences

Using a bag-of-words representation or its normalized version TF-IDF (short for Term Frequency–Inverse Document Frequency) is simple using scikit-learn, as you can see here:

```
# Create an instance of a tfidf vectorizer,
# We could use CountVectorizer for a non normalized version
vectorizer = TfidfVectorizer()

# Fit our vectorizer to questions in our dataset
# Returns an array of vectorized text
bag_of_words = vectorizer.fit_transform(df[df["is_question"]]["Text"])
```

Multiple novel text vectorization methods have been developed over the years, starting in 2013 with Word2Vec (see the paper, "Efficient Estimation of Word Representations in Vector Space," by Mikolov et al.) (*https://oreil.ly/gs-AC*) and more recent approaches such as fastText (see the paper, "Bag of Tricks for Efficient Text Classification," by Joulin et al.) (*https://arxiv.org/abs/1607.01759*). These vectorization techniques produce word vectors that attempt to learn a representation that captures similarities between concepts better than a TF-IDF encoding. They do this by learning which words tend to appear in similar contexts in large bodies of text such as Wikipedia. This approach is based on the distributional hypothesis, which claims that linguistic items with similar distributions have similar meanings.

Concretely, this is done by learning a vector for each word and training a model to predict a missing word in a sentence using the word vectors of words around it. The number of neighboring words to take into account is called the *window size*. In Figure 4-6, you can see a depiction of this task for a window size of two. On the left, the word vectors for the two words before and after the target are fed to a simple model. This simple model and the values of the word vectors are then optimized so that the output matches the word vector of the missing word.

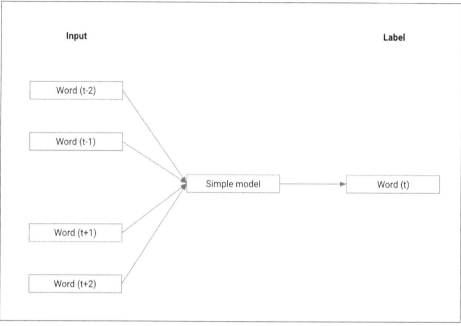

Figure 4-6. Learning word vectors, from the Word2Vec paper "Efficient Estimation of Word Representations in Vector Space" by Mikolov et al. (https://oreil.ly/gs-AC)

Many open source pretrained word vectorizing models exist. Using vectors produced by a model that was pretrained on a large corpus (oftentimes Wikipedia or an archive of news stories) can help our models leverage the semantic meaning of common words better.

For example, the word vectors mentioned in the Joulin et al. fastText (*https://fast text.cc/*) paper are available online in a standalone tool. For a more customized approach, spaCy (*https://spacy.io*) is an NLP toolkit that provides pretrained models for a variety of tasks, as well as easy ways to build your own.

Here is an example of using spaCy to load pretrained word vectors and using them to get a semantically meaningful sentence vector. Under the hood, spaCy retrieves the pretrained value for each word in our dataset (or ignores it if it was not part of its pretraining task) and averages all vectors in a question to get a representation of the question.

```
import spacy

# We load a large model, and disable pipeline unnecessary parts for our task
# This speeds up the vectorization process significantly
```

```
# See https://spacy.io/models/en#en_core_web_lg for details about the model
nlp = spacy.load('en_core_web_lg', disable=["parser", "tagger", "ner",
    "textcat"])

# We then simply get the vector for each of our questions
# By default, the vector returned is the average of all vectors in the sentence
# See https://spacy.io/usage/vectors-similarity for more
spacy_emb = df[df["is_question"]]["Text"].apply(lambda x: nlp(x).vector)
```

To see a comparison of a TF-IDF model with pretrained word embeddings for our dataset, please refer to the vectorizing text notebook in the book's GitHub repository (*https://oreil.ly/ml-powered-applications*).

Since 2018, word vectorization using large language models on even larger datasets has started producing the most accurate results (see the papers "Universal Language Model Fine-Tuning for Text Classification" (*https://arxiv.org/abs/1801.06146*), by J. Howard and S. Ruder, and "BERT: Pre-training of Deep Bidirectional Transformers for Language Understanding" (*https://arxiv.org/abs/1810.04805*), by J. Devlin et al.). These large models, however, do come with the drawback of being slower and more complex than simple word embeddings.

Finally, let's examine vectorization for another commonly used type of data, images.

Image data.   Image data is already vectorized, as an image is nothing more but a multidimensional array of numbers, often referred to in the ML community as tensors (*https://oreil.ly/w7jQi*). Most standard three-channel RGB images, for example, are simply stored as a list of numbers of length equal to the height of the image in pixels, multiplied by its width, multiplied by three (for the red, green, and blue channels). In Figure 4-7, you can see how we can represent an image as a tensor of numbers, representing the intensity of each of the three primary colors.

While we can use this representation as is, we would like our tensors to capture a little more about the semantic meaning of our images. To do this, we can use an approach similar to the one for text and leverage large pretrained neural networks.

Models that have been trained on massive classification datasets such as VGG (see the paper by A. Simonyan and A. Zimmerman, "Very Deep Convolutional Networks for Large-Scale Image Recognition") (*https://oreil.ly/TVHID*) or Inception (see the paper by C. Szegedy et al., "Going Deeper with Convolutions") (*https://oreil.ly/nbetp*) on the ImageNet dataset (*http://www.image-net.org/*) end up learning very expressive representations in order to classify well. These models mostly follow a similar high-level structure. The input is an image that passes through many successive layers of computation, each generating a different representation of said image.

Finally, the penultimate layer is passed to a function that generates classification probabilities for each class. This penultimate layer thus contains a representation of the image that is sufficient to classify which object it contains, which makes it a useful representation for other tasks.

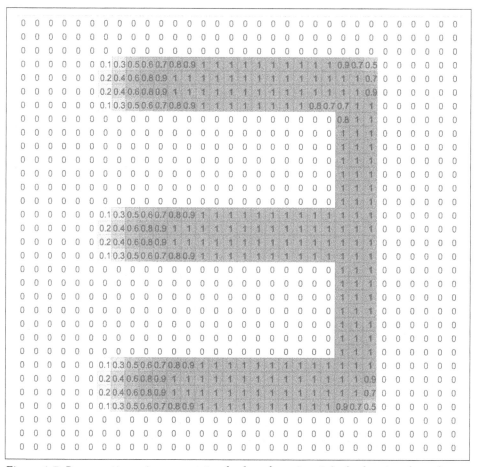

Figure 4-7. Representing a 3 as a matrix of values from 0 to 1 (only showing the red channel)

Extracting this representation layer proves to work extremely well at generating meaningful vectors for images. This requires no custom work other than loading the pretrained model. In Figure 4-8 each rectangle represents a different layer for one of those pretrained models. The most useful representation is highlighted. It is usually located just before the classification layer, since that is the representation that needs to summarize the image best for the classifier to perform well.

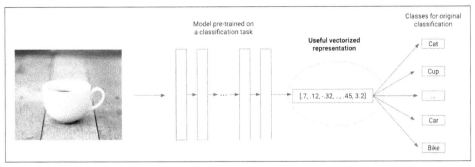

Figure 4-8. Using a pretrained model to vectorize images

Using modern libraries such as Keras makes this task much easier. Here is a function that loads images from a folder and transforms them into semantically meaningful vectors for downstream analysis, using a pretrained network available in Keras:

```python
import numpy as np

from keras.preprocessing import image
from keras.models import Model
from keras.applications.vgg16 import VGG16
from keras.applications.vgg16 import preprocess_input


def generate_features(image_paths):
    """
    Takes in an array of image paths
    Returns pretrained features for each image
    :param image_paths: array of image paths
    :return: array of last-layer activations,
    and mapping from array_index to file_path
    """

    images = np.zeros(shape=(len(image_paths), 224, 224, 3))

    # loading a  pretrained model
    pretrained_vgg16 = VGG16(weights='imagenet', include_top=True)

    # Using only the penultimate layer, to leverage learned features
    model = Model(inputs=pretrained_vgg16.input,
                  outputs=pretrained_vgg16.get_layer('fc2').output)

    # We load all our dataset in memory (works for small datasets)
    for i, f in enumerate(image_paths):
        img = image.load_img(f, target_size=(224, 224))
        x_raw = image.img_to_array(img)
        x_expand = np.expand_dims(x_raw, axis=0)
        images[i, :, :, :] = x_expand

    # Once we've loaded all our images, we pass them to our model
```

```
inputs = preprocess_input(images)
images_features = model.predict(inputs)
return images_features
```

Transfer Learning

Pretrained models are useful to vectorize our data, but they can also sometimes be entirely adapted to our task. Transfer learning is the process of using a model that was previously trained on one dataset or task for a different dataset or task. More than simply reusing the same architecture or pipeline, transfer learning uses the previously learned weights of a trained model as a starting point for a new task.

Transfer learning can in theory work from any task to any other, but it is commonly used to improve performance on smaller datasets, by transferring weights from large datasets such as ImageNet for computer vision or WikiText (*https://oreil.ly/voPkP*) for NLP.

While transfer learning often improves performance, it also may introduce an additional source of unwanted bias. Even if you clean your current dataset carefully, if you use a model that was pretrained on the entirety of Wikipedia, for example, it could carry over the gender bias shown to be present there (see the article "Gender Bias in Neural Natural Language Processing," by K. Lu et al.) (*https://oreil.ly/kPy1l*).

Once you have a vectorized representation, you can cluster it or pass your data to a model, but you can also use it to more efficiently inspect your dataset. By grouping data points with similar representations together, you can more quickly look at trends in your dataset. We'll see how to do this next.

Dimensionality reduction

Having vector representations is necessary for algorithms, but we can also leverage those representations to visualize data directly! This may seem challenging, because the vectors we described are often in more than two dimensions, which makes them challenging to display on a chart. How could we display a 14-dimensional vector?

Geoffrey Hinton, who won a Turing Award for his work in deep learning, acknowledges this problem in his lecture with the following tip: "To deal with hyper-planes in a 14-dimensional space, visualize a 3D space and say *fourteen* to yourself very loudly. Everyone does it." (See slide 16 from G. Hinton et al.'s lecture, "An Overview of the Main Types of Neural Network Architecture" here (*https://oreil.ly/wORb-*).) If this seems hard to you, you'll be excited to hear about dimensionality reduction, which is the technique of representing vectors in fewer dimensions while preserving as much about their structure as possible.

Dimensionality reduction techniques such as t-SNE (see the paper by L. van der Maaten and G. Hinton, PCA (*https://oreil.ly/kXwvH*), "Visualizing Data Using t-SNE") (*https://oreil.ly/x8S2b*), and UMAP (see the paper by L. McInnes et al, "UMAP: Uniform Manifold Approximation and Projection for Dimension Reduction") (*https://oreil.ly/IYrHH*) allow you to project high-dimensional data such as vectors representing sentences, images, or other features on a 2D plane.

These projections are useful to notice patterns in data that you can then investigate. They are approximate representations of the real data, however, so you should validate any hypothesis you make from looking at such a plot by using other methods. If you see clusters of points all belonging to one class that seem to have a feature in common, check that your model is actually leveraging that feature, for example.

To get started, plot your data using a dimensionality reduction technique and color each point by an attribute you are looking to inspect. For classification tasks, start by coloring each point based on its label. For unsupervised tasks, you can color points based on the values of given features you are looking at, for example. This allows you to see whether any regions seem like they will be easy for your model to separate, or trickier.

Here is how to do this easily using UMAP, passing it embeddings we generated in "Vectorizing" on page 69:

```
import umap

# Fit UMAP to our data, and return the transformed data
umap_emb = umap.UMAP().fit_transform(embeddings)

fig = plt.figure(figsize=(16, 10))
color_map = {
    True: '#ff7f0e',
    False:'#1f77b4'
}
plt.scatter(umap_emb[:, 0], umap_emb[:, 1],
            c=[color_map[x] for x in sent_labels],
            s=40, alpha=0.4)
```

As a reminder, we decided to start with using only data from the writers' community of Stack Exchange. The result for this dataset is displayed on Figure 4-9. At first glance, we can see a few regions we should explore, such as the dense region of unanswered questions on the top left. If we can identify which features they have in common, we may discover a useful classification feature.

After data is vectorized and plotted, it is generally a good idea to start systematically identifying groups of similar data points and explore them. We could do this simply by looking at UMAP plots, but we can also leverage clustering.

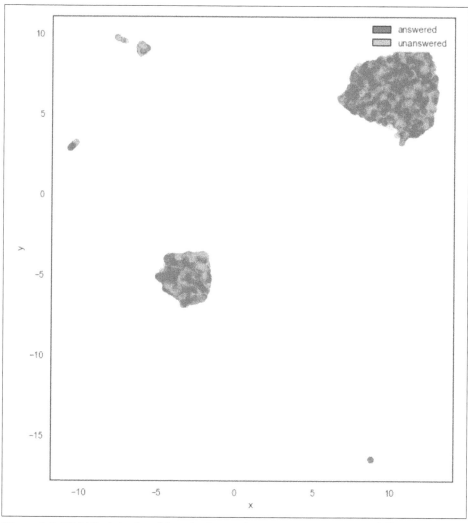

Figure 4-9. UMAP plot colored by whether a given question was successfully answered

Clustering

We mentioned clustering earlier as a method to extract structure from data. Whether you are clustering data to inspect a dataset or using it to analyze a model's performance as we will do in Chapter 5, clustering is a core tool to have in your arsenal. I use clustering in a similar fashion as dimensionality reduction, as an additional way to surface issues and interesting data points.

A simple method to cluster data in practice is to start by trying a few simple algorithms such as k-means (*https://oreil.ly/LKdYP*) and tweak their hyperparameters such as the number of clusters until you reach a satisfactory performance.

Clustering performance is hard to quantify. In practice, using a combination of data visualization and methods such as the elbow method (*https://oreil.ly/k98SV*) or a silhouette plot (*https://oreil.ly/QGky6*) is sufficient for our use case, which is not to perfectly separate our data but to identify regions where our model may have issues.

The following is an example snippet of code for clustering our dataset, as well as visualizing our clusters using a dimensionality technique we described earlier, UMAP.

```
from sklearn.cluster import KMeans
import matplotlib.cm as cm

# Choose number of clusters and colormap
n_clusters=3
cmap = plt.get_cmap("Set2")

# Fit clustering algorithm to our vectorized features
clus = KMeans(n_clusters=n_clusters, random_state=10)
clusters = clus.fit_predict(vectorized_features)

# Plot the dimentionality reduced features on a 2D plane
plt.scatter(umap_features[:, 0], umap_features[:, 1],
            c=[cmap(x/n_clusters) for x in clusters], s=40, alpha=.4)
plt.title('UMAP projection of questions, colored by clusters', fontsize=14)
```

As you can see in Figure 4-10, the way we would instinctively cluster the 2D representation does not always match with the clusters our algorithm finds on the vectorized data. This can be because of artifacts in our dimensionality reduction algorithm or a complex data topology. In fact, adding a point's assigned cluster as a feature can sometimes improve a model's performance by letting it leverage said topology.

Once you have clusters, examine each cluster and try to identify trends in your data on each of them. To do so, you should select a few points per cluster and act as if you were the model, thus labeling those points with what you think the correct answer should be. In the next section, I'll describe how to do this labeling work.

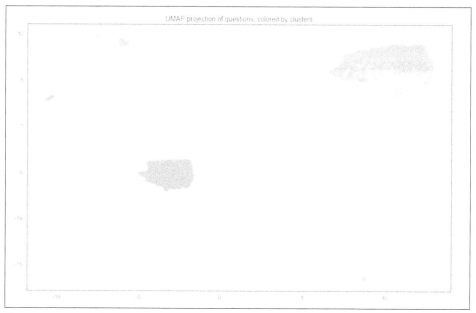

Figure 4-10. Visualizing our questions, colored by cluster

Be the Algorithm

Once you've looked at aggregate metrics and cluster information, I'd encourage you to follow the advice in "Monica Rogati: How to Choose and Prioritize ML Projects" on page 20 and try to do your model's job by labeling a few data points in each cluster with the results you would like a model to produce.

If you have never tried doing your algorithm's job, it will be hard to judge the quality of its results. On the other side, if you spend some time labeling data yourself, you will often notice trends that will make your modeling task much easier.

You might recognize this advice from our previous section about heuristics, and it should not surprise you. Choosing a modeling approach involves making almost as many assumptions about our data as building heuristics, so it makes sense for these assumptions to be data driven.

You should label data even if your dataset contains labels. This allows you to validate that your labels do capture the correct information and that they are correct. In our case study, we use a question's score as a measure of its quality, which is a weak label. Labeling a few examples ourselves will allow us to validate the assumption that this label is appropriate.

Once you label a few examples, feel free to update your vectorization strategy by adding any features you discover to help make your data representation as informative as possible, and go back to labeling. This is an iterative process, as illustrated in Figure 4-11.

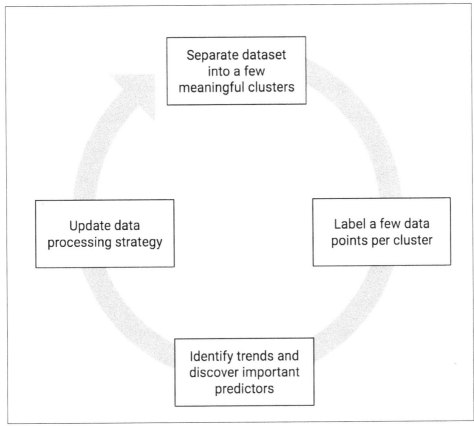

Figure 4-11. The process of labeling data

To speed up your labeling, make sure to leverage your prior analysis by labeling a few data points in each cluster you have identified and for each common value in your feature distribution.

One way to do this is to leverage visualization libraries to interactively explore your data. Bokeh (*https://oreil.ly/6eORd*) offers the ability to make interactive plots. One quick way to label data is to go through a plot of our vectorized examples, labeling a few examples for each cluster.

Figure 4-12 shows a representative individual example from a cluster of mostly unanswered questions. Questions in this cluster tended to be quite vague and hard to answer objectively and did not receive answers. These are accurately labeled as poor questions. To see the source code for this plot and an example of its use for the ML

Editor, navigate to the exploring data to generate features notebook in this book's Git-Hub repository (*https://oreil.ly/ml-powered-applications*).

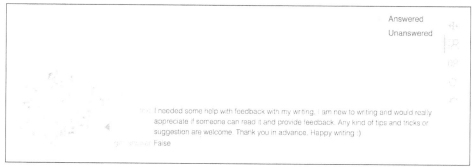

Figure 4-12. Using Bokeh to inspect and label data

When labeling data, you can choose to store labels with the data itself (as an additional column in a DataFrame, for example) or separately using a mapping from file or identifier to label. This is purely a matter of preference.

As you label examples, try to notice which process you are using to make your decisions. This will help with identifying trends and generating features that will help your models.

Data Trends

After having labeled data for a while, you will usually identify trends. Some may be informative (short tweets tend to be simpler to classify as positive or negative) and guide you to generate useful features for your models. Others may be irrelevant correlations because of the way data was gathered.

Maybe all of the tweets we collected that are in French happen to be negative, which would likely lead a model to automatically classify French tweets as negative. I'll let you decide how inaccurate that might be on a broader, more representative sample.

If you notice anything of the sort, do not despair! These kinds of trends are crucial to identify *before* you start building models, as they would artificially inflate accuracy on training data and could lead you to put a model in production that does not perform well.

The best way to deal with such biased examples is to gather additional data to make your training set more representative. You could also try to eliminate these features from your training data to avoid biasing your model, but this may not be effective in practice, as models frequently pick up on bias by leveraging correlations with other features (see Chapter 8).

Once you've identified some trends, it is time to use them. Most often, you can do this in one of two ways, by creating a feature that characterizes that trend or by using a model that will easily leverage it.

Let Data Inform Features and Models

We would like to use the trends we discover in the data to inform our data processing, feature generation, and modeling strategy. To start, let's look at how we could generate features that would help us capture these trends.

Build Features Out of Patterns

ML is about using statistical learning algorithms to leverage patterns in the data, but some patterns are easier to capture for models than others. Imagine the trivial example of predicting a numerical value using the value itself divided by 2 as a feature. The model would simply have to learn to multiply by 2 to predict the target perfectly. On the other hand, predicting the stock market from historical data is a problem that requires leveraging much more complex patterns.

This is why a lot of the practical gains of ML come from generating additional *features* that will help our models identify useful patterns. The ease with which a model identifies patterns depends on the way we represent data and how much of it we have. The more data you have and the less noisy your data is, the less feature engineering work you usually have to do.

It is often valuable to start by generating features, however; first because we will usually be starting with a small dataset and second because it helps encode our beliefs about the data and debug our models.

Seasonality is a common trend that benefits from specific feature generation. Let's say that an online retailer noticed that most of their sales happens on the last two weekends of the month. When building a model to predict future sales, they want to make sure that it has the potential to capture this pattern.

As you'll see, depending on how they represent dates, the task could prove quite difficult for their models. Most models are only able to take numerical inputs (see "Vectorizing" on page 69 for methods to transform text and images into numerical inputs), so let's examine a few ways to represent dates.

Raw datetime

The simplest way to represent time is in Unix time (*https://oreil.ly/hMlX3*), which represents "the number of seconds that have elapsed since 00:00:00 Thursday, 1 January 1970."

While this representation is simple, our model would need to learn some pretty complex patterns to identify the last two weekends of the month. The last weekend of 2018, for example (from 00:00:00 on the 29th to 23:59:59 on the 30th of December), is represented in Unix time as the range from 1546041600 to 1546214399 (you can verify that if you take the difference between both numbers, which represents an interval of 23 hours, 59 minutes, and 59 seconds measured in seconds).

Nothing about this range makes it particularly easy to relate to other weekends in other months, so it will be quite hard for a model to separate relevant weekends from others when using Unix time as an input. We can make the task easier for a model by generating features.

Extracting day of week and day of month

One way to make our representation of dates clearer would be to extract the day of the week and day of the month into two separate attributes.

The way we would represent 23:59:59 on the 30th of December, 2018, for example, would be with the same number as earlier, and two additional values representing the day of the week (0 for Sunday, for example) and day of the month (30).

This representation will make it easier for our model to learn that the values related to weekends (0 and 6 for Sunday and Saturday) and to later dates in the month correspond to higher activity.

It is also important to note that representations will often introduce bias to our model. For example, by encoding the day of the week as a number, the encoding for Friday (equal to five) will be five times greater than the one for Monday (equal to one). This numerical scale is an artifact of our representation and does not represent something we wish our model to learn.

Feature crosses

While the previous representation makes the task easier for our models, they would still have to learn a complex relationship between the day of the week and the day of the month: high traffic does not happen on weekends early in the month or on weekdays late in the month.

Some models such as deep neural networks leverage nonlinear combinations of features and can thus pick up on these relationships, but they often need a significant amount of data. A common way to address this problem is by making the task even easier and introducing *feature crosses*.

A feature cross is a feature generated simply by multiplying (crossing) two or more features with each other. This introduction of a nonlinear combination of features allows our model to discriminate more easily based on a combination of values from multiple features.

In Table 4-5, you can see how each of the representations we described would look for a few example data points.

Table 4-5. Representing your data in a clearer way will make it much easier for your algorithms to perform well

Human representation	Raw data (Unix datetime)	Day of week (DoW)	Day of month (DoM)	Cross (DoW / DoM)
Saturday, December 29, 2018, 00:00:00	1,546,041,600	7	29	174
Saturday, December 29, 2018, 01:00:00	1,546,045,200	7	29	174
...	...	...	...	...
Sunday, December 30, 2018, 23:59:59	1,546,214,399	1	30	210

In Figure 4-13, you can see how these feature values change with time and which ones make it simpler for a model to separate specific data points from others.

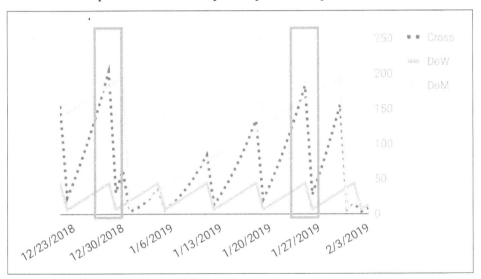

Figure 4-13. The last weekends of the month are easier to separate using feature crosses and extracted features

There is one last way to represent our data that will make it even easier for our model to learn the predictive value of the last two weekends of the month.

Giving your model the answer

It may seem like cheating, but if you know for a fact that a certain combination of feature values is particularly predictive, you can create a new binary feature that takes a nonzero value only when these features take the relevant combination of values. In our case, this would mean adding a feature called "is_last_two_weekends", for example, that will be set to one only during the last two weekends of the month.

If the last two weekends are as predictive as we had supposed they were, the model will simply learn to leverage this feature and will be much more accurate. When building ML products, never hesitate to make the task easier for your model. Better to have a model that works on a simpler task than one that struggles on a complex one.

Feature generation is a wide field, and methods exist for most types of data. Discussing every feature that is useful to generate for different types of data is outside the scope of this book. If you'd like to see more practical examples and methods, I recommend taking a look at *Feature Engineering for Machine Learning* (O'Reilly), by Alice Zheng and Amanda Casari.

In general, the best way to generate useful features is by looking at your data using the methods we described and asking yourself what the easiest way is to represent it in a way that will make your model learn its patterns. In the following section, I'll describe a few examples of features I generated using this process for the ML Editor.

ML Editor Features

For our ML Editor, using the techniques described earlier to inspect our dataset (see details of the exploration in the exploring data to generate features notebook, in this book's GitHub repository (*https://oreil.ly/ml-powered-applications*)), we generated the following features:

- Action verbs such as *can* and *should* are predictive of a question being answered, so we added a binary value that checks whether they are present in each question.

- Question marks are good predictors as well, so we have generated a `has_ques tion` feature.

- Questions about correct use of the English language tended not to get answers, so we added a `is_language_question` feature.

- The length of the text of the question is another factor, with very short questions tending to go unanswered. This led to the addition of a normalized question length feature.

- In our dataset, the title of the question contains crucial information as well, and looking at titles when labeling made the task much easier. This led to include the title text in all the earlier feature calculations.

Once we have an initial set of features, we can start building a model. Building this first model is the topic of the next chapter, Chapter 5.

Before moving on to models, I wanted to dive deeper on the topic of how to gather and update a dataset. To do that, I sat down with Robert Munro, an expert in the field.

I hope you enjoy the summary of our discussion here, and that it leaves you excited to move on to our next part, building our first model!

Robert Munro: How Do You Find, Label, and Leverage Data?

Robert Munro has founded several AI companies, building some of the top teams in artificial intelligence. He was chief technology officer at Figure Eight, a leading data labeling company during their biggest growth period. Before that, Robert ran product for AWS's first native natural language processing and machine translation services. In our conversation, Robert shares some lessons he learned building datasets for ML.

Q: *How do you get started on an ML project?*

A: The best way is to start with the business problem, as it will give you boundaries to work with. In your ML editor case study example, are you editing text that someone else has written after they submit it, or are you suggesting edits live as somebody writes? The first would let you batch process requests with a slower model, while the second one would require something quicker.

In terms of models, the second approach would invalidate sequence-to-sequence models as they would be too slow. In addition, sequence-to-sequence models today do not work beyond sentence-level recommendations and require a lot of parallel text to be trained. A faster solution would be to leverage a classifier and use the important features it extracts as suggestions. What you want out of this initial model is an easy implementation and results you can have confidence in, starting with naive Bayes on bag of words features, for example.

Finally, you need to spend some time looking at some data and labeling it yourself. This will give you an intuition for how hard the problem is and which solutions might be a good fit.

Q: *How much data do you need to get started?*

A: When gathering data, you are looking to guarantee that you have a representative and diverse dataset. Start by looking at the data you have and seeing if any types are unrepresented so that you can gather more. Clustering your dataset and looking for outliers can be helpful to speed up this process.

For labeling data, in the common case of classification, we've seen that labeling on the order of 1,000 examples of your rarer category works well in practice. You'll at least get enough signal to tell you whether to keep going with your current modeling approach. At around 10,000 examples, you can start to trust in the confidence of the models you are building.

As you get more data, your model's accuracy will slowly build up, giving you a curve of how your performance scales with data. At any point you only care about the last part of the curve, which should give you an estimate of the current value more data will give you. In the vast majority of cases, the improvement you will get from labeling more data will be more significant than if you iterated on the model.

Q: *What process do you use to gather and label data?*

A: You can look at your current best model and see what is tripping it up. Uncertainty sampling is a common approach: identify examples that your model is the most uncertain about (the ones closest to its decision boundary), and find similar examples to add to the training set.

You can also train an "error model" to find more data your current model struggles on. Use the mistakes your model makes as labels (labeling each data point as "predicted correctly" or "predicted incorrectly"). Once you train an "error model" on these examples, you can use it on your unlabeled data and label the examples that it predicts your model will fail on.

Alternatively, you can train a "labeling model" to find the best examples to label next. Let's say you have a million examples, of which you've labeled only 1,000. You can create a training set of 1,000 randomly sampled labeled images, and 1,000 unlabeled, and train a binary classifier to predict which images you have labeled. You can then use this labeling model to identify data points that are most different from what you've already labeled and label those.

Q: *How do you validate that your models are learning something useful?*

A: A common pitfall is to end up focusing labeling efforts on a small part of the relevant dataset. It may be that your model struggles with articles that are about basketball. If you keep annotating more basketball articles, your model may become great at basketball but bad at everything else. This is why while you should use strategies to gather data, you should always randomly sample from your test set to validate your model.

Finally, the best way to do it is to track when the performance of your deployed model drifts. You could track the uncertainty of the model or ideally bring it back to the business metrics: are your usage metrics gradually going down? This could be caused by other factors, but is a good trigger to investigate and potentially update your training set.

Conclusion

In this chapter, we covered important tips to efficiently and effectively examine a dataset.

We started by looking at the quality of data and how to decide whether it is sufficient for our needs. Next, we covered the best way to get familiar with the type of data you have: starting with summary statistics and moving on to clusters of similar points to identify broad trends.

We then covered why it is valuable to spend some significant time labeling data to identify trends that we can then leverage to engineer valuable features. Finally, we got to learn from Robert Munro's experience helping multiple teams build state-of-the-art datasets for ML.

Now that we've examined a dataset and generated features we hope to be predictive, we are ready to build our first model, which we will do in Chapter 5.

## PART III

Iterate on Models

Part I covered best practices to set up an ML project and track its progress. In Part II, we saw the value of building an end-to-end pipeline as fast as possible along with exploring an initial dataset.

Because of its experimental nature, ML is very much an iterative process. You should plan to repeatedly iterate on models and data, following an experimental loop as pictured in Figure III-1.

Figure III-1. The ML loop

Part III will describe one iteration of the loop. When working on ML projects, you should plan to go through multiple such iterations before expecting to reach satisfying performance. Here is an overview of the chapters in this part of the book:

Chapter 5

In this chapter, we will train a first model and benchmark it. Then, analyze its performance in depth and identify how it could be improved.

Chapter 6

This chapter covers techniques to build and debug models quickly and avoid time-consuming errors.

Chapter 7

In this chapter, we will use the ML Editor as a case study to show how to leverage a trained classifier to provide suggestions to users and build a fully functioning suggestion model.

## CHAPTER 5

Train and Evaluate Your Model

In the previous chapters we've covered how to identify the right problem to tackle, make a plan to tackle it, build a simple pipeline, explore a dataset, and generate an initial set of features. These steps have allowed us to gather enough information to begin training an adequate model. An adequate model here means a model that is a good fit for the task at hand and that has good chances of performing well.

In this chapter, we will start by briefly going over some concerns when choosing a model. Then, we will describe best practices to separate your data, which will help evaluate your models in realistic conditions. Finally, we'll look at methods to analyze modeling results and diagnose errors.

The Simplest Appropriate Model

Now that we are ready to train a model, we need to decide which model to start with. It may be tempting to try every possible model, benchmark them all, and pick the one with the best results on a held-out test set according to some metrics.

In general, this is not the best approach. Not only is it computationally intensive (there are many sets of models and many parameters for each model, so realistically you will only be able to test a suboptimal subset), it also treats models as predictive black boxes and entirely ignores that *ML models encode implicit assumptions about the data in the way they learn*.

Different models make different assumptions about the data and so are suited for different tasks. In addition, since ML is an iterative field, you'll want to pick models that you can build and evaluate quickly.

Let's first define how to identify simple models. Then, we will cover some examples of data patterns and appropriate models to leverage them.

Simple Models

A simple model should be quick to implement, understandable, and deployable: quick to implement because your first model will likely not be your last, understandable because it will allow you to debug it more easily, and deployable because that is a fundamental requirement for an ML-powered application. Let's start by exploring what I mean by quick to implement.

Quick to implement

Choose a model that will be simple for you to implement. Generally, this means picking a well-understood model that has multiple tutorials written about it and that people will be able to help you with (especially if you ask well-formulated questions using our ML Editor!). For a new ML-driven application, you will have enough challenges to tackle in terms of processing data and deploying a reliable result that you should initially do your best to avoid all model headaches.

If possible, start by using models from popular libraries such as Keras or scikit-learn, and hold off before diving into an experimental GitHub repository that has no documentation and hasn't been updated in the last nine months.

Once your model is implemented, you'll want to inspect and understand how it is leveraging your dataset. To do so, you need a model that is understandable.

Understandable

Model *explainability* and *interpretability* describe the ability for a model to expose reasons (such as a given combination of predictors) that caused it to make predictions. Explainability can be useful for a variety of reasons, such as verifying that our models are not biased in undesirable ways or explaining to a user what they could do to improve prediction results. It also makes iterating and debugging much easier.

If you can extract the features a model relies on to make decisions, you'll have a clearer view of which features to add, tweak, or remove, or which model could make better choices.

Unfortunately, model interpretability is often complex even for simple models and sometimes intractable for larger ones. In "Evaluate Feature Importance" on page 121, we will see ways to tackle this challenge and help you identify points of improvement for your model. Among other things, we will use black-box explainers that attempt to provide explanations of a model's prediction regardless of its internal workings.

Simpler models such as logistic regression or decision trees tend to be easier to explain as they provide some measure of feature importance, which is another reason they are usually good models to try first.

Deployable

As a reminder, the end goal of your model is to provide a valuable service to people who will use it. This means when you think of which model to train, you should always consider whether you will be able to deploy it.

We will cover deployment in Part IV, but you should already be thinking about questions such as the following:

- How long will it take a trained model to make a prediction for a user? When thinking of prediction latency, you should include not only the time it takes for a model to output a result, but the delay in between when a user submits a prediction request and receives the result. This includes any preprocessing steps such as feature generation, any network calls, and any postprocessing steps that happen in between a model's output and the data that is presented to a user.
- Is this inference pipeline fast enough for our use case if we take into account the number of concurrent users we expect?
- How long does it take to train the model, and how often do we need to train it? If training takes 12 hours and you need to retrain your model every 4 hours to be fresh, not only will your compute bill be quite expensive, but your model will always be out of date.

We can compare how simple models are by using a table such as Figure 5-1. As the field of ML evolves and new tooling is built, models that may be complex to deploy or hard to interpret today may become simpler to use, and this table will need to be updated. For this reason, I suggest you build your own version based on your particular problem domain.

Model name	Ease of implementation		Understandability		Deployability		Total "Simplicity score"
	Well understood model	Vetted implementation	Easy to extract feature importance	Easy to debug	Inference time	Training time	
Decision tree (from scikit-learn)	5/5	5/5	4/5	4/5	5/5	5/5	28/30
CNN (From Keras)	4/5	5/5	3/5	3/5	3/5	2/5	20/30
Transformer (Fom a personal github repository)	2/5	1/5	0/5	0/5	2/5	1/5	6/30

Figure 5-1. Scoring models based on their simplicity

Even among models that are simple, interpretable, and deployable, there are still many potential candidates. To choose a model, you should also take into account the patterns you identified in Chapter 4.

From Patterns to Models

The patterns we have identified and the features we have generated should guide our model choice. Let's cover a few examples of patterns in the data and appropriate models to leverage them.

We want to ignore feature scale

Many models will leverage larger features more heavily than smaller ones. This can be fine in some cases, but undesirable in others. For models using optimization procedures like gradient descent such as neural networks, differences in feature scale can sometimes lead to instability in the training procedure.

If you want to use both age in years (ranging from one to a hundred) and income in dollars (let's say our data reaches up to nine figures) as two predictors, you need to make sure that your model is able to leverage the most predictive features, regardless of their scale.

You can ensure this by preprocessing features to normalize their scale to have zero mean and unit variance. If all features are normalized to the same range, a model will consider each of them equally (at least initially).

Another solution is to turn to models that are not affected by differences in feature scale. The most common practical examples are decision trees, random forests, and gradient-boosted decision trees. XGBoost (*https://oreil.ly/CWpnk*) is an implementation of gradient-boosted trees commonly used in production because of its robustness, as well as its speed.

Our predicted variable is a linear combination of predictors

Sometimes, there is good reason to believe that we can make good predictions using only a linear combination of our features. In these cases, we should use a linear model such as a linear regression for continuous problems or a logistic regression or naive Bayes classifier for classification problems.

These models are simple, efficient, and often allow for a direct interpretation of their weights that can help us identify important features. If we believe the relationships between our features and our predicted variable are more complex, using a nonlinear model such as a multilayer neural network or generating feature crosses (see the beginning of "Let Data Inform Features and Models" on page 85) can help.

Our data has a temporal aspect

If we are dealing with time series of data points where the value at a given time depends on previous values, we would want to leverage models that explicitly encode this information. Examples of such models include statistical models such as autoregressive integrated moving average (ARIMA) or recurrent neural networks (RNN).

Each data point is a combination of patterns

When tackling problems in the image domain, for example, convolutional neural networks (CNNs) have proven useful through their ability to learn *translation-invariant filters*. This means that they are able to extract local patterns in an image regardless of their position. Once a CNN learns how to detect an eye, it can detect it anywhere in an image, not just in the places that it appeared in the training set.

Convolutional filters have proven useful in other fields that contain local patterns, such as speech recognition or text classification, where CNNs have been used successfully for sentence classification. For an example, see the implementation by Yoon Kim in the paper, "Convolutional Neural Networks for Sentence Classification" (*https://arxiv.org/abs/1408.5882*).

There are many additional points to consider when thinking of the right models to use. For most classical ML problems, I recommend using this handy flowchart (*https://oreil.ly/tUsD6*) that the scikit-learn team helpfully provides. It provides model suggestions for many common use cases.

ML Editor model

For the ML Editor, we would like our first model to be fast and reasonably easy to debug. In addition, our data consists of individual examples, without a need to consider a temporal aspect (such as a series of questions, for example). For that reason, we will start with a popular and resilient baseline, a random forest classifier.

Once you've identified a model that seems reasonable, it is time to train it. As a general guideline, you should not train your model on the entirety of the dataset you gathered in Chapter 4. You'll want to start by holding out some data from your training set. Let's cover why and how you should do that.

Split Your Dataset

The main goal of our model is to provide valid predictions for data that our users will submit. This means that our model will eventually have to perform well on data that it has *never seen before*.

When you train a model on a dataset, measuring its performance on the same dataset only tells you how good it is at making predictions on data it has already seen. If you only train a model on a subset of your data, you can then use the data the model was not trained on to estimate how well it would perform on unseen data.

In Figure 5-2, you can see an example of a split into three separate sets (train, validation, and test) based on an attribute of our dataset (the author of a question). In this chapter, we will cover what each of these sets means, and how to think about them.

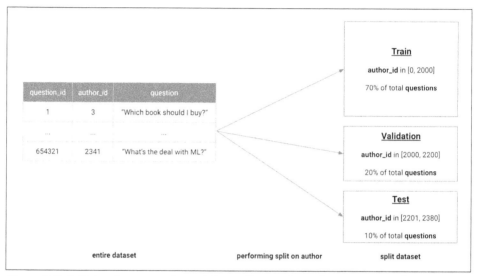

Figure 5-2. Splitting data on author while attributing the right proportion of questions to each split

The first held-out set to consider is the validation set.

Validation set

To estimate how our model performs on unseen data, we purposefully hold out part of our dataset from training and then use the performance on this held-out dataset as a proxy for our model's performance in production. The held-out set allows us to validate that our model can generalize to unseen data and thus is often called a *validation set*.

You can choose different sections of your data to hold out as a validation set to evaluate your model and train it on the remaining data. Doing multiple rounds of this process helps control for any variance due to a particular choice of validation set and is called *cross-validation*.

As you change your data preprocessing strategy and the type of model you use or its hyperparameters, your model's performance on the validation set will change (and ideally improve). Using the validation set allows you to tune hyperparameters the same way that using a training set allows a model to tune its parameters.

After multiple iterations of using the validation set to make model adjustments, your modeling pipeline can become tailored specifically to performing well on your validation data. This defeats the purpose of the validation set, which is supposed to be a proxy for unseen data. For this reason, you should hold out an additional test set.

Test set

Since we will go through multiple cycles of iteration on our model and measure its performance on a validation set at each cycle, we may bias our model so that it performs well on the validation set. This helps our model generalize beyond the training set but also carries the risk of simply learning a model that performs well only on our particular validation sets. Ideally, we would want to have a model that works well on new data that is hence not contained in the validation set.

For this reason, we usually hold out a third set called a *test set*, which serves as a final benchmark of our performance on unseen data, once we are satisfied with our iterations. While using a test set is a best practice, practitioners sometimes use the validation set as a test set. This increases the risk of biasing a model toward the validation set but can be appropriate when running only a few experiments.

It is important to avoid using performance on the test set to inform modeling decisions, as this set is supposed to represent the unseen data we will face in production. Adapting a modeling approach to perform well on the test set risks leading to overestimating the performance of the model.

To have a model that performs in production, the data you train on should resemble data produced by users who will interact with your product. Ideally, any kind of data you could receive from users should be represented in your dataset. If that is not the case, then keep in mind that your test set performance is indicative of performance for only a subset of your users.

For the ML Editor, this means that users who do not conform to the demographics of *writers.stackoverflow.com* may not be as well served by our recommendations. If we wanted to address this problem, we should expand the dataset to contain questions more representative of these users. We could start by incorporating questions from other Stack Exchange websites to cover a broader set of topics, or different question and answering websites altogether.

Correcting a dataset in such a manner can be challenging for a side project. When building consumer-grade products, however, it is necessary to help model weaknesses be caught early before users are exposed to them. Many of the failure modes we will cover in Chapter 8 could have been avoided with a more representative dataset.

Relative proportions

In general, you should maximize the amount of data the model can use to learn from, while holding out large enough validation and test sets to provide accurate performance metrics. Practitioners often use 70% of the data for training, 20% for validation, and 10% for testing, but this depends entirely on the quantity of data. For very large datasets, you can afford to use a larger proportion of data for training while still having enough data to validate models. For smaller datasets, you may need to use a smaller proportion for training in order to have a validation set that is large enough to provide an accurate performance measurement.

Now you know why you'd want to split data, and which splits to consider, but how should you decide which datapoint goes in each split? The splitting methods you use have a significant impact on modeling performance and should depend on the particular features of your dataset.

Data leakage

The method you use to separate your data is a crucial part of validation. You should aim to make your validation/test set close to what you expect unseen data to be like.

Most often, train, validation, and test sets are separated by sampling data points randomly. In some cases, this can lead to *data leakage*. Data leakage happens when (because of our training procedure) a model receives information during training that it won't have access to when being used in front of real users in production.

Data leakage should be avoided at all costs, because it leads to an inflated view of the performance of our model. A model trained on a dataset exhibiting data leakage is able to leverage information to make predictions that it will not have when it encounters different data. This makes the task artificially easier for the model, but only due to the leaked information. The model's performance appears high on the held-out data but will be much worse in production.

In Figure 5-3, I've drawn a few common causes where randomly splitting your data into sets will cause data leakage. There are many potential causes of data leakage, and we will explore two frequent ones next.

To start our exploration, let's tackle the example at the top of Figure 5-3, temporal data leakage. Then, we will move on to sample contamination, a category that encompasses the bottom two examples in Figure 5-3.

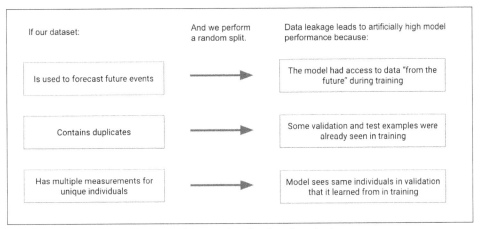

Figure 5-3. Splitting data randomly can often lead to data leakage

Temporal data leakage. In time-series forecasting, a model needs to learn from data points in the past to predict events that have not happened yet. If we perform a random split on a forecasting dataset, we will introduce data leakage: a model that is trained on a random set of points and evaluated on the rest will have access to training data that happens *after* events it is trying to predict.

The model will perform artificially well on the validation and test sets but fail in production, because all it has learned is to leverage future information, which is unavailable in the real world.

Once you are aware of it, temporal data leakage is usually easy to catch. Other types of data leakage can give a model access to information it should not have during training and artificially inflate its performance by "contaminating" its training data. They can often be much harder to detect.

Sample contamination. A common source of data leakage lies in the level at which the randomness occurs. When building a model to predict the grade students' essays will receive, a data scientist I was assisting once found that his model performed close to perfect on a held-out test set.

On such a hard task, a model that performs so well should be closely examined as it frequently indicates the presence of a bug or *data leakage*. Some would say that the ML equivalent of Murphy's law is that the more pleasantly surprised you are by the performance of your model on your test data, the more likely you are to have an error in your pipeline.

In this example, because most students had written multiple essays, splitting data randomly led to essays by the same students being present both in the training and in the test sets. This allowed the model to pick up on features that identified students and use that information to make accurate predictions (students in this dataset tended to have similar grades across all their essays).

If we were to deploy this essay score predictor for future use, it would not be able to predict useful scores for students it hadn't seen before and would simply predict historical scores for students whose essays it has been trained on. This would not be useful at all.

To solve the data leakage in this example, a new split was made at the student rather than the essay level. This meant that each student appeared either only in the training set or only in the validation set. Since the task became much harder, this led to a decrease in model accuracy. However, since the training task was now much closer to what it would be in production, this new model was much more valuable.

Sample contamination can happen in nuanced ways in common tasks. Let's take the example of an apartment rental booking website. This website incorporates a click prediction model that, given a user query and an item, predicts whether the user will click on the item. This model is used to decide which listings to display to users.

To train such a model, this website could use a dataset of user features such as their number of previous bookings, paired with apartments that were presented to them and whether they clicked on them. This data is usually stored in a production database that can be queried to produce such pairs. If engineers of this website were to simply query the database to build such a dataset, they would likely be faced with a case of data leakage. Can you see why?

In Figure 5-4, I've sketched out an illustration of what can go wrong by depicting a prediction for a specific user. At the top, you can see the features that a model could use in production to provide a click prediction. Here, a new user with no previous bookings is presented with a given apartment. At the bottom, you can see the state of the features a few days later when engineers extract data from the database.

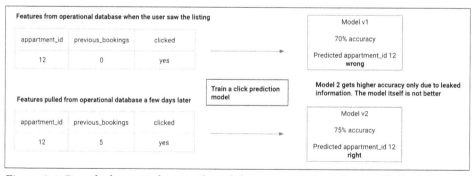

Figure 5-4. Data leakage can happen for subtle reasons, such as due to a lack of data versioning

Notice the difference in `previous_bookings`, which is due to user activity that happened after they were initially presented with the listing. By using a snapshot of a database, information about future actions of the user was leaked into the training set. We now know that the user will eventually book five apartments! Such leakage can lead a model trained with information at the bottom to output a correct prediction on the incorrect training data. The accuracy of the model on the generated dataset will be high because it is leveraging data it will not have access to in production. When the model is deployed, it will perform worse than expected.

If you take anything away from this anecdote, it is to always investigate the results of a model, especially if it shows surprisingly strong performance.

ML Editor Data Split

The dataset we are using to train our ML Editor contains questions asked on Stack Overflow, as well as their answers. At first glance, a random split can seem sufficient and is quite simple to implement in scikit-learn. We could, for example, write a function like the one shown here:

```
from sklearn.model_selection import train_test_split

def get_random_train_test_split(posts, test_size=0.3, random_state=40):
    """
    Get train/test split from DataFrame
    Assumes the DataFrame has one row per question example
    :param posts: all posts, with their labels
    :param test_size: the proportion to allocate to test
    :param random_state: a random seed
    """
    return train_test_split(
        posts, test_size=test_size, random_state=random_state
    )
```

There is a potential reach for leakage with such an approach; can you identify it?

If we think back to our use case, we know we would like our model to work on questions it has not seen before, only looking at their content. On a question and answering website, however, many other factors can play into whether a question is answered successfully. One of these factors is the identity of the author.

If we split our data randomly, a given author could appear both in our training and validation sets. If certain popular authors have a distinctive style, our model could overfit on this style and reach artificially high performance on our validation set due to data leakage. To avoid this, it would be safer for us to make sure each author appears only in training or validation. This is the same type of leakage we described in the student grading example earlier.

Using scikit-learn's `GroupShuffleSplit` class and passing the feature representing an author's unique ID to its split method, we can guarantee that a given author appears in only one of the splits.

```
from sklearn.model_selection import GroupShuffleSplit

def get_split_by_author(
    posts, author_id_column="OwnerUserId", test_size=0.3, random_state=40
):
    """
    Get train/test split
    Guarantee every author only appears in one of the splits
    :param posts: all posts, with their labels
    :param author_id_column: name of the column containing the author_id
    :param test_size: the proportion to allocate to test
    :param random_state: a random seed
    """
    splitter = GroupShuffleSplit(
        n_splits=1, test_size=test_size, random_state=random_state
    )
    splits = splitter.split(posts, groups=posts[author_id_column])
    return next(splits)
```

To see a comparison between both splitting methods, refer to the splitting data note-book in this book's GitHub repository (*https://oreil.ly/ml-powered-applications*).

Once a dataset is split, a model can be fit to the training set. We've covered the required parts of a training pipeline in "Start with a Simple Pipeline" on page 38. In the training of a simple model notebook in the GitHub repository for this book (*https://oreil.ly/ml-powered-applications*), I show an example of an end-to-end training pipeline for the ML Editor. We will analyze the results of this pipeline.

We've covered the main risks we want to keep in mind when splitting data, but what should we do once our dataset is split and we've trained a model on the training split? In the next section, we'll talk about different practical ways to evaluate trained models and how to leverage them best.

Judge Performance

Now that we have split our data, we can train our model and judge how it performed. Most models are trained to minimize a cost function, which represents how far a model's predictions are from the true labels. The smaller the value of the cost function, the better the model fits the data. Which function you minimize depends on your model and your problem, but it is generally a good idea to take a look at its value both on the training set and on the validation set.

This commonly helps estimate the *bias-variance trade-off* of our model, which measures the degree to which our model has learned valuable generalizable information from the data, without memorizing the details of our training set.

I'm assuming familiarity with standard classification metrics, but here is a short reminder just in case. For classification problems, accuracy represents the proportion of examples a model predicts correctly. In other words, it is the proportion of true results, which are both true positives and true negatives. In cases with a strong imbalance, a high accuracy can mask a poor model. If 99% of cases are positive, a model that always predicts the positive class will have 99% accuracy but may not be very useful. Precision, recall, and f1 score address this limitation. Precision is the proportion of true positives among examples predicted as positive. Recall is the proportion of true positives among elements that had a positive label. The f1 score is the harmonic mean of precision and recall.

In the training of a simple model notebook in this book's GitHub repository (*https:// oreil.ly/ml-powered-applications*), we train a first version of a random forest using TF-IDF vectors and the features we identified in "ML Editor Features" on page 88.

Here are the accuracy, precision, recall, and f1 scores for our training set and our validation set.

```
Training accuracy = 0.585, precision = 0.582, recall = 0.585, f1 = 0.581
Validation accuracy = 0.614, precision = 0.615, recall = 0.614, f1 = 0.612
```

Taking a quick look at these metrics allows us to notice two things:

- Since we have a balanced dataset consisting of two classes, picking a class at random for every example would give us roughly 50% accuracy. Our model's accuracy reaches 61%, better than a random baseline.

- Our accuracy on the validation set is higher than on the training set. It seems our model works well on unseen data.

Let's dive deeper to find out more about the performance of the model.

Bias variance trade-off

Weak performance on the training set is a symptom of high bias, also called *underfitting*, which means a model has failed to capture useful information: it is not even able to perform well on data points it has already been given the label for.

Strong performance on the training set but weak performance on the validation set is a symptom of high variance, also called *overfitting*, meaning that a model has found ways to learn the input/output mapping for the data it has been trained on, but what it has learned does not generalize to unseen data.

Underfitting and overfitting are two extreme cases of the bias-variance trade-off, which describes how the types of errors a model makes change as its complexity increases. As model complexity grows, variance increases and bias decreases, and the model goes from underfitting to overfitting. You can see this depicted in Figure 5-5.

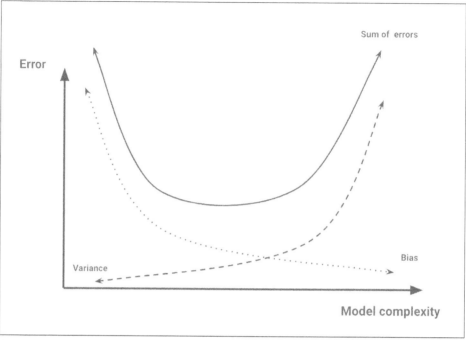

Figure 5-5. As complexity increases, bias decreases but variance increases as well

In our case, since our validation performance is better than our training performance, we can see that our model is not overfitting the training data. We can likely increase the complexity of our model or features to improve performance. Fighting the bias-variance trade-off requires finding an optimal point between reducing bias, which increases a model's performance on the training set, and reducing variance, which increases its performance on the validation set (often worsening training performance as a byproduct).

Performance metrics help generate an aggregate perspective of a model's performance. This is helpful to guess how a model is doing but does not provide much intuition as to what precisely a model is succeeding or failing at. To improve our model, we need to dive deeper.

Going beyond aggregate metrics

A performance metric helps determine whether a model has learned correctly from a dataset or whether it needs to be improved. The next step is to examine results further in order to understand in which way a model is failing or succeeding. This is crucial for two reasons:

Performance validation

Performance metrics can be very deceptive. When working on a classification problem with severely imbalanced data such as predicting a rare disease that appears in fewer than 1% of patients, any model that always predicts that a patient is healthy will reach an accuracy of 99%, even though it has no predictive power at all. There exists performance metrics suited for most problems (the f1 score (*https://oreil.ly/fQAq9*) would work better for the previous problem), but the key is to remember that they are aggregate metrics and paint an incomplete picture of the situation. To trust the performance of a model, you need to inspect results at a more granular level.

Iteration

Model building is an iterative process, and the best way to start an iteration loop is by identifying both what to improve and how to improve it. Performance metrics do not help identify where a model is struggling and which part of the pipeline needs improvement. Too often, I've seen data scientists try to improve model performance by simply trying many other models or hyperparameters, or building additional features haphazardly. This approach amounts to throwing darts at the wall while blindfolded. The key to building successful models quickly is to identify and address specific reasons models are failing.

With these two motivations in mind, we will cover a few ways to dive deeper into the performance of a model.

Evaluate Your Model: Look Beyond Accuracy

There are a myriad of ways to inspect how a model is performing, and we will not cover every potential evaluation method. We will focus on a few that are often helpful to tease out what might be happening below the surface.

When it comes to investigating model performance, think of yourself as a detective and each of the methods covered next as different ways to surface clues. We'll start by covering multiple techniques that contrast a model's prediction with the data to uncover interesting patterns.

Contrast Data and Predictions

The first step to evaluating a model in depth is to find more granular ways than aggregate metrics to contrast data and predictions. We'd like to break down aggregate performance metrics such as accuracy, precision, or recall on different subsets of our data. Let's see how to do this for the common ML challenge of classification.

You can find all the code examples in the comparing data to predictions notebook in this book's GitHub repository (*https://oreil.ly/ml-powered-applications*).

For classification problems, I usually recommend starting by looking at a confusion matrix, shown in Figure 5-6, whose rows represent each true class, and columns represent the predictions of our model. A model with perfect predictions will have a confusion matrix with zeros everywhere except in the diagonal going from the top left to the bottom right. In reality, that is rarely the case. Let's take a look at why a confusion matrix is often very useful.

Confusion Matrix

A confusion matrix allows us at a glance to see whether our model is particularly successful on certain classes and struggles on some others. This is particularly useful for datasets with many different classes or classes that are imbalanced.

Oftentimes, I've seen models with impressive accuracy show a confusion matrix with one column entirely empty, meaning that there is a class that the model never predicts. This often happens for rare classes and can sometimes be harmless. If the rare class represents an important outcome, however, such as a borrower defaulting on a loan, a confusion matrix will help us notice the problem. We can then correct it by weighing the rare class more heavily in our model's loss function, for example.

The top row of Figure 5-6 shows that the initial model we've trained does well when it comes to predicting low-quality questions. The bottom row shows that the model struggles to detect all high-quality questions. Indeed, out of all the questions that received a high score, our model only predicts their class correctly half of the time. Looking at the right column, however, we can see that when the model predicts that a question is high quality, its prediction tends to be accurate.

Confusion matrices can be even more useful when working on problems with more than two classes. For example, I once worked with an engineer who was trying to classify words from speech utterances who plotted a confusion matrix for his latest model. He immediately noticed two symmetrical, off-diagonal values that were abnormally high. These two classes (which each represented a word) were confusing the model and the cause of a majority of its errors. Upon further inspection, it turns out that the words that were confusing the model were *when* and *where*. Gathering additional data for these two examples was enough to help the model better differentiate these similar-sounding words.

A confusion matrix allows us to compare a model's predictions with the true classes for each class. When debugging models, we may want to look deeper than their predictions and examine the probabilities output by the model.

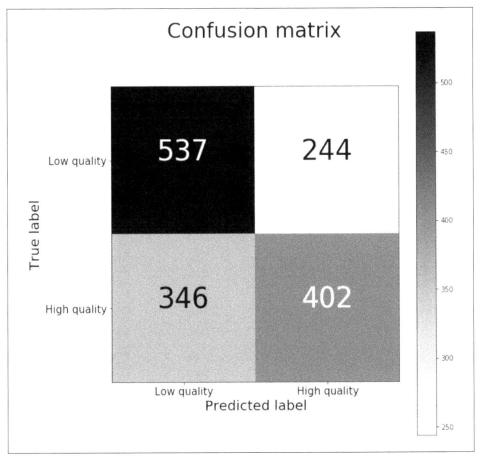

Figure 5-6. Confusion matrix for an initial baseline on our question classification task

ROC Curve

For binary classification problems, receiver operating characteristic (ROC) curves can also be very informative. An ROC curve plots the true positive rate (TPR) as a function of the false positive rate (FPR).

The vast majority of models used in classification return a probability score that a given example belongs to a certain class. This means that at inference time, we can choose to attribute an example to a certain class if the probability given by the model is above a certain threshold. This is usually called the *decision threshold*.

By default, most classifiers use a probability of 50% for their decision threshold, but this is something we can change based on our use case. By varying the threshold regularly from 0 to 1 and measuring the TPR and FPR at each point, we obtain an ROC curve.

Once we have a model's prediction probability and the associated true labels, getting FPRs and TPRs is simple using scikit-learn. We can then generate an ROC curve.

```
from sklearn.metrics import roc_curve

fpr, tpr, thresholds = roc_curve(true_y, predicted_proba_y)
```

Two details are important to understand for ROC curves such as the one plotted in Figure 5-7. First, the diagonal line going between the bottom left to the top right represents guessing randomly. This means that to beat a random baseline, a classifier/threshold pair should be above this line. In addition, the perfect model would be represented by the green dotted line on the top left.

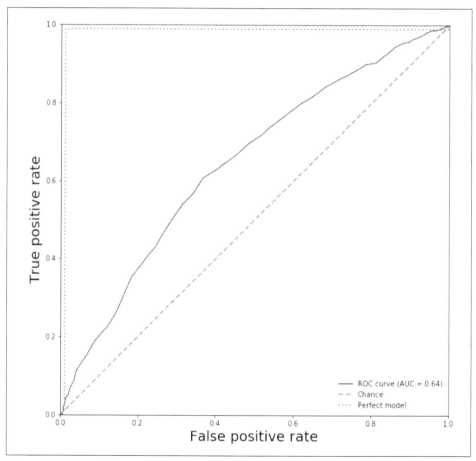

Figure 5-7. ROC curve for an initial model

Because of these two details, classification models often use the area under the curve (AUC) to represent performance. The larger the AUC, the closer to a "perfect" model our classifier could be. A random model will have an AUC of 0.5, while a perfect model has an AUC of 1. When concerning ourselves with a practical application, however, we should choose one specific threshold that gives us the most useful TPR/FPR ratio for our use case.

For that reason, I recommend adding vertical or horizontal lines to an ROC curve that represent our product needs. When building a system that routes customer requests to staff if it is deemed urgent enough, the FPR you can afford is then entirely determined by the capacity of your support staff and the number of users you have. This means that any models with an FPR higher than that limit should not even be considered.

Plotting a threshold on an ROC curve allows you to have a more concrete goal than simply getting the largest AUC score. Make sure your efforts count toward your goal!

Our ML Editor model classifies questions as good or bad. In this context, the TPR represents the proportion of high-quality questions our model correctly judges as good. The FPR is the proportion of bad questions our model claims is good. If we do not help our users, we'd like to at least guarantee we don't harm them. This means that we should not use any model that risks recommending bad questions too frequently. We should thus set a threshold for our FPR, such as 10%, for example, and use the best model we can find under that threshold. In Figure 5-8, you can see this requirement represented on our ROC curve; it has significantly reduced the space of acceptable decision thresholds for models.

An ROC curve gives us a more nuanced view of how a model's performance changes as we make its predictions more or less conservative. Another way to look at a model's prediction probability is to compare its distributions with the true class distributions to see whether it is well calibrated.

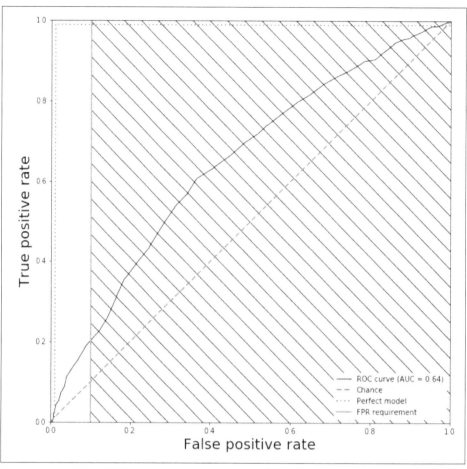

Figure 5-8. Adding ROC lines representing our product need

Calibration Curve

Calibration plots are another informative plot for binary classification tasks, as they can help us get a sense for whether our model's outputted probability represents its confidence well. A calibration plot shows the fraction of true positive examples as a function of the confidence of our classifier.

For example, out of all the data points our classifier gives a probability of being classified as positive that is higher than 80%, how many of those data points are actually positive? A calibration curve for a perfect model will be a diagonal line from bottom left to top right.

In Figure 5-9, we can see at the top that our model is well calibrated between .2 and .7, but not for probabilities outside of that range. Taking a look at the histogram of predicted probabilities below reveals that our model very rarely predicts probabilities outside of that range, which is likely leading to the extreme results shown earlier. The model is rarely confident in its predictions.

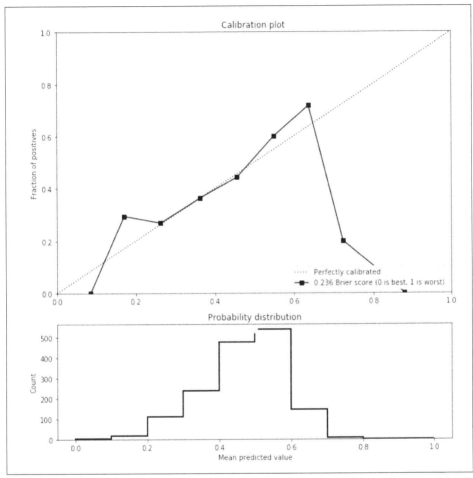

Figure 5-9. A calibration curve: the diagonal line represents a perfect model (top); histogram of predicted values (bottom)

For many problems, such as predicting CTR in ad serving, the data will lead to our models being quite skewed when probabilities get close to 0 or 1, and a calibration curve will help us see this at a glance.

To diagnose the performance of a model, it can be valuable to visualize individual predictions. Let's cover methods to make this visualization process efficient.

Dimensionality Reduction for Errors

We described vectorization and dimensionality reduction techniques for data exploration in "Vectorizing" on page 69 and "Dimensionality reduction" on page 78. Let's see how the same techniques can be used to make error analysis more efficient.

When we first covered how to use dimensionality reduction methods to visualize data, we colored each point in a dataset by its class to observe the topology of labels. When analyzing model errors, we can use different color schemes to identify errors.

To identify error trends, color each data point by whether a model's prediction was correct or not. This will allow you to identify types of similar data points a model performs poorly on. Once you identify a region in which a model performs poorly, visualize a few data points in it. Visualizing hard examples is a great way to generate features represented in these examples to help a model fit them better.

To help surface trends in hard examples, you can also use the clustering methods from "Clustering" on page 80. After clustering data, measure model performance on each cluster and identify clusters where the model performs worst. Inspect data points in these clusters to help you generate more features.

Dimensionality reduction techniques are one way of surfacing challenging examples. To do so, we can also directly use a model's confidence score.

The Top-k Method

Finding dense error regions helps identify failure modes for a model. Above, we used dimensionality reduction to help us find such regions, but we can also directly use a model itself. By leveraging prediction probabilities, we can identify data points that were most challenging or for which a model was most uncertain. Let's call this approach the *top-k method*.

The top-k method is straightforward. First, pick a manageable number of examples to visualize that we will call k. For a personal project where a single person will be visualizing results, start with ten to fifteen examples. For each class or cluster you have previously found, visualize:

- The k best performing examples
- The k worst performing examples
- The k most uncertain examples

Visualizing these examples will help you identify examples that are easy, hard, or confusing to your model. Let's dive into each category in more detail.

The k best performing examples

First, display the k examples your model predicted correctly and was most confident about. When visualizing those examples, aim to identify any commonality in feature value among them that could explain model performance. This will help you identify features that are successfully leveraged by a model.

After visualizing successful examples to identify features leveraged by a model, plot unsuccessful ones to identify features it fails to pick up on.

The k worst performing examples

Display the k examples your model predicted incorrectly and was most confident about. Start with k examples in training data and then validation.

Just like visualizing error clusters, visualizing k examples that a model performs the worst on in a training set can help identify trends in data points the model fails on. Display these data points to help you identify additional features that would make them easier for a model.

When exploring an initial model's error for the ML Editor, for example, I found that some questions posted received a low score because they did not contain an actual question. The model was not initially able to predict a low score for such questions, so I added a feature to count question marks in the body of the text. Adding this feature allowed the model to make accurate predictions for these "nonquestion" questions.

Visualizing the k worst examples in the validation data can help identify examples that significantly differ from the training data. If you do identify examples in the validation set that are too hard, refer to tips in "Split Your Dataset" on page 99 to update your data splitting strategy.

Finally, models are not always confidently right or wrong; they can also output uncertain predictions. I'll cover those next.

The k most uncertain examples

Visualizing the k most uncertain examples consists of displaying examples for which a model was least confident in its predictions. For a classification model, which this book focuses mostly on, uncertain examples are ones where a model outputs as close to an equal probability as possible for each class.

If a model is well calibrated (see "Calibration Curve" on page 114 for an explanation of calibration), it will output uniform probabilities for examples that a human labeler would be uncertain about as well. For a cat versus dog classifier, for example, a picture containing both a dog and a cat would fall into that category.

Uncertain examples in the training set are often a symptom of conflicting labels. Indeed, if a training set contains two duplicate or similar examples that are each labeled a different class, a model will minimize its loss during training by outputting an equal probability for each class when presented with this example. Conflicting labels thus lead to uncertain predictions, and you can use the top-k method to attempt to find these examples.

Plotting the top-k most uncertain examples in your validation set can help find gaps in your training data. Validation examples that a model is uncertain about but are clear to a human labeler are often a sign that the model has not been exposed to this kind of data in its training set. Plotting the top-k uncertain examples for a validation set can help identify data types that should be present in the training set.

Top-k evaluation can be implemented in a straightforward manner. In the next section, I'll share a working example.

Top-k implementation tips

The following is a simple top-k implementation that works with pandas DataFrames. The function takes as input a DataFrame containing predicted probabilities and labels and returns each of the top-k above. It can be found in this book's GitHub repository (*https://oreil.ly/ml-powered-applications*).

```python
def get_top_k(df, proba_col, true_label_col, k=5, decision_threshold=0.5):
    """
    For binary classification problems
    Returns k most correct and incorrect example for each class
    Also returns k most unsure examples
    :param df: DataFrame containing predictions, and true labels
    :param proba_col: column name of predicted probabilities
    :param true_label_col: column name of true labels
    :param k: number of examples to show for each category
    :param decision_threshold: classifier decision boundary to classify as
            positive
    :return: correct_pos, correct_neg, incorrect_pos, incorrect_neg, unsure
    """
    # Get correct and incorrect predictions
    correct = df[
        (df[proba_col] > decision_threshold) == df[true_label_col]
    ].copy()
    incorrect = df[
        (df[proba_col] > decision_threshold) != df[true_label_col]
    ].copy()

    top_correct_positive = correct[correct[true_label_col]].nlargest(
        k, proba_col
    )
    top_correct_negative = correct[~correct[true_label_col]].nsmallest(
        k, proba_col
    )
```

```
top_incorrect_positive = incorrect[incorrect[true_label_col]].nsmallest(
    k, proba_col
)
top_incorrect_negative = incorrect[~incorrect[true_label_col]].nlargest(
    k, proba_col
)

# Get closest examples to decision threshold
most_uncertain = df.iloc[
    (df[proba_col] - decision_threshold).abs().argsort()[:k]
]

return (
    top_correct_positive,
    top_correct_negative,
    top_incorrect_positive,
    top_incorrect_negative,
    most_uncertain,
)
```

Let's illustrate the top-k method by using it for the ML Editor.

Top-k method for the ML Editor

We'll apply the top-k method to the first classifier that we trained. A notebook containing usage examples for the top-k method is available in this book's GitHub repository (*https://oreil.ly/ml-powered-applications*).

Figure 5-10 shows the top two most correct examples for each class for our first ML Editor model. The feature that differs the most between both classes is text_len, which represents the length of the text. The classifier has learned that good questions tend to be long, and poor ones are short. It relies heavily on text length to discriminate between classes.

```
In [166]:  1  # Most confident correct positive predictions
           2  top_pos.to_display
```

Out[166]:

Id	predicted_proba	true_label	Title	body_text	text_len	action_verb_full	question_mark_full	language_question
38358	0.84	True	Punctuation when using inline dialogue	I am a bit crazy about punctuation and I have a question that I'm struggling to find a consensus...	277	False	True	False
7602	0.81	True	Is it unusual for a flashback to have a very long dialogue?	This flashback is from a short story I'm writing (unedited first draft):\n\n met Limei last sum...	870	True	True	False

```
In [167]:  1  # Most confident correct negative predictions
           2  top_neg.to_display
```

Out[167]:

Id	predicted_proba	true_label	Title	body_text	text_len	action_verb_full	question_mark_full	language_question
7878	0.20	False	When quoting a person's informal speech, how much liberty do you have to make changes to what th...	Even during a formal interview for a news article, people speak informally. They say "uhm", they...	116	True	True	False
16453	0.21	False	Printing by the Publisher	My first book was published through Xlibris. They have reported no sales from numerous authors, ...	131	True	True	False

Figure 5-10. Top-k most correct

Figure 5-11 confirms this hypothesis. The unanswered questions our classifier predicts as most likely to be answered are the longest ones, and vice versa. This observation also corroborates what we found in "Evaluate Feature Importance" on page 121, where we saw text_len was the most important feature.

```
In [168]:  1  # Most confident incorrect negative predictions
           2  worst_pos.to_display
```

Out[168]:

Id	predicted_proba	true_label	Title	body_text	text_len	action_verb_full	question_mark_full	language_question
18735	0.23	True	What do I need to know about publishing a book which I have illustrated, not written?	I recently went to the market to buy books for my 2 year old kid and found many expensive books ...	184	True	True	False
19509	0.25	True	How to copyright a book without lawyer and outside USA?	I would like to publish an ebook with amazon and i dont have time/money to keep copyrights with ...	56	True	True	False

```
In [169]:  1  # Most confident incorrect positive predictions
           2  worst_neg.to_display
```

Out[169]:

Id	predicted_proba	true_label	Title	body_text	text_len	action_verb_full	question_mark_full	language_question
12574	0.86	False	When does repetition start becoming tedious (especially metaphors)?	I always find myself using CTRL + F to remove the words/phrases I think I'm repeating too much (...	361	False	True	False
42039	0.78	False	How do I write a MODERN combat/violence scene without being dry?	Warning: I have ADHD and this might be a little ramble-y, sorry.\n\ I'm completely stumped. I'm tr...	770	True	True	False

Figure 5-11. Top-k most incorrect

We've established that the classifier leverages text_len to easily identify answered and unanswered questions, but that this feature is not sufficient and leads to misclassifications. We should add more features to improve our model. Visualizing more than two examples would help identify more candidate features.

Using the top-k method on both training and validation data helps identify limits of both our model and dataset. We've covered how it can help identify whether a model has the capacity to represent data, whether a dataset is balanced enough, and whether it contains enough representative examples.

We mostly covered evaluation methods for classification models, since such models are applicable for many concrete problems. Let's briefly take a look at ways to inspect performance when not doing classification.

Other Models

Many models can be evaluated using a classification framework. In object detection, for example, where the goal is for a model to output bounding boxes around objects of interest in an image, accuracy is a common metric. Since each image can have multiple bounding boxes representing objects and predictions, calculating an accuracy requires an additional step. First, computing the overlap between predictions and labels (often using the Jaccard index (*https://oreil.ly/eklQm*)) allows each prediction to be marked as correct or incorrect. From there, one can calculate accuracy and use all the previous methods in this chapter.

Similarly, when building models aiming to recommend content, the best way to iterate is often to test the model on a variety of categories and report its performance. The evaluation then becomes similar to a classification problem, where each category represents a class.

For types of problems where such methods may prove tricky, such as with generative models, you can still use your previous exploration of data to separate a dataset in multiple categories and generate performance metrics for each category.

When I worked with a data scientist building a sentence simplification model, examining the model's performance conditioned on sentence length showed that longer sentences proved much harder for the model. This took inspection and hand labeling but led to a clear next action step of augmenting the training data with longer sentences, which helped improve performance significantly.

We've covered many ways to inspect a model's performance by contrasting its predictions with labels, but we can also inspect the model itself. If a model isn't performing well at all, it may be worthwhile to try to interpret its predictions.

Evaluate Feature Importance

An additional way to analyze a model's performance is to inspect which features of the data it is using to make predictions. Doing so is called feature importance analysis. Evaluating feature importance is helpful to eliminate or iterate on features that are currently not helping the model. Feature importance can also help identify features that are suspiciously predictive, which is often a sign of data leakage. We will start by generating feature importance for models that can do so easily and then cover cases where such features may not be easy to extract directly.

Directly from a Classifier

To validate that a model is working correctly, visualize which features the model is using or ignoring. For simple models such as regression or decision trees, extracting the importance of features is straightforward by looking at the learned parameters of the model.

For the first model we used in the ML Editor case study, which is a random forest, we can simply use scikit-learn's API to obtain a ranked list of the importance of all features. The feature importance code and its usages can be found in the feature importance notebook in this book's GitHub repository (*https://oreil.ly/ml-powered-applications*).

```
def get_feature_importance(clf, feature_names):
    importances = clf.feature_importances_
    indices_sorted_by_importance = np.argsort(importances)[::-1]
    return list(
        zip(
            feature_names[indices_sorted_by_importance],
            importances[indices_sorted_by_importance],
        )
    )
```

If we use the function above on our trained model, with some simple list processing we can get a simple list of the ten most informative features:

```
Top 10 importances:

text_len: 0.0091
are: 0.006
what: 0.0051
writing: 0.0048
can: 0.0043
ve: 0.0041
on: 0.0039
not: 0.0039
story: 0.0039
as: 0.0038
```

There are a few things to notice here:

- The length of the text is the most informative feature.

- The other features we generated do not appear at all, with importances more than an order of magnitude lower than others. The model was not able to leverage them to meaningfully separate classes.

- The other features represent either very common words, or nouns relevant to the topic of writing.

Because our model and features are simple, these results can actually give us ideas for new features to build. We could, for example, add a feature that counts the usage of common and rare words to see if they are predictive of an answer receiving a high score.

If features or models become complex, generating feature importances requires using model explainability tools.

Black-Box Explainers

When features become complicated, feature importances can become harder to interpret. Some more complex models such as neural networks may not even be able to expose their learned feature importances. In such situations, it can be useful to leverage black-box explainers, which attempt to explain a model's predictions independently of its inner workings.

Commonly, these explainers identify predictive features for a model on a given data point instead of globally. They do this by changing each feature value for a given example and observing how the model's predictions change as a consequence. LIME (*https://github.com/marcotcr/lime*) and SHAP (*https://github.com/slundberg/shap*) are two popular black-box explainers.

For an end-to-end example of using these, see the black-box explainer notebook in the book's GitHub repository (*https://oreil.ly/ml-powered-applications*).

Figure 5-12 shows an explanation provided by LIME around which words were most important in deciding to classify this example question as high quality. LIME generated these explanations by repeatedly removing words from the input question and seeing which words make our model lean more towards one class or another.

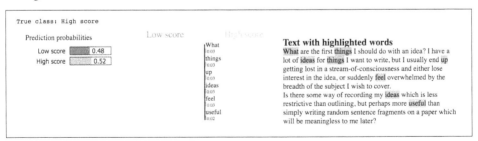

Figure 5-12. Explaining one particular example

We can see that the model correctly predicted that the question would receive a high score. However, the model was not confident, outputting only a 52% probability. The right side of Figure 5-12 shows the most impactful words for the prediction. These words do not seem like they should be particularly relevant to a question being of high quality, so let's examine more examples to see if the model leverages more useful patterns.

To get a quick sense of trends, we can use LIME on a larger sample of questions. Running LIME on each question and aggregating the results can give us an idea of which word our model finds predictive overall to make its decisions.

In Figure 5-13 we plot the most important predictions across 500 questions in our dataset. We can see the trend of our model leveraging common words is apparent in this larger sample as well. It seems that the model is having a hard time generalizing beyond leveraging frequent words. The bag of words features representing rare words most often have a value of zero. To improve on this, we could either gather a larger dataset to expose our models to a more varied vocabulary, or create features that will be less sparse.

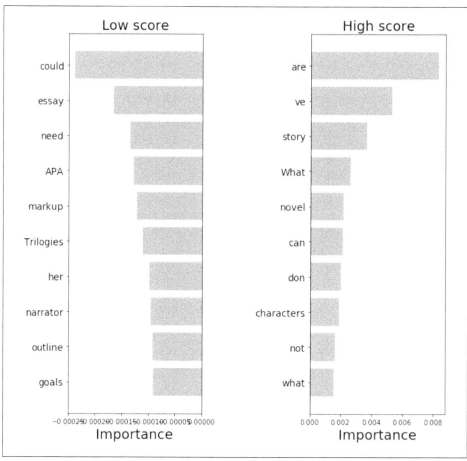

Figure 5-13. Explaining multiple examples

You'll often be surprised by the predictors your model ends up using. If any features are more predictive for the model than you'd expect, try to find examples containing these features in your training data and examine them. Use this opportunity to double check how you split your dataset and watch for data leakage.

When building a model to automatically classify emails into different topics based on their content, for example, an ML Engineer I was mentoring once found that the best predictor was a three-letter code at the top of the email. It turns out this was an internal code to the dataset that mapped almost perfectly to the labels. The model was entirely ignoring the content of the email, and memorizing a pre-existing label. This was a clear example of data leakage, which was only caught by looking at feature importance.

Conclusion

We started this chapter by covering criteria to decide on an initial model based on all we've learned so far. Then, we covered the importance of splitting data into multiple sets, and methods to avoid data leakage.

After training an initial model, we took a deep dive into ways to judge how well it is performing by finding different ways to compare and contrast its predictions to the data. Finally, we went on to inspect the model itself by displaying feature importances and using a black-box explainer to gain an intuition for the feature it uses to make predictions.

By now, you should have some intuition about improvements you could make to your modeling. This takes us to the topic of Chapter 6 where we will take a deeper dive on methods to tackle the problems we've surfaced here, by debugging and troubleshooting an ML pipeline.

Debug Your ML Problems

In the previous chapter, we trained and evaluated our first model.

Getting a pipeline to a satisfactory level of performance is hard and requires multiple iterations. The goal of this chapter is to guide you through one such iteration cycle. In this chapter, I will cover tools to debug modeling pipelines and ways to write tests to make sure they stay working once we start changing them.

Software best practices encourage practitioners to regularly test, validate, and inspect their code, especially for sensitive steps such as security or input parsing. This should be no different for ML, where errors in a model can be much harder to detect than in traditional software.

We will cover some tips that will help you make sure that your pipeline is robust and that you can try it out without causing your entire system to fail, but first let's dig into software best practices!

Software Best Practices

For most ML projects, you will repeat the process of building a model, analyzing its shortcomings, and addressing them multiple times. You are also likely to change each part of your infrastructure more than once, so it is crucial to find methods to increase iteration speed.

In ML just like with any other software project, you should follow time-tested software best practices. Most of them can be applied to ML projects with no modifications, such as building only what you need, often referred to as the Keep It Stupid Simple (KISS (*https://oreil.ly/ddzav*)) principle.

ML projects are iterative in nature and go through many different iterations of data cleaning and feature generation algorithms, as well as model choices. Even when following these best practices, two areas often end up slowing down iteration speed: debugging and testing. Speeding up debugging and test writing can have a significant impact on any projects but is even more crucial for ML projects, where the stochastic nature of models often turns a simple error into a days-long investigation.

Many resources exist to help you learn how to debug general programs, such as the University of Chicago's concise debugging guide (*https://oreil.ly/xwfYn*). If, like most ML practitioners, your language of choice is Python, I recommend looking through the Python documentation for pdb (*https://oreil.ly/CBldR*), the standard library debugger.

More than most pieces of software, however, ML code can often execute seemingly correctly but produce entirely absurd results. This means that while these tools and tips apply as is to most ML code, they are not sufficient to diagnose common problems. I illustrate this in Figure 6-1: while in most software applications, having strong test coverage can give us a high level of confidence that our application is functioning well, ML pipelines can pass many tests but still give entirely incorrect results. An ML program doesn't just have to run—it should produce accurate predictive outputs.

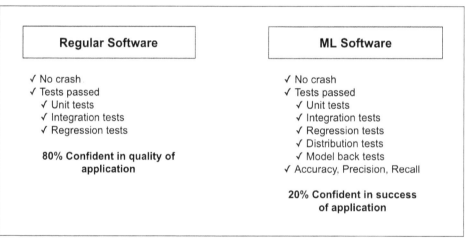

Figure 6-1. An ML pipeline can execute with no errors and still be wrong

Because ML presents an additional set of challenges when it comes to debugging, let's cover a few specific methods that help.

ML-Specific Best Practices

When it comes to ML more than any type of software, merely having a program execute end-to-end is not sufficient to be convinced of its correctness. An entire pipeline can run with no errors and produce an entirely useless model.

Let's say your program loads data and passes it to a model. Your model takes in these inputs and optimizes the model's parameters based on a learning algorithm. Finally, your trained model produces outputs from a different set of data. Your program has run without any visible bugs. The problem is that just by having your program run, you have no guarantee at all that your model's predictions are correct.

Most models simply take a numerical input of a given shape (say a matrix representing an image) and output data of a different shape (a list of coordinates of key points in the input image, for example). This means that most models will still run even if a data processing step corrupted the data before passing it to the model, as long as the data is still numeric and of a shape the model can take as input.

If your modeling pipeline performs poorly, how can you know whether it is due to the quality of a model or the presence of a bug earlier in the process?

The best way to tackle these problems in ML is to follow a progressive approach. Start by validating the data flow, then the learning capacity, and finally generalization and inference. Figure 6-2 shows an overview of the process we will cover in this chapter.

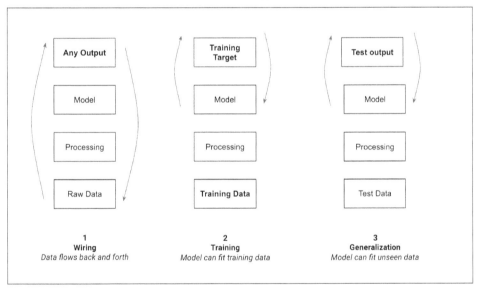

Figure 6-2. The order in which to debug a pipeline

This chapter will take you through each of these three steps, explaining each one in depth. It can be tempting to skip steps in this plan when faced with a perplexing bug, but the vast majority of times I've found that following this principled approach is the fastest way to identify and correct errors.

Let's start by validating the data flow. The simplest way to do this is by taking a very small subset of data and verifying that it can flow all the way through your pipeline.

Debug Wiring: Visualizing and Testing

This first step is simple and will make life dramatically simpler once you adopt it: start by making your pipelines work for a small subset of examples in your dataset. This corresponds to the wiring step in Figure 6-2. Once you've made sure your pipeline works for a few examples, you'll be able to write tests to make sure your pipeline keeps functioning as you make changes.

Start with One Example

The goal of this initial step is to verify that you are able to ingest data, transform it in the right format, pass it to a model, and have the model output something correct. At this stage, you aren't judging whether your model can learn something, just whether the pipeline can let data through.

Concretely this means:

- Selecting a few examples in your dataset
- Getting your model to output a prediction for these examples
- Getting your model to update its parameters to output the correct predictions for these examples

The first two items are focused on verifying that our model can ingest input data and produce a reasonable-looking output. This initial output will most likely be wrong from a modeling perspective but will allow us to check that the data is flowing all the way through.

The last item aims to make sure our model has the ability to learn a mapping from a given input to the associated output. Fitting a few data points will not produce a useful model and will likely lead to overfitting. This process simply allows us to validate that the model can update its parameters to fit a set of inputs and outputs.

Here is how this first step would look in practice: if you are training a model to predict whether Kickstarter campaigns will be successful, you may be planning on training it on all campaigns from the last few years. Following this tip, you should start by checking whether your model can output a prediction for two campaigns. Then, use the label for these campaigns (whether they were successful or not) to optimize the model's parameters until it predicts the correct outcome.

If we have chosen our model appropriately, it should have the capacity to learn from our dataset. And if our model can learn from our entire dataset, it should have the capacity to memorize a data point. The ability to learn from a few examples is a necessary condition for a model to learn from an entire dataset. It is also much easier to validate than the entire learning process, so starting with one allows us to quickly narrow down any potential future problems.

The vast majority of errors that can come up at this initial stage relate to data mismatch: the data you are loading and preprocessing is fed to your model in a format that it cannot accept. Since most models accept only numerical values, for example, they may fail when a given value is left empty and has a null value.

Some cases of mismatch can be more elusive and lead to silent failure. A pipeline fed values that are not in the correct range or shape may still run but would produce a poorly performing model. Models that require normalized data will often still train on nonnormalized data: they simply will not be able to fit it in a useful manner. Similarly, feeding a matrix of the wrong shape to a model can cause it to misinterpret the input and produce incorrect outputs.

Catching such errors is harder, because they will manifest later in the process once we evaluate the performance of a model. The best way to proactively detect them is to visualize data as you build your pipeline and build tests to encode assumptions. We will see how to do this next.

Visualization steps

As we've seen in previous chapters, while metrics are a crucial part of modeling work, regularly inspecting and investigating our data is equally important. Observing just a few examples to start makes it easier to notice changes or inconsistencies.

The goal of this process is to inspect changes at regular intervals. If you think of a data pipeline as an assembly line, you'd want to inspect the product *after every meaningful change*. This means checking the value of your datapoint at every line is probably too frequent, and looking only at the input and output values is definitely not informative enough.

In Figure 6-3, I illustrate a few example inspection points you could use to take a look at a data pipeline. In this example, we inspect the data at multiple steps, starting with raw data all the way to model outputs.

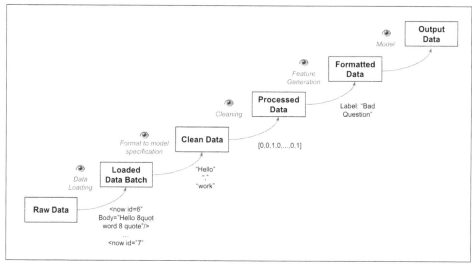

Figure 6-3. Potential inspection points

Next, we'll cover a few key steps that are often worth inspecting. We'll start with data loading and move on to cleaning, feature generation, formatting, and model outputs.

Data loading

Whether you are loading your data from disk or through an API call, you will want to verify that it is formatted correctly. This process is similar to the one you go through when doing EDA but is done here within the context of the pipeline you have built to verify that no error has led to the data becoming corrupted.

Does it contain all the fields you expect it to? Are any of these fields null or of constant value? Do any of the values lie in a range that seems incorrect, such as an age variable sometimes being negative? If you are working with text or speech or images, do the examples match your expectations of what they would look, sound, or read like?

Most of our processing steps rely on assumptions we make about the structure of our input data, so it is crucial to validate this aspect.

Because the goal here is to identify inconsistencies between our expectation of the data and reality, you may want to visualize more than one or two data points. Visualizing a representative sample will assure we do not only observe a "lucky" example and wrongly assume all data points are of the same quality.

Figure 6-4 shows an example for our case study from the dataset exploration notebook in this book's GitHub repository (*https://oreil.ly/ml-powered-applications*). Here, hundreds of posts in our archive are of an undocumented post type and thus need to be filtered out. In the figure, you can see rows with a PostTypeId of 5, which is not referenced in the dataset documentation and that we thus remove from the training data.

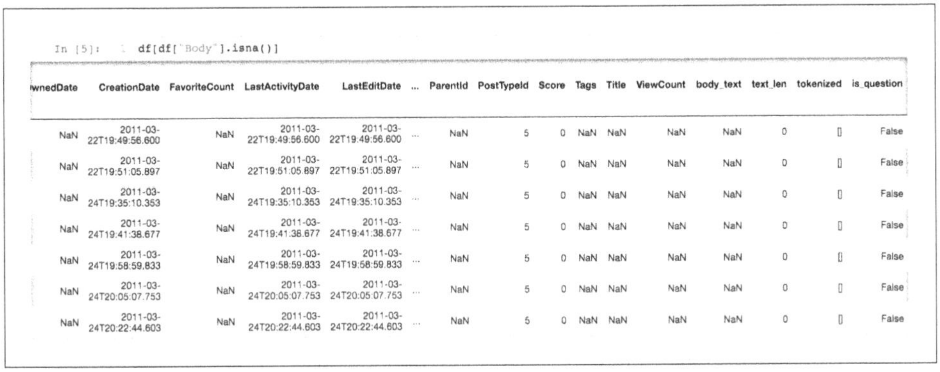

```
In [5]:    df[df["Body"].isna()]
```

wnedDate	CreationDate	FavoriteCount	LastActivityDate	LastEditDate	...	ParentId	PostTypeId	Score	Tags	Title	ViewCount	body_text	text_len	tokenized	is_question
NaN	2011-03-22T19:49:56.600	NaN	2011-03-22T19:49:56.600	2011-03-22T19:49:56.600	...	NaN	5	0	NaN	NaN	NaN	NaN	0	[]	False
NaN	2011-03-22T19:51:05.897	NaN	2011-03-22T19:51:05.897	2011-03-22T19:51:05.897	...	NaN	5	0	NaN	NaN	NaN	NaN	0	[]	False
NaN	2011-03-24T19:35:10.353	NaN	2011-03-24T19:35:10.353	2011-03-24T19:35:10.353	...	NaN	5	0	NaN	NaN	NaN	NaN	0	[]	False
NaN	2011-03-24T19:41:38.677	NaN	2011-03-24T19:41:38.677	2011-03-24T19:41:38.677	...	NaN	5	0	NaN	NaN	NaN	NaN	0	[]	False
NaN	2011-03-24T19:58:59.833	NaN	2011-03-24T19:58:59.833	2011-03-24T19:58:59.833	...	NaN	5	0	NaN	NaN	NaN	NaN	0	[]	False
NaN	2011-03-24T20:05:07.753	NaN	2011-03-24T20:05:07.753	2011-03-24T20:05:07.753	...	NaN	5	0	NaN	NaN	NaN	NaN	0	[]	False
NaN	2011-03-24T20:22:44.603	NaN	2011-03-24T20:22:44.603	2011-03-24T20:22:44.603	...	NaN	5	0	NaN	NaN	NaN	NaN	0	[]	False

Figure 6-4. Visualizing a few rows of data

Once you've verified that the data conforms to expectations laid out in the dataset documentation, it is time to start processing it for modeling purposes. This starts with data cleaning.

Cleaning and feature selection

The next step in most pipelines is to remove any unnecessary information. This can include fields or values that are not going to be used by the model but also any fields that may contain information about our label that our model would not have access to in production (see "Split Your Dataset" on page 99).

Remember that each feature you remove is a potential predictor for your model. The task of deciding which features to keep and which features to remove is called *feature selection* and is an integral part of iterating on models.

You should verify that no crucial information is lost, that all unneeded values are removed, and that you have not left any extra information in our dataset that will artificially boost our model's performance by leaking information (see "Data leakage" on page 102).

Once the data is cleaned, you'll want to generate some features for your model to use.

Feature generation

When generating a new feature, such as adding the frequency of references to a product name in the description of a kickstarter campaign, for example, it is important to inspect its values. You need to check that the feature values are populated and that the values seem reasonable. This is a challenging task, as it requires not only identifying all features but estimating reasonable values for each of these features.

At this point, you do not need to analyze it any deeper, as this step is focusing on validating assumptions about data flowing through the model, not the usefulness of the data or the model yet.

Once features have been generated, you should make sure they can be passed to the model in a format it can understand.

Data formatting

As we've discussed in earlier chapters, before passing data points to a model, you will need to transform them to a format it can understand. This can include normalizing input values, vectorizing text by representing it in a numerical fashion, or formatting a black and white video as a 3D tensor (see "Vectorizing" on page 69).

If you are working on a supervised problem, you'll use a label in addition to the input, such as class names in classification, or a segmentation map in image segmentation. These will also need to be transformed to a model-understandable format.

In my experience working on multiple image segmentation problems, for example, data mismatch between labels and model predictions is one of the most common causes of errors. Segmentation models use segmentation masks as labels. These masks are the same size as the input image, but instead of pixel values, they contain class labels for each pixel. Unfortunately, different libraries use different conventions to represent these masks, so the labels often end up in the wrong format, preventing the model from learning.

I've illustrated this common pitfall in Figure 6-5. Let's say a model expects segmentation masks to be passed with a value of 255 for pixels that are of a certain class, and 0 otherwise. If a user instead assumes that pixels contained within the mask should have a value of 1 instead of 255, they may pass their labeled masks in the format seen in "provided." This would lead the mask to be considered as almost entirely empty, and the model would output inaccurate predictions.

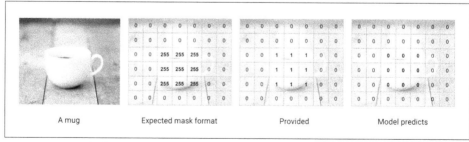

Figure 6-5. Poorly formatted labels will prevent a model from learning

Similarly, classification labels are often represented as a list of zeros with a single one at the index of the true class. A simple off-by-one error can lead to labels being shifted and a model learning to always predict the shifted-by-one label. This kind of error can be hard to troubleshoot if you do not take the time to look at your data.

Because ML models will manage to fit to most numerical outputs regardless of whether they have an accurate structure or content, this stage is where many tricky bugs occur and where this method is useful to find them.

Here is an example of what such a formatting function looks like for our case study. I generate a vectorized representation of our question text. Then, I append additional features to this representation. Since the function consists of multiple transformations and vector operations, visualizing the return value of this function will allow me to verify that it does format data the way we intend it to.

```
def get_feature_vector_and_label(df, feature_names):
    """
    Generate input and output vectors using the vectors feature and
     the given feature names
    :param df: input DataFrame
    :param feature_names: names of feature columns (other than vectors)
    :return: feature array and label array
    """
    vec_features = vstack(df["vectors"])
    num_features = df[feature_names].astype(float)
    features = hstack([vec_features, num_features])
    labels = df["Score"] > df["Score"].median()
    return features, labels

features = [
    "action_verb_full",
    "question_mark_full",
    "text_len",
    "language_question",
]

X_train, y_train = get_feature_vector_and_label(train_df, features)
```

When working with text data especially, there are usually multiple steps involved before data is properly formatted for a model. Going from a string of text to a tokenized list to a vectorized representation including potential additional features is an error-prone process. Even inspecting the shape of the objects at each step can help catch many simple mistakes.

Once the data is in the appropriate format, you can pass it to a model. The last step is to visualize and validate the model's outputs.

Model output

At first, looking at outputs helps us see whether our model's predictions are the right type or shape (if we are predicting house price and duration on market, is our model outputting an array of two numbers?).

In addition, when fitting a model to only a couple data points, we should see its outputs start matching the true label. If the model doesn't fit the data points, this may be an indication of the data being incorrectly formatted or becoming corrupted.

If the output of the model does not change at all during training, this may mean that our model is actually not leveraging the input data. In such a case, I recommend referring to "Stand on the Shoulders of Giants" on page 32 to validate that the model is being used correctly.

Once we've gone through the entire pipeline for a few examples, it is time to write a few tests to automate some of this visualization work.

Systematizing our visual validation

Going through the visualization work described earlier helps catch a significant amount of bugs and is a good time investment for every novel pipeline. Validating assumptions about how data is flowing through the model helps save a significant amount of time down the line, which can now be spent focusing on training and generalization.

Pipelines change often, however. As you update different aspects iteratively to improve your model and modify some of the processing logic, how can you guarantee that everything is still working as intended? Going through the pipeline and visualizing an example at all steps each time you make any change would quickly get tiring.

This is where the software engineering best practices we talked about earlier come into play. It is time to isolate each part of this pipeline, and encode our observations into tests that we will be able to run as our pipeline changes, to validate it.

Separate your concerns

Just like regular software, ML benefits greatly from a modular organization. To make current and future debugging easier, separate each function so that you can check that it individually works before looking at the broader pipeline.

Once a pipeline is broken down into individual functions, you'll be able to write tests for them.

Test Your ML Code

Testing a model's behavior is hard. The majority of code in an ML pipeline is not about the training pipeline or the model itself, however. If you look back to our pipeline example in "Start with a Simple Pipeline" on page 38, most functions behave in a deterministic way and can be tested.

In my experience, helping engineers and data scientists debug their models, I've learned that the vast majority of errors come from the way data is acquired, processed, or fed to the model. Testing data processing logic is thus crucial in order to build a successful ML product.

For even more information about potential tests of an ML system, I recommend the paper by E. Breck et al., "The ML Test Score: A Rubric for ML Production Readiness and Technical Debt Reduction" (*https://oreil.ly/OjYVl*), which contains many more examples and lessons learned from deploying such systems at Google.

In this next section, we will describe useful tests to write for three key areas. In Figure 6-6, you can see each of these areas, along with a few examples of tests that we will describe next.

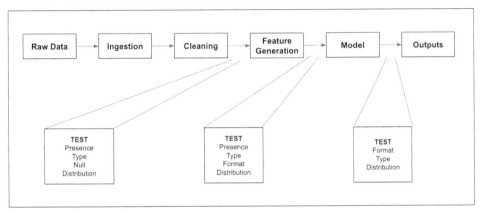

Figure 6-6. The three key areas to test

Pipelines start by ingesting data, so we'll want to test that part first.

Test data ingestion

Data usually lives serialized on a disk or in a database. When moving data from storage to our pipeline, we should make sure to verify the integrity and correctness of the data. We can start by writing tests that verify that the data points we load possess every feature we'll need.

The following are three tests validating that our parser returns the right type (a dataframe), that all important columns are defined, and that features are not all null. You can find the tests we'll cover in this chapter (and additional ones) in the tests folder on this book's GitHub repository (*https://oreil.ly/ml-powered-applications*).

```
def test_parser_returns_dataframe():
    """
    Tests that our parser runs and returns a DataFrame
    """
    df = get_fixture_df()
```

```
    assert isinstance(df, pd.DataFrame)


def test_feature_columns_exist():
    """
    Validate that all required columns are present
    """
    df = get_fixture_df()
    for col in REQUIRED_COLUMNS:
        assert col in df.columns


def test_features_not_all_null():
    """
    Validate that no features are missing every value
    """
    df = get_fixture_df()
    for col in REQUIRED_COLUMNS:
        assert not df[col].isnull().all()
```

We can also test each feature for its type and validate that it is not null. Finally, we can encode assumptions we have about the distribution and ranges of these values by testing their average, minimum, and maximum values. Recently, libraries such as Great Expectations (*https://oreil.ly/VG6b1*) have emerged to test the distributions of features directly.

Here, you can see how you could write a simple mean test:

```
ACCEPTABLE_TEXT_LENGTH_MEANS = pd.Interval(left=20, right=2000)

def test_text_mean():
    """
    Validate that text mean matches with exploration expectations
    """
    df = get_fixture_df()
    df["text_len"] = df["body_text"].str.len()
    text_col_mean = df["text_len"].mean()
    assert text_col_mean in ACCEPTABLE_TEXT_LENGTH_MEANS
```

These tests allow us to verify that no matter which changes are made on the storage side or with the API of our data source, we can know that our model has access to the same kind of data it was first trained on. Once we're confident as to the consistency of the data we ingest, let's look at the next step in the pipeline, data processing.

Test data processing

After testing that the data that makes it to the beginning of our pipeline conforms to our expectations, we should test that our cleaning and feature generation steps do what we expect. We can start by writing tests for the preprocessing function we have, verifying that it does indeed do what we intend it to. Also, we can write similar tests to the data ingestion ones and focus on guaranteeing that our assumptions about the state of the data going into our model are valid.

This means testing for the presence, type, and characteristics of the data points after our processing pipeline. The following are examples of tests for the presence of generated features, their type, and minimum, maximum, and mean values:

```
def test_feature_presence(df_with_features):
    for feat in REQUIRED_FEATURES:
        assert feat in df_with_features.columns

def test_feature_type(df_with_features):
    assert df_with_features["is_question"].dtype == bool
    assert df_with_features["action_verb_full"].dtype == bool
    assert df_with_features["language_question"].dtype == bool
    assert df_with_features["question_mark_full"].dtype == bool
    assert df_with_features["norm_text_len"].dtype == float
    assert df_with_features["vectors"].dtype == list

def test_normalized_text_length(df_with_features):
    normalized_mean = df_with_features["norm_text_len"].mean()
    normalized_max = df_with_features["norm_text_len"].max()
    normalized_min = df_with_features["norm_text_len"].min()
    assert normalized_mean in pd.Interval(left=-1, right=1)
    assert normalized_max in pd.Interval(left=-1, right=1)
    assert normalized_min in pd.Interval(left=-1, right=1)
```

These tests allow us to notice any changes to our pipelines that impact the input to our model without having to write any additional tests. We will only need to write new tests when we add new features or change the input to our model.

We can now feel confident both in the data we ingest and in the transformations we apply to it, so it is time to test the next part of the pipeline, the model.

Test model outputs

Similarly to the two previous categories, we will write tests to validate that the values the model outputs have the correct dimensions and ranges. We will also test predictions for specific inputs. This helps proactively detect regressions in prediction quality in new models and guarantee that any model we use always produces the expected output on these example inputs. When a new model shows better aggregate performance, it can be hard to notice whether its performance worsened on specific types of inputs. Writing such tests helps detect such issues more easily.

In the following examples, I start by testing the shape of the predictions of our model, as well as their values. The third test aims to prevent regressions by guaranteeing that the model classifies a specific poorly worded input question as low quality.

```
def test_model_prediction_dimensions(
    df_with_features, trained_v1_vectorizer, trained_v1_model
```

```
):
    df_with_features["vectors"] = get_vectorized_series(
        df_with_features["full_text"].copy(), trained_v1_vectorizer
    )

    features, labels = get_feature_vector_and_label(
        df_with_features, FEATURE_NAMES
    )

    probas = trained_v1_model.predict_proba(features)
    # the model makes one prediction per input example
    assert probas.shape[0] == features.shape[0]
    # the model predicts probabilities for two classes
    assert probas.shape[1] == 2


def test_model_proba_values(
    df_with_features, trained_v1_vectorizer, trained_v1_model
):
    df_with_features["vectors"] = get_vectorized_series(
        df_with_features["full_text"].copy(), trained_v1_vectorizer
    )

    features, labels = get_feature_vector_and_label(
        df_with_features, FEATURE_NAMES
    )

    probas = trained_v1_model.predict_proba(features)
    # the model's probabilities are between 0 and 1
    assert (probas >= 0).all() and (probas <= 1).all()


def test_model_predicts_no_on_bad_question():
    input_text = "This isn't even a question. We should score it poorly"
    is_question_good = get_model_predictions_for_input_texts([input_text])
    # The model classifies the question as poor
    assert not is_question_good[0]
```

We first visually inspected the data to verify it remained useful and usable throughout our pipeline. Then, we wrote tests to guarantee these assumptions remain correct as our processing strategy evolves. It is now time to tackle the second part of Figure 6-2, debugging the training procedure.

Debug Training: Make Your Model Learn

Once you've tested your pipeline and validated that it works for one example, you know a few things. Your pipeline takes in data and successfully transforms it. It then passes this data to a model in the right format. Finally, the model can take a few data points and learn from them, outputting the correct results.

It is now time to see whether your model can work on more than a few data points and learn from your training set. The focus of this next section is on being able to train your model on many examples and have it *fit to all of your training data*.

To do so, you can now pass your entire training set to your model and measure its performance. Alternatively, if you have a large amount of data, you can instead gradually increase the quantity of data you feed to your model while keeping an eye on aggregate performance.

One advantage of progressively increasing the size of your training dataset is that you'll be able to measure the effect of additional data on the performance of your model. Start with a few hundred examples, and then move to a few thousand, before passing in your whole dataset (if your dataset is smaller than a thousand examples, feel free to skip straight to using it in its entirety).

At each step, fit your model on the data and evaluate its performance *on the same data*. If your model has the capacity to learn from the data you are using, its performance on the training data should stay relatively stable.

To contextualize model performance, I recommend generating an estimate of what an acceptable error level for your task is by labeling a few examples yourself, for example, and comparing your predictions to the true label. Most tasks also come with an irreducible error, representing the best performance given the complexity of the task. See Figure 6-7 for an illustration of usual training performance compared to such metrics.

A model's performance on the whole dataset should be worse than when using only one example, since memorizing an entire training set is harder than a single example, but should still remain within the boundaries defined earlier.

If you are able to feed your entire training set and the performance of your model reaches the requirement you defined when looking at your product goal, feel free to move on to the next section! If not, I've outlined a couple common reasons a model can struggle on a training set in the next section.

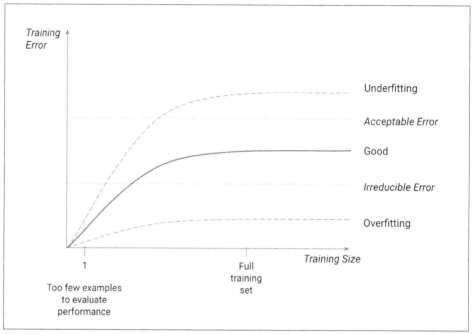

Figure 6-7. Training accuracy as a function of dataset size

Task Difficulty

If a model's performance is drastically lower than expected, the task may be too difficult. To evaluate how hard a task is, consider:

- The quantity and diversity of data you have
- How predictive the features you have generated are
- The complexity of your model

Let's look at each of those in a little more detail.

Data quality, quantity, and diversity

The more diverse and complex your problem is, the more data you will need for a model to learn from it. For your model to learn patterns, you should aim to have many examples of each type of data you have. If you are classifying pictures of cats as one of a hundred possible breeds, for example, you'd need many more pictures than if you were simply trying to tell cats apart from dogs. In fact, the quantity of data you need often scales exponentially with the number of classes, as having more classes means more opportunities for misclassification.

In addition, the less data you have, the more impact any errors in your labels or any missing values have. This is why it is worth spending the time to inspect and verify features and labels of your dataset.

Finally, most datasets contain *outliers*, data points that are radically different from others and very hard for a model to handle. Removing outliers from your training set can often improve the performance of a model by simplifying the task at hand, but it is not always the right approach: if you believe that your model may encounter similar data points in production, you should keep outliers and *focus on improving your data and model* so that the model can successfully fit to them.

The more complex a dataset is, the more helpful it can be to work on ways to represent your data that will make it easier for a model to learn from it. Let's look at what this means.

Data representation

How easy is it to detect the patterns you care about using only the representation you give your model? If a model is struggling to perform well on training data, you should add features that make the data more expressive and thus help the model learn better.

This can consist of novel features we had previously decided to ignore but that may be predictive. In our ML Editor example, a first iteration of the model only took into account the text in the body of a question. After exploring the dataset further, I noticed that question titles are often very informative as to whether a question is good or not. Incorporating that feature back into the dataset allowed the model to perform better.

New features can often be generated by iterating on existing ones or combining them in a creative manner. We saw an example of this in "Let Data Inform Features and Models" on page 85, when we looked at ways to combine the day of the week and day of the month to generate a feature that was relevant to a particular business case.

In some cases, the problem lies with your model. Let's look at these cases next.

Model capacity

Increasing data quality and improving features often provides the largest benefits. When a model is the cause for poor performance, it can often mean that it is not adequate to the task at hand. As we saw in "From Patterns to Models" on page 98, specific datasets and problems call for specific models. A model that is not appropriate for a task will struggle to perform on it, even if it was able to overfit a few examples.

If a model struggles on a dataset that seems to have many predictive features, start by asking yourself whether you are using the right type of model. If possible, use a simpler version of the given model to more easily inspect it. For example, if a random forest model isn't performing at all, try a decision tree on the same task and visualize its splits to examine whether they use the features you thought would be predictive.

On the other hand, the model you are using may be too simple. Starting with the simplest model is good to quickly iterate, but some tasks are entirely out of reach of some models. To tackle them, you may need to add complexity to your model. To verify that a model is indeed adapted to a task, I recommend looking at prior art as we described in "Stand on the Shoulders of Giants" on page 32. Find examples of similar tasks, and examine which models were used to tackle them. Using one of those models should be a good starting point.

If the model seems appropriate for the task, its lackluster performance could be due to the training procedure.

Optimization Problems

Starting by validating that a model can fit a small set of examples makes us confident that data can flow back and forth. We do not know, however, whether our training procedure can adequately fit a model to the entire dataset. The method that our model is using to update its weights may be inadequate for our current dataset. Such problems often occur in more complex models such as neural networks, where hyperparameter choice can have a significant impact on training performance.

When dealing with models that are fit using gradient descent techniques such as neural networks, using visualization tools such as TensorBoard (*https://oreil.ly/xn2tY*) can help surface training problems. When plotting the loss during your optimization process, you should see it decline steeply initially and then gradually. In Figure 6-8, you can see an example of a TensorBoard dashboard depicting a loss function (cross-entropy in this case) as training progresses.

Such a curve can show that the loss is decreasing very slowly, indicating that a model may be learning too slowly. In such a case, you could increase the learning rate and plot the same curve to see whether the loss decreases faster. If a loss curve looks very unstable, on the other hand, it may be due to the learning rate being too large.

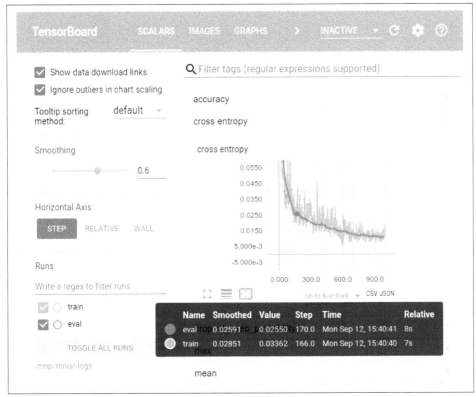

Figure 6-8. TensorBoard dashboard screenshot from the TensorBoard documentation

In addition to the loss, visualizing weight values and activations can help you identify if a network is not learning properly. In Figure 6-9, you can see a change in the distribution of the weights as training progresses. If you see the distributions remain stable for a few epochs, it may be a sign that you should increase the learning rate. If they vary too much, lower it instead.

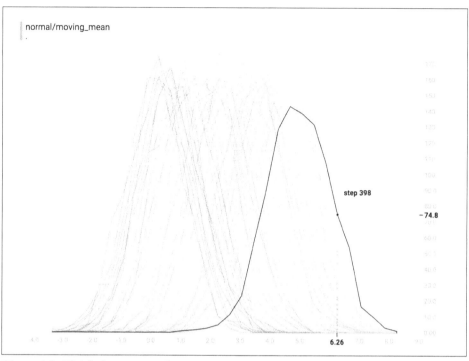

Figure 6-9. Weight histograms changing as training progresses

Successfully fitting a model to the training data is an important milestone in an ML project, but it is not the last step. The end goal of building an ML product is to build a model that can perform well on examples it has never seen before. To do this, we need a model that can generalize well to unseen examples, so I'll cover generalization next.

Debug Generalization: Make Your Model Useful

Generalization is the third and final part of Figure 6-2 and focuses on getting an ML model to work well on data it has not seen before. In "Split Your Dataset" on page 99, we saw the importance of creating separate training, validation, and test splits to evaluate a model's ability to generalize to unseen examples. In "Evaluate Your Model: Look Beyond Accuracy" on page 109, we covered methods to analyze the performance of a model and identify potential additional features to help improve it. Here, we'll cover some recommendations when a model still fails to perform on the validation set after multiple iterations.

Data Leakage

We covered data leakage in more detail in "Data leakage" on page 102, but I want to mention it here within the context of generalization. A model will often initially perform worse on the validation set than the training set. This is to be expected since it is harder to make predictions on data that a model has not been exposed to before than on data it was trained to fit.

 When looking at validation loss and training loss during training before it is complete, validation performance may appear better than training performance. This is because the training loss accumulates over the epoch as the model is trained, while the validation loss is calculated after the epoch has completed, using the latest version of the model.

If validation performance is better than training performance, it can sometimes be due to data leakage. If examples in the training data contain information about others in the validation data, a model will be able to leverage this information and perform well on the validation set. If you are surprised by validation performance, inspect the features a model uses and see if they show data leakage. Fixing such a leakage issue will lead to a lower validation performance, but a better model.

Data leakage can lead us to believe that a model is generalizing when it really isn't. In other cases, it is clear from looking at performance on a held-out validation set that the model performs well only on training. In those kinds of cases, the model may be overfitting.

Overfitting

In "Bias variance trade-off" on page 107, we saw that when a model is struggling to fit the training data, we say the model is underfitting. We also saw that the opposite of *underfitting* is *overfitting*, and this is when our model fits our training data *too well*.

What does fitting data too well mean? It means that instead of learning generalizable trends that correlate with good or poor writing, for example, a model may pick up on specific patterns present in individual examples in a training set that are not present in different data. Those patterns help it get a high score on the training set but aren't useful to classify other examples.

Figure 6-10 shows a practical example of overfitting and underfitting for a toy dataset. The overfit model fits the training data perfectly but doesn't accurately approximate the underlying trend; thus, it fails to accurately predict unseen points. The underfit model does not capture the trend of the data at all. The model labeled reasonable fit performs worse on the training data than the overfit model but better on unseen data.

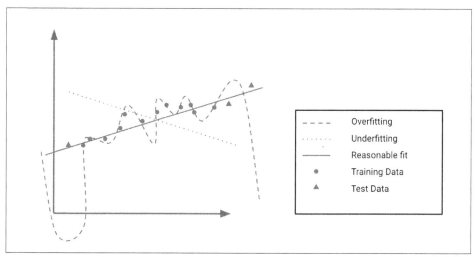

Figure 6-10. Overfitting versus underfitting

When a model performs drastically better on the training set than on the test set, that usually means that it is overfit. It has learned the specific details of the training data but is not able to perform on unseen data.

Since overfitting is due to a model learning too much about training data, we can prevent it by reducing the ability of a model to learn from a dataset. There are a few ways to do that, which we'll cover here.

Regularization

Regularization adds a penalty on a model's capacity to represent information. Regularizing aims to limit the ability of a model to focus on many irrelevant patterns and encourages it to pick fewer, more predictive features.

A common way to regularize a model is to impose a penalty on the absolute value of its weights. For models such as linear and logistic regression, for example, L1 and L2 regularization add an additional term to the loss function that penalizes large weights. In the case of L1, this term is the sum of the absolute value of weights. For L2, it is the sum of the squared values of weight.

Different regularization methods have different effects. L1 regularization can help select informative features by setting uninformative ones to zero (read more on the "Lasso (statistics)" Wikipedia page (*https://oreil.ly/Su9Bf*)). L1 regularization is also useful when some features are correlated by encouraging the model to leverage only one of them.

Regularization methods can also be model specific. Neural networks often use dropout as a regularization method. Dropout randomly ignores some proportion of neurons in a network during training. This prevents a single neuron from becoming excessively influential, which could enable the network to memorize aspects of training data.

For tree-based models such as random forests, reducing the maximum depth of trees reduces the ability of each tree to overfit to the data and thus helps regularize the forest. Increasing the number of trees used in a forest also regularizes it.

Another way to prevent a model from overfitting to training data is to make the data itself harder to overfit to. We can do this through a process called *data augmentation*.

Data augmentation

Data augmentation is the process of creating new training data by slightly altering existing data points. The goal is to artificially produce data points that are different from existing ones in order to expose a model to a more varied type of input. Augmentation strategies depend on the type of data. In Figure 6-11, you can see a few potential augmentations for images.

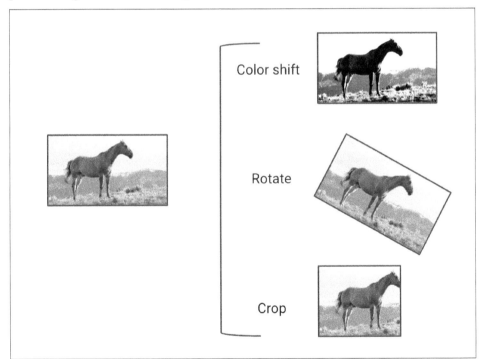

Figure 6-11. A few examples of data augmentation for images

Data augmentation makes a training set less homogeneous and thus more complex. This makes fitting the training data harder but exposes a model to a wider range of inputs during training. Data augmentation often leads to lower performance on the training set but higher performance on unseen data such as a validation set and examples in production. This strategy is especially effective if we can use augmentation to make our training set more similar to examples in the wild.

I once helped an engineer use satellite imagery to detect flooded roads after a hurricane. The project was challenging, since he only had access to labeled data for non-flooded cities. To help improve his model's performance on hurricane imagery, which is significantly darker and lower quality, they built augmentation pipelines that made training images look darker and blurrier. This lowered training performance since the roads were now harder to detect. On the other hand, it increased the model's performance on the validation set because the augmentation process exposed the model to images that were more similar to the ones it would encounter in the validation set. Data augmentation helped make the training set more representative and thus made the model more robust.

If after using the methods described earlier a model still performs poorly on a validation set, you should iterate on the dataset itself.

Dataset redesign

In some cases, a difficult training/validation split can lead to a model underfitting and struggling on the validation set. If a model is exposed to only easy examples in its training set and only challenging ones in its validation set, it will be unable to learn from difficult data points. Similarly, some categories of examples may be underrepresented in the training set, preventing a model ever from learning from them. If a model is trained to minimize an aggregate metric, it risks fitting mostly the majority of classes, ignoring minority ones.

While augmentation strategies can help, redesigning a training split to make it more representative is often the best path forward. When doing this, we should carefully control for data leakage and make the splits as balanced as possible in terms of difficulty. If the new data split allocates all the easy examples to the validation set, the model's performance on the validation set will be artificially high, but it will not translate to results in production. To alleviate concerns that data splits may be of unequal quality, we can use k-fold cross-validation (*https://oreil.ly/NkhZa*), where we perform k successive different splits, and measure the performance of the model on each split.

Once we've balanced our training and validation set to make sure that they are of similar complexity, our model's performance should improve. If the performance is still not satisfactory, we may be simply tackling a really hard problem.

Consider the Task at Hand

A model can struggle to generalize because the task is too complex. The input we are using may not be predictive of the target, for example. To make sure the task you are tackling is of appropriate difficulty for the current state of ML, I suggest referring once more to "Stand on the Shoulders of Giants" on page 32, where I described how to explore and evaluate the current state of the art.

In addition, having a dataset does not mean that a task is solvable. Consider the impossible task of accurately predicting random outputs from random inputs. You could build a model that performs well on a training set by memorizing it, but this model would not be able to accurately predict other random outputs from random inputs.

If your models aren't generalizing, your task may be too hard. There may not be enough information in your training examples to learn *meaningful features* that will be informative for future data points. If that is the case, then the problem you have is not well suited for ML, and I would invite you to revisit Chapter 1 to find a better framing.

Conclusion

In this chapter, we covered the three successive steps you should follow to get a model to work. First, debug the wiring of your pipeline by inspecting the data and writing tests. Then, get a model to perform well on a training test to validate that it has the capacity to learn. Finally, verify that it is able to generalize and produce useful outputs on unseen data.

This process will help you debug models, build them faster, and make them more robust. Once you have built, trained, and debugged your first model, the next step is to judge its performance and either iterate on it or deploy it.

In Chapter 7, we will cover how to use a trained classifier to provide actionable recommendations for users. We will then compare candidate models for the ML Editor and decide which one should be used to power these recommendations.

Using Classifiers for Writing Recommendations

The best way to make progress in ML is through repeatedly following the iterative loop depicted in Figure 7-1, which we saw in the introduction to Part III. Start by establishing a modeling hypothesis, iterate on a modeling pipeline, and perform detailed error analysis to inform your next hypothesis.

Figure 7-1. The ML loop

The previous chapters described multiple steps in this loop. In Chapter 5, we covered how to train and score a model. In Chapter 6, we shared advice on how to build models faster and troubleshoot ML-related errors. This chapter closes an iteration of the loop by first showcasing methods to use trained classifiers to provide suggestions to users, then selecting a model to use for the ML Editor, and finally combining both to build a working ML Editor.

In "ML Editor Planning" on page 36 we outlined our plan for the ML Editor, which consists of training a model that classifies questions into high- and low-score categories and use this trained model to guide users to write better questions. Let's see how we can use such a model to provide writing advice to users.

Extracting Recommendations from Models

The goal of the ML Editor is to provide writing recommendations. Classifying a question as good or bad is a first step in this direction since it makes it possible to display the current quality of a question to a user. We'd like to go one step beyond this and help users improve the formulation of their questions by providing them with actionable recommendations.

This section covers methods to provide such recommendations. We will start with simple approaches that rely on aggregate feature metrics and do not require the use of a model at inference time. Then, we will see how to both use a model's score and its sensitivity to perturbations to generate more personalized recommendations. You can find examples of each of the methods showcased in this chapter applied to the ML Editor in the generating recommendations notebook on this book's GitHub site (*https://oreil.ly/ml-powered-applications*).

What Can We Achieve Without a Model?

Training a model that performs well is achieved through multiple iterations of the ML loop. Each iteration helps create a better set of features through researching prior art, iterating on potential datasets, and examining model results. To provide users with recommendations, you can leverage this feature iteration work. This approach does not necessarily require running a model on each question a user submits and focuses instead on making general recommendations.

You can do so either by using the features directly or by incorporating a trained model to help select relevant ones.

Using feature statistics

Once predictive features have been identified, they can be directly communicated to a user without using a model. If the mean value of a feature is significantly different for each class, you can share this information directly to help users nudge their examples in the direction of the target class.

One of the features we identified early on for the ML Editor was the presence of question marks. Inspecting the data showed that questions with high scores tend to have fewer question marks. To use this information to generate recommendations, we can write a rule that warns a user if the proportion of question marks in their question is much larger than in highly rated questions.

Visualizing average feature values for each label can be done in a few lines of code using pandas.

```
class_feature_values = feats_labels.groupby("label").mean()
class_feature_values = class_feature_values.round(3)
class_feature_values.transpose()
```

Running the previous code produces the result shown in Table 7-1. In these results, we can see that many of the features we've generated have significantly different values for high- and low-score questions, labeled True and False here.

Table 7-1. Differences in feature values between classes

Label	False	True
num_questions	0.432	0.409
num_periods	0.814	0.754
num_commas	0.673	0.728
num_exclam	0.019	0.015
num_quotes	0.216	0.199
num_colon	0.094	0.081
num_stops	10.537	10.610
num_semicolon	0.013	0.014
num_words	21.638	21.480
num_chars	822.104	967.032

Using feature statistics is a simple way to provide robust recommendations. It is in many ways similar to the heuristic approach that we first built in "The Simplest Approach: Being the Algorithm" on page 17.

When comparing feature values between classes, it can be hard to identify which features contribute the most to a question being classified a certain way. To estimate this better, we can use feature importance.

Extracting Global Feature Importance

We first showed examples of generating feature importance in the context of model evaluation in "Evaluate Feature Importance" on page 121. Feature importances can also be used to prioritize feature-based recommendations. When displaying recommendations to users, features that are most predictive for a trained classifier should be prioritized.

Next, I've displayed the results of a feature importance analysis for a question classification model that uses a total of 30 features. Each of the top features has a much larger importance than the bottom features. Guiding users to act based on these top features first will help them improve their questions faster according to the model.

```
Top 5 importances:

num_chars: 0.053
num_questions: 0.051
num_periods: 0.051
ADV: 0.049
ADJ: 0.049

Bottom 5 importances:

X: 0.011
num_semicolon: 0.0076
num_exclam: 0.0072
CONJ: 0
SCONJ: 0
```

Combining feature statistics and feature importance can make recommendations more actionable and focused. The first approach provides target values for each feature, while the latter prioritizes a smaller subset of the most important features to display. These approaches also provide recommendations quickly, since they do not require running a model at inference time, only checking an input against feature statistics for the most important features.

As we saw in "Evaluate Feature Importance" on page 121, extracting feature importances can be more difficult for complex models. If you are using a model that does not expose feature importances, you can leverage a black-box explainer on a large sample of examples to attempt to infer their values.

Feature importance and feature statistics come with another drawback, which is that they do not always provide accurate recommendations. Since recommendations are based on statistics aggregated over the entire dataset, they will not be applicable to each individual example. Feature statistics only provide general recommendations, such as "questions that contain more adverbs tend to receive higher ratings." However, there exists examples of questions with a below average proportion of adverbs that receive a high score. Such recommendations are not useful for these questions.

In the next two sections, we will cover methods to provide more granular recommendations that work at the level of individual examples.

Using a Model's Score

Chapter 5 described how classifiers output a score for each example. The example is then assigned a class based on whether this score is above a certain threshold. If a model's score is well calibrated (see "Calibration Curve" on page 114 for more on calibration), then it can be used as an estimate of the probability of an input example belonging to the given class.

To display a score instead of a class for a scikit-learn model, use the `predict_proba` function and select the class for which you'd like to display a score.

```
# probabilities is an array containing one probability per class
probabilities = clf.predict_proba(features)

# Positive probas contains only the score of the positive class
positive_probs = clf[:,1]
```

If it is well calibrated, presenting a score to users allows them to track improvements in their question as they follow recommendations to modify it, leading to it receiving a higher score. Quick feedback mechanisms like a score help users have an increased sense of trust in the recommendations provided by a model.

On top of a calibrated score, a trained model can also be used to provide recommendations to improve a specific example.

Extracting Local Feature Importance

Recommendations can be generated for an individual example by using a black-box explainer on top of a trained model. In "Evaluate Feature Importance" on page 121, we saw how black-box explainers estimate the importance of feature values for a specific example by repeatedly applying slight perturbations to input features and observing changes in the model's predicted score. This makes such explainers a great tool to provide recommendations.

Let's demonstrate this using the LIME (*https://github.com/marcotcr/lime*) package to generate explanations for an example. In the following code example, we first instantiate a tabular explainer, and then we choose an example to explain in our test data. We show the explanations in the generating recommendations notebook on this book's GitHub repository (*https://oreil.ly/ml-powered-applications*), and display them in array format.

```
from lime.lime_tabular import LimeTabularExplainer

explainer = LimeTabularExplainer(
    train_df[features].values,
    feature_names=features,
    class_names=["low", "high"],
    discretize_continuous=True,
)
```

```
idx = 8
exp = explainer.explain_instance(
    test_df[features].iloc[idx, :],
    clf.predict_proba,
    num_features=10,
    labels=(1,),
)

print(exp_array)
exp.show_in_notebook(show_table=True, show_all=False)
exp_array = exp.as_list()
```

Running the previous code produces the plot shown in Figure 7-2 as well as the array of feature importances shown in the following code. The model's predicted probabilities are displayed on the left side of the figure. In the middle of the figure, feature values are ranked by their contributions to the prediction.

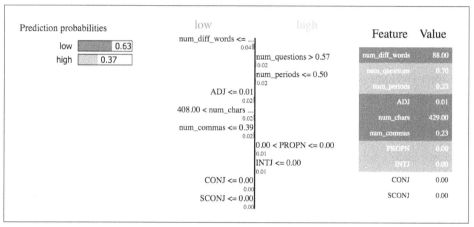

Figure 7-2. Explanations as recommendations

Those values are identical to the ones in the more readable console output below. Each row in this output represents a feature value and its impact on the score of the model. For example, the fact that the feature num_diff_words had a value lower than 88.00 lowered the score of the model by about .038. According to this model, increasing the length of the input question beyond this number would increase its quality.

```
[('num_diff_words <= 88.00', -0.038175093133182826),
 ('num_questions > 0.57', 0.022220445063244717),
 ('num_periods <= 0.50', 0.018064270196074716),
 ('ADJ <= 0.01', -0.01753028452563776),
 ('408.00 < num_chars <= 655.00', -0.01573650444507041),
 ('num_commas <= 0.39', -0.015551364531963608),
 ('0.00 < PROPN <= 0.00', 0.011826217792851488),
 ('INTJ <= 0.00', 0.011302327527387477),
```

```
    ('CONJ <= 0.00', 0.0),
    ('SCONJ <= 0.00', 0.0)]
```

For more usage examples, please refer to the generating recommendations notebook in the book's GitHub repository (*https://oreil.ly/ml-powered-applications*).

Black-box explainers can generate accurate recommendations for an individual model, but they do come with a drawback. These explainers generate estimates by perturbing input features and running a model on each perturbed input, so using them to generate recommendations is slower than the methods discussed. For example, the default number of perturbations that LIME uses to evaluate feature importance is 500. This makes this method two orders of magnitude slower than methods that need to run a model only once and even slower than ones that do not need to run a model at all. On my laptop, running LIME on an example question takes a little over 2 seconds. Such a delay could prevent us from serving recommendations to users as they are typing and require them to submit questions manually instead.

Just like many ML models, the recommendation methods we've seen here present a trade-off between accuracy and latency. The right recommendation for a product depends on its requirements.

Every recommendation method we've covered relies on features that were generated during model iteration, and some of them leverage the models that were trained as well. In the next section, we'll compare different model options for the ML Editor and decide which one is the most appropriate for recommendations.

Comparing Models

"Measuring Success" on page 23 covered important metrics to judge the success of a product. "Judge Performance" on page 106 described methods to evaluate models. Such methods can also be used to compare successive iterations of models and features to identify top-performing ones.

In this section we will choose a subset of key metrics and use them to evaluate three successive iterations of the ML Editor in terms of model performance and usefulness of recommendations.

The goal of the ML Editor is to provide recommendations using the techniques mentioned. To power such recommendations, a model should match the following requirements. It should be well calibrated so that its predicted probabilities represent a meaningful estimate of the quality of a question. As we covered in "Measuring Success" on page 23, it should have high precision so that the recommendations it makes are accurate. The features it uses should be understandable to a user, since they will serve as the basis for recommendations. Finally, it should be fast enough to allow us to use a black-box explainer to provide recommendations.

Let's describe a few successive modeling approaches for the ML Editor and compare their performance. The code for these performance comparisons can be found in the comparing models notebook in this book's GitHub repository (*https://oreil.ly/ml-powered-applications*).

Version 1: The Report Card

In Chapter 3, we built a first version of the editor that was entirely based on heuristics. This first version used hard-coded rules meant to encode readability and displayed results to users in a structured format. Building this pipeline allowed us to modify our approach and focus ML efforts on providing clearer recommendations, rather than a set of measurements.

Since this initial prototype was built in order to develop an intuition for the problem we were tackling, we won't be comparing it to other models here.

Version 2: More Powerful, More Unclear

After building a heuristic-based version and exploring the Stack Overflow dataset, we settled on an initial modeling approach. The simple model we trained can be found in the simple model notebook in this book's GitHub repository (*https://oreil.ly/ml-powered-applications*).

This model used a combination of features generated by vectorizing text using the methods described in "Vectorizing" on page 69 and manually created features that were surfaced during data exploration. When first exploring the dataset, I noticed a few patterns:

- Longer questions received higher scores.
- Questions that were specifically about use of the English language received lower scores.
- Questions that contained at least one question mark received higher scores.

I created features to encode these assumptions by counting the length of the text, the presence of words such as *punctuate* and *abbreviate*, and the frequency of question marks.

In addition to these features, I vectorized input questions using TF-IDF. Using a simple vectorization scheme allows me to tie a model's feature importances back to individual words, which can allow for word-level recommendations using the methods described earlier.

This first approach showed acceptable aggregate performance, with a precision of 0.62. Its calibration, however, left much to be desired, as you can see in Figure 7-3.

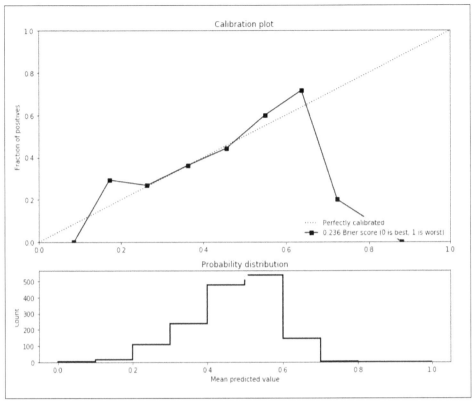

Figure 7-3. V2 model calibration

After inspecting this model's feature importances, I realized the only predictive manually created feature was question length. Other generated features had no predictive power. Exploring the dataset once more revealed a few more features that seemed predictive:

- A restrained usage of punctuation seemed to be predictive of high scores.
- Questions that were more emotionally charged seemed to receive a lower score.
- Questions that were descriptive and used more adjectives seemed to receive a higher score.

To encode these new hypotheses, I generated a new set of features. I created counts for each possible punctuation element. I then created counts that for each part-of-speech category, such as verb or adjective, measured how many words in a question belonged to that category. Finally, I added a feature to encode the emotional sentiment of a question. For more details about these features, refer to the second model notebook in this book's GitHub repository (*https://oreil.ly/ml-powered-applications*).

This updated version of the model performed slightly better in aggregate, with a precision of 0.63. Its calibration did not improve upon the previous model. Displaying the feature importances for this model revealed that this model exclusively relies on the manually crafted features, revealing that these features have some predictive power.

Having a model rely on such understandable features makes it easier to explain recommendations to a user than when using vectorized word-level features. For example, the most important word-level features for this model are the words *are* and *what*. We can guess why these words may be correlated with question quality, but recommending to a user that they should reduce or increase the occurrence of arbitrary words in their question does not make for clear recommendations.

To address this limitation of a vectorized representation and recognizing that the manually crafted features were predictive, I attempted to build a simpler model that does not use any vectorization features.

Version 3: Understandable Recommendations

The third model contains only the features described earlier (counts of punctuation and parts of speech, question sentiment, and question length). The model thus only uses 30 features, as opposed to more than 7,000 when using vectorized representations. See the third model notebook in this book's GitHub repository (*https://oreil.ly/ml-powered-applications*) for more details. Removing vectorized features and keeping manual ones allows the ML Editor to only leverage features that are explainable to a user. However, it may lead to a model performing more poorly.

In terms of aggregate performance, this model does perform worse than previous ones with a precision of 0.597. However, it is significantly better calibrated than previous models. In Figure 7-4, you can see that model 3 is well calibrated for most probabilities, even ones above .7 that other models struggle with. The histogram shows that this is due to this model predicting such probabilities more often than other models as well.

Because of the increased range of scores it produces and the improved calibration of scores, this model is the best choice when it comes to displaying a score to guide users. When it comes to making clear recommendations, this model is also the best choice since it only relies on explainable features. Finally, because it relies on fewer features than other models, it is also the fastest to run.

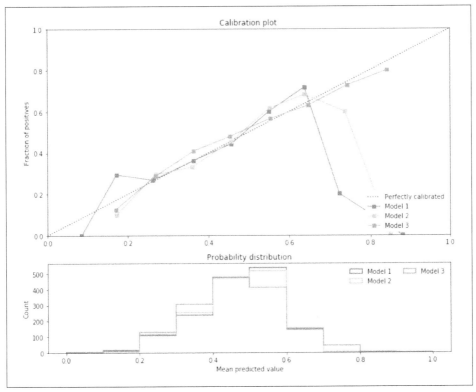

Figure 7-4. Calibration comparison

Model 3 is the best choice for the ML Editor and is thus the model we should deploy for an initial version. In the next section, we will briefly cover how to use this model with the recommendation techniques to provide editing recommendations to users.

Generating Editing Recommendations

The ML Editor can benefit from any of the four methods we described to generate recommendations. In fact, all of these methods are showcased in the generating recommendations notebook in the book's GitHub repository (*https://oreil.ly/ml-powered-applications*). Because the model we are using is fast, we will illustrate the most elaborate approach here, using black-box explainers.

Let's start by taking a look at the entire recommendation function that takes in a question and provides editing advice based on a trained model. Here is what this function looks like:

```
def get_recommendation_and_prediction_from_text(input_text, num_feats=10):
    global clf, explainer
    feats = get_features_from_input_text(input_text)
```

```
    pos_score = clf.predict_proba([[feats]])[0][1]

    exp = explainer.explain_instance(
        feats, clf.predict_proba, num_features=num_feats, labels=(1,)
    )
    parsed_exps = parse_explanations(exp.as_list())
    recs = get_recommendation_string_from_parsed_exps(parsed_exps)
    return recs, pos_score
```

Calling this function on an example input and pretty printing its results produces recommendations such as the following ones. We can then display these recommendations to users to allow them to iterate on their question.

```
>> recos, score = get_recommendation_and_prediction_from_text(example_question)
>> print("%s score" % score)
0.4 score
>> print(*recos, sep="\n")
Increase question length
Increase vocabulary diversity
Increase frequency of question marks
No need to increase frequency of periods
Decrease question length
Decrease frequency of determiners
Increase frequency of commas
No need to decrease frequency of adverbs
Increase frequency of coordinating conjunctions
Increase frequency of subordinating conjunctions
```

Let's break this function down. Starting with its signature, the function takes as arguments an input string representing a question, as well as an optional argument determining how many of the most important features to make recommendations for. It returns recommendations, as well as a score representing the current quality of the question.

Diving into the body of the question, the first line refers to two globally defined variables, the trained model and an instance of a LIME explainer like the one we defined in "Extracting Local Feature Importance" on page 157. The next two lines generate features from the input text and pass these features to the classifier for it to predict. Then, exp is defined by using LIME to generate explanations.

The last two function calls turn these explanations into human-readable recommendations. Let's see how by looking at the definitions of these functions, starting with parse_explanations.

```
def parse_explanations(exp_list):
    global FEATURE_DISPLAY_NAMES
    parsed_exps = []
    for feat_bound, impact in exp_list:
        conditions = feat_bound.split(" ")

        # We ignore doubly bounded conditions , e.g. 1 <= a < 3 because
```

```
        # they are harder to formulate as a recommendation
        if len(conditions) == 3:
            feat_name, order, threshold = conditions

            simple_order = simplify_order_sign(order)
            recommended_mod = get_recommended_modification(simple_order, impact)

            parsed_exps.append(
                {
                    "feature": feat_name,
                    "feature_display_name": FEATURE_DISPLAY_NAMES[feat_name],
                    "order": simple_order,
                    "threshold": threshold,
                    "impact": impact,
                    "recommendation": recommended_mod,
                }
            )
    return parsed_exps
```

This function is long, but it is accomplishing a relatively simple goal. It takes the array of feature importances returned by LIME and produces a more structured dictionary that can be used in recommendations. Here is an example of this transformation:

```
# exps is in the format of LIME explanations
>> exps = [('num_chars <= 408.00', -0.03908691525058592),
 ('DET > 0.03', -0.014685507408497802)]

>> parse_explanations(exps)

[{'feature': 'num_chars',
  'feature_display_name': 'question length',
  'order': '<',
  'threshold': '408.00',
  'impact': -0.03908691525058592,
  'recommendation': 'Increase'},
 {'feature': 'DET',
  'feature_display_name': 'frequency of determiners',
  'order': '>',
  'threshold': '0.03',
  'impact': -0.014685507408497802,
  'recommendation': 'Decrease'}]
```

Notice that the function call converted the threshold value displayed by LIME to a recommendation of whether a feature value should be increased or decreased. This is done using the get_recommended_modification function displayed here:

```
def get_recommended_modification(simple_order, impact):
    bigger_than_threshold = simple_order == ">"
    has_positive_impact = impact > 0

    if bigger_than_threshold and has_positive_impact:
        return "No need to decrease"
    if not bigger_than_threshold and not has_positive_impact:
```

```
        return "Increase"
    if bigger_than_threshold and not has_positive_impact:
        return "Decrease"
    if not bigger_than_threshold and has_positive_impact:
        return "No need to increase"
```

Once the explanations are parsed to recommendations, all that is left is to display them in an appropriate format. This is accomplished by the last function call in get_recommendation_and_prediction_from_text, which is displayed here:

```
def get_recommendation_string_from_parsed_exps(exp_list):
    recommendations = []
    for feature_exp in exp_list:
        recommendation = "%s %s" % (
            feature_exp["recommendation"],
            feature_exp["feature_display_name"],
        )
        recommendations.append(recommendation)
    return recommendations
```

If you'd like to experiment with this editor and iterate on it, feel free to refer to the generating recommendations notebook in this book's GitHub repository (*https://oreil.ly/ml-powered-applications*). At the end of the notebook, I've included an example of using the model recommendations to rephrase a question multiple times and increase its score. I'm reproducing this example here to demonstrate how such recommendations can be used to guide users' editing questions.

```
// First attempt at a question
>> get_recommendation_and_prediction_from_text(
    """
I want to learn how models are made
    """
)


0.39 score
Increase question length
Increase vocabulary diversity
Increase frequency of question marks
No need to increase frequency of periods
No need to decrease frequency of stop words

// Following the first three recommendations
>> get_recommendation_and_prediction_from_text(
    """
I'd like to learn about building machine learning products.
Are there any good product focused resources?
Would you be able to recommend educational books?
    """
)


0.48 score
Increase question length
```

```
Increase vocabulary diversity
Increase frequency of adverbs
No need to decrease frequency of question marks
Increase frequency of commas

// Following the recommendations once more
>> get_recommendation_and_prediction_from_text(
    """
I'd like to learn more about ML, specifically how to build ML products.
When I attempt to build such products, I always face the same challenge:
how do you go beyond a model?
What are the best practices to use a model in a concrete application?
Are there any good product focused resources?
Would you be able to recommend educational books?
    """
)

0.53 score
```

Voilà, we now have a pipeline that can take in a question and provide actionable recommendations to users. This pipeline is by no means perfect, but we now have a working end-to-end ML-powered editor. If you'd like to try your hand at improving it, I encourage you to interact with this current version and identify failure modes to address. Interestingly, while models can always be iterated upon, I would argue that the most promising aspect to improve for this editor would be to generate new features that are even clearer to users.

Conclusion

In this chapter, we've covered different methods to generate suggestions from a trained classification model. With these methods in mind, we compared different modeling approaches for the ML Editor and chose the one that would optimize our product goal of helping users ask better questions. We then built an end-to-end pipeline for the ML Editor and used it to provide recommendations.

The model we settled on still has much room for improvement and can benefit from more iteration cycles. If you'd like to practice using the concepts we outlined in Part III, I encourage you to go through these cycles yourself. Overall, every chapter in Part III represents one aspect of the ML iteration loop. To progress on ML projects, repeatedly go through the steps outlined in this section until you estimate that a model is ready to be deployed.

In Part IV, we will cover risks that come with deploying models, how to mitigate them, and methods to monitor and react to model performance variability.

Deploy and Monitor

Once we have built a model and validated it, we would like to give users access to it. There are many different methods to surface ML models. The simplest case involves building a small API, but in order to guarantee that your models run well for all of your users, you will need more.

See Figure IV-1 for an illustration of some of the systems we will cover in the next few chapters and that usually accompany a model in production.

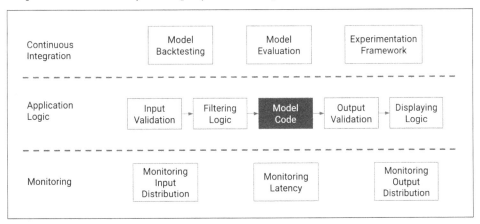

Figure IV-1. Typical production modeling pipeline

Production ML pipelines need to be able to detect data and model failures and handle them with grace. Ideally, you should also aim to proactively predict any failure and have a strategy to deploy updated models. If any of this sounds challenging to you, worry not! This is what we will cover in Part IV.

Chapter 8

Before deploying, we should always perform a final round of validation. The goal is to thoroughly examine potential abuse and negative uses of our models and do our best to anticipate and build safeguards around them.

Chapter 9

We will cover different methods and platforms to deploy models and how you would go about choosing one versus the other.

Chapter 10

In this chapter, we will learn how to build a robust production environment that can support models. This includes detecting and addressing model failure, optimizing model performance, and systematizing retraining.

Chapter 11

In this final chapter, we will tackle the crucial step of monitoring. In particular, we will cover why we need to monitor models, the best ways to monitor models, and how we can couple our monitoring setup to our deployment strategy.

## CHAPTER 8

Considerations When Deploying Models

The previous chapters covered model training and generalization performance. These are necessary steps to deploy a model, but they are not sufficient to guarantee the success of an ML-powered product.

Deploying a model requires a deeper dive into failure modes that could impact users. When building products that learn from data, here are a few questions you should answer:

- How was the data you are using collected?
- What assumptions is your model making by learning from this dataset?
- Is this dataset representative enough to produce a useful model?
- How could the results of your work be misused?
- What is the intended use and scope of your model?

The field of data ethics aims to answer some of these questions, and the methods used are constantly evolving. If you'd like to dive deeper, O'Reilly has a comprehensive report on the subject, *Ethics and Data Science*, by Mike Loukides et al.

In this chapter, we will discuss some concerns around data collection and usage and the challenges involved with making sure models keep working well for everyone. We will conclude the section with a practical interview covering tips to translate model predictions to user feedback.

Let's start by looking at data, first covering ownership concerns and then moving on to bias.

Data Concerns

In this section, we will start by outlining tips to keep in mind when you store, use, and generate data. We will start by covering data ownership and the responsibilities that come with storing data. Then, we will discuss common sources of bias in datasets and methods to take this bias into account when building models. Finally, we'll cover examples of the negative consequences of such biases and why they are important to mitigate.

Data Ownership

Data ownership refers to the requirements associated with the collection and use of data. Here are a few important aspects to consider with regard to data ownership:

- *Data collection:* Are you legally authorized to collect and use the dataset you want to train your model on?

- *Data usage and permission:* Have you clearly explained to your users why you needed their data and how you wanted to use it, and did they agree?

- *Data storage:* How are you storing your data, who has access to it, and when will you delete it?

Collecting data from users can help personalize and tailor product experiences. It also implies both moral and legal responsibilities. While there has always been a moral obligation to safe-keep data provided by users, new regulations increasingly make it a legal one. In Europe, for example, the GDPR regulation now sets strict guidelines regarding data collection and processing.

For organizations storing large amounts of data, data breaches represent a significant liability risk. Such breaches both erode the trust of users in the organization and often lead to legal action. Limiting the amount of data collected thus limits legal exposure.

For our ML editor, we will start by using publicly available datasets, which were collected with the agreement of users and are stored online. If we wanted to record additional data, such as records of how our service is used in order to improve it, we would have to clearly define a data collection policy and share it with users.

In addition to data collection and storage, it is important to consider whether using collected data may lead to poor performance. A dataset is appropriate to use in some cases, but not in others. Let's explore why.

Data Bias

Datasets are the result of specific data collection decisions. These decisions lead to datasets presenting a biased view of the world. ML models learn from datasets and thus will reproduce these biases.

For example, let's say a model is trained on historical data to predict leadership skills by forecasting the likelihood of a person becoming a CEO based on information including their gender. Historically, according to the "The Data on Women Leaders" fact sheet (*https://oreil.ly/vTLkH*) compiled by the Pew Research Center, most Fortune 500 CEOs have been male. Using this data to train a model will lead to it learning that being male is a valuable predictor of leadership. Being male and being a CEO are correlated in the chosen dataset due to societal reasons, which led to fewer opportunities for women to even be considered for such roles. By blindly training a model on this data and using it to make predictions, we would simply be reinforcing biases of the past.

It can be tempting to consider data as ground truth. In reality, most datasets are a collection of approximate measurements that ignore a larger context. We should start with the assumption that any dataset is biased and estimate how this bias will affect our model. We can then take steps to improve a dataset by making it more representative and adjust models to limit their ability to propagate existing bias.

Here are a few examples of common sources of errors and biases in datasets:

- *Measurement errors or corrupted data:* Each data point comes with uncertainty due to the method used to produce it. Most models ignore such uncertainty and can thus propagate systematic measurement errors.

- *Representation:* Most datasets present an unrepresentative view of a population. Many early face recognition datasets mostly contained images of white men. This led to models performing well for this demographic but failing on others.

- *Access:* Some datasets can be harder to find than others. For example, English text is easier to gather online than other languages. This ease of access leads to most of the state-of-the-art language models being trained exclusively on English data. As a consequence, English speakers will have access to better ML-powered services than non-English speakers. This disparity often is self-reinforcing, as the additional volume of users for English products helps make those models even better compared to ones for other languages.

Test sets are used to evaluate the performance of models. For this reason, you should take special care to make sure that your test set is as accurate and representative as possible.

Test sets

Representation appears in every ML problem. In "Split Your Dataset" on page 99, we covered the value of separating data in different sets to evaluate a model's performance. When doing this, you should attempt to build a test set that is inclusive, representative, and realistic. This is because a test set serves as a proxy for performance in production.

To do this, when designing your test set, think of every user that could interact with your model. To improve the chances that every user has an equally positive experience, try to include examples representative of every type of user in your test set.

Design your test set to encode product goals. When building a diagnosis model, you'll want to make sure that it performs adequately for all genders. To evaluate whether that is the case, you'll need to have them all represented in your test set. Gathering a diverse set of point of views can help with this endeavor. If you can, before deploying a model, give a diverse set of users an opportunity to examine it, interact with it, and share feedback.

I want to make a final point when it comes to bias. Models are often trained on historical data, which represents the state of the world in the past. Because of this, bias most often affects populations that are already disenfranchised. Working to eliminate bias is thus an endeavor that can help make systems fairer for the people who need it most.

Systemic Bias

Systemic bias refers to institutional and structural policies that have led to some populations being unfairly discriminated against. Because of this discrimination, such populations are often over- or underrepresented in historical datasets. For example, if societal factors have contributed to some populations being historically overrepresented in criminal arrest databases, an ML model trained from that data will encode this bias and carry it forward to modern-day predictions.

This can have disastrous consequences and lead to the marginalization of subsets of the population. For a concrete example, see J. Angwin et al.'s "Machine Bias" ProPublica report (*https://oreil.ly/6UE3z*), on ML bias for crime prediction.

Removing or limiting bias in a dataset is challenging. When trying to prevent a model from being biased against certain features such as ethnicity or gender, some have tried to remove the attribute in question from the list of features that a model uses to make predictions.

In practice, simply removing a feature does not prevent a model from being biased against it, because most datasets contain many other features that are strongly correlated with it. For example, ZIP code and income are highly correlated with ethnicity in the United States. If you remove only one feature, a model may be just as biased, albeit in ways that are harder to detect.

Instead, you should be explicit about which fairness constraints you are trying to enforce. For example, you could follow the approach outlined in the paper by M. B. Zafar et al., "Fairness Constraints: Mechanisms for Fair Classification" (*https://oreil.ly/JWlIi*), where the fairness of a model is measured using the p% rule. The p% rule is defined as "the ratio between the percentage of subjects having a certain sensitive attribute value receiving a positive outcome and the percentage of subjects not having that value receiving the same outcome should be no less than p:100." Using such a rule allows us to quantify bias and thus address it better, but it requires keeping track of the feature we'd like a model not to be biased against.

In addition to evaluating risk, biases, and errors in a dataset, ML requires evaluating models.

Modeling Concerns

How can we minimize the risk of a model introducing undesirable bias?

There are multiple ways that models can impact users negatively. First, we'll tackle runaway feedback loops, and then we'll explore the risks of a model discreetly failing on a small segment of the population. We will then discuss the importance of contextualizing ML predictions appropriately for users and end this section by covering the risk of having nefarious actors abusing models.

Feedback Loops

In most ML-powered systems, having a user follow a model's recommendation will make it more likely for future models to make the same recommendation. When left unchecked, this phenomenon can lead to models entering a self-reinforcing feedback loop.

For example, if we train a model to recommend videos to users and our first version of the model is slightly more likely to recommend videos of cats than dogs, then users will watch more cat videos than dog videos on average. If we train a second version of the model using a dataset of historical recommendations and clicks, we will incorporate the first model's bias into our dataset, and our second model will favor cats much more heavily.

Since content recommendation models often get updated multiple times a day, it would not take long before our most recent version of the model recommends exclusively cat videos. You can see an example of this in Figure 8-1. Due to an initial popularity of a cat video, the model progressively learns to recommend more cat videos, until it reaches the state on the right, only ever recommending cat videos.

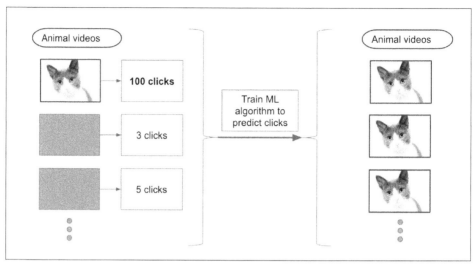

Figure 8-1. Example of a feedback loop

Filling the internet up with cat videos might not seem like a tragedy, but you can imagine how these mechanisms can rapidly reinforce negative biases and recommend inappropriate or dangerous content to unsuspecting users. In fact, models that attempt to maximize the probability of a user clicking will learn to recommend click-bait content, content that is very tempting to click but does not provide any value to the user.

Feedback loops also tend to introduce bias to favor a minority of very active users. If a video platform uses the number of clicks on each video to train its recommendation algorithm, it risks having its recommendation overfit to its most active users who represent the vast majority of clicks. Every other user of the platform would then be exposed to the same videos regardless of their individual preferences.

To limit negative effects of feedback loops, choose a label that is less prone to creating such a loop. Clicks only measure whether a user opens a video, not whether they enjoy it. Using clicks as an optimization goal leads to recommending more eye-catching content, without any concerns for its relevance. Replacing the target metric with watch time, which is more correlated with the user satisfaction, would help alleviate such a feedback loop.

Even then, recommendation algorithms that optimize for engagement of any sort always carry the risk of degenerating into a feedback loop since their only objective is to maximize a practically limitless metric. For example, even if an algorithm optimizes for watch time to encourage more engaging content, the state of the world that would maximize this metric is one where every user spent their entire day watching videos. Using such engagement metrics may help increase usage, but this raises the question of whether that is always a worthwhile goal to optimize for.

In addition to the risk of creating feedback loops, models can also exhibit poorer performance than expected in production despite receiving convincing scores on offline validation metrics.

Inclusive Model Performance

In "Evaluate Your Model: Look Beyond Accuracy" on page 109, we covered a variety of evaluation metrics that attempt to judge performance on different subsets of a dataset. This type of analysis is helpful to ensure that a model performs equally well for different types of users.

This is especially important when training new versions of existing models and deciding whether to deploy them. If you only compare aggregate performance, you could fail to notice a significant degradation of performance on a segment of the data.

Failure to notice such degradation of performance has led to catastrophic product failures. In 2015, an automated photo-tagging system categorized photos of African American users as gorillas (see this 2015 BBC article (*https://oreil.ly/nVkZv*)). This is an appalling failure and a consequence of not validating a model on a representative set of inputs.

This sort of issue can arise when updating an existing model. Say you are updating a facial recognition model, for example. The previous model had an accuracy of 90%, and the new one has an accuracy of 92%. Before deploying this new model, you should benchmark its performance on a few different subsets of users. You may find that while the performance has slightly improved in aggregate, the new model's accuracy is performing very poorly for photos of women over the age of 40, so you should abstain from deploying it. Instead, you should modify the training data to add more representative examples and retrain a model that can perform well for every category.

Omitting such benchmarks can lead to models not working for a significant proportion of their intended audience. Most models will never work for every possible input, but it is important to validate that they work for all expected ones.

Considering Context

Users will not always be aware that a given piece of information originated as a prediction from a ML model. Whenever possible, you should share the context of a prediction with a user, so they can make an informed decision as to how to leverage it. To do so, you can start by describing to them how the model was trained.

There is no industry-standard "model disclaimer" format yet, but active research in this area has shown promising formats, such as model cards (see this article by M. Mitchell et al., "Model Cards for Model Reporting" (*https://arxiv.org/abs/1810.03993*)), a documentation system for transparent model reporting. In the proposed approach, a model is accompanied by metadata about how it was trained, which data it was tested on, what its intended use is, and more.

In our case study, the ML Editor provides feedback based on a specific dataset of questions. If we were to deploy it as a product, we would include a disclaimer about the types of inputs the model is expected to perform well on. Such a disclaimer could be as simple as "This product attempts to recommend better ways to phrase a question. It was trained on questions from the writing Stack Exchange and may thus reflect the particular preferences of that community."

Keeping well-meaning users informed is important. Now, let's look at potential challenges that can come from less-friendly users.

Adversaries

Some ML projects need to consider the risk of having models be defeated by adversaries. Fraudsters may attempt to fool a model that is tasked with detecting suspicious credit card transactions. Alternatively, adversaries may want to probe a trained model to glean information they should not be allowed to access about the underlying training data, such as sensitive user information.

Defeating a model

Many ML models are deployed to protect accounts and transactions from fraudsters. In turn, fraudsters attempt to defeat these models by fooling them into believing they are legitimate users.

If you are trying to prevent fraudulent logins to an online platform, for example, you may want to consider sets of features that would include the user's country of origin (many large-scale attacks use multiple servers from the same region). If you train a model on such features, you risk introducing bias against nonfraudulent users in countries where fraudsters live. In addition, relying only on such a feature will make it easy for malicious actors to fool your systems by faking their location.

To defend against adversaries, it is important to regularly update models. As attackers learn existing patterns of defense and adapt their behavior to defeat them, update your models so that they can quickly classify this new behavior as fraudulent. This requires monitoring systems so that we can detect changes of patterns in activity. We will cover this in more detail in Chapter 11. In many cases, defending against attackers requires generating new features to better detect their behavior. Feel free to refer to "Let Data Inform Features and Models" on page 85 for a refresher on feature generation.

The most common type of attack on models aims to fool them into a wrong prediction, but other types of attacks exist. Some attacks aim to use a trained model to learn about the data it was trained on.

Exploiting a model

More than simply fooling a model, attackers could use it to learn private information. A model reflects the data it was trained on, so one could use its predictions to infer patterns in the original dataset. To illustrate this idea, consider the example of a classification model trained on a dataset containing two examples. Each example is of a different class, and both examples differ only by a single feature value. If you gave an attacker access to a model trained on this dataset and allowed them to observe its predictions to arbitrary inputs, they could eventually infer that this feature is the only predictive one in the dataset. Similarly, an attacker could infer the distribution of features within the training data. These distributions often receive sensitive or private information.

In the fraudulent login detection example, let's imagine that ZIP code is one of the required fields at login. An attacker could attempt to log in with many different accounts, testing different ZIP codes to see which values lead to a successful login. Doing so would allow them to estimate the distribution of ZIP codes in the training set and thus the geographical distribution of this website's customers.

The simplest way to limit the efficiency of such attacks is to limit the number of requests a given user can make, thereby limiting their ability to explore feature values. This is not a silver bullet, as sophisticated attackers may be able to create multiple accounts to circumvent such a limit.

The adversaries described in this section are not the only nefarious users you should be concerned with. If you choose to share your work with the wider community, you should also ask yourself whether it could be used for dangerous applications.

Abuse Concerns and Dual-Use

Dual-use describes technologies that are developed for one purpose but can be used for others. Because of ML's ability to perform well on datasets of similar types (see Figure 2-3), ML models often present a dual-use concern.

If you build a model that allows people to change their voice to sound like their friends', could it be misused to impersonate others without their consent? If you do choose to build it, how could you include the proper guidance and resources to make sure that users understand the proper use of your model?

Similarly, any model that can accurately classify faces has dual-use implications for surveillance. While such a model may originally be built to enable a smart doorbell, it could then be used to automatically track individuals across a city-wide network of cameras. Models are built using a given dataset but can present risks when retrained on other similar datasets.

There are currently no clear best practices on considering dual-use. If you believe your work could be exploited for unethical uses, I encourage you to consider making it harder to reproduce for that purpose or to engage in thoughtful discussion with the community. Recently, OpenAI made the decision to not release its most powerful language model because of concerns that it may make spreading disinformation online much easier (see OpenAI's announcement post, "Better Language Models and Their Implications" (*https://oreil.ly/W1Y6f*)). While this was a relatively novel decision, I wouldn't be surprised if such concerns are raised more often going forward.

To conclude this chapter, in the next section I am sharing a discussion with Chris Harland, currently director of engineering at Textio, who has an abundance of experience deploying models to users and presenting the results with enough context to make them useful.

Chris Harland: Shipping Experiments

Chris has a Ph.D. in physics and worked on a variety of ML tasks including computer vision to extract structured information from receipts for expensing software. He worked on the search team at Microsoft, where he realized the value of ML engineering. Chris then joined Textio, a company that builds augmented writing products to help users write more compelling job descriptions. Chris and I sat down to discuss his experience shipping ML-powered products and how he approaches validating results beyond accuracy metrics.

Q: *Textio uses ML to directly guide users. How is that different from other ML tasks?*

A: When you only focus on predictions, such as when to buy gold or who to follow on Twitter, you can tolerate some amount of variance. When you do guidance for writing, that is not the case, because your recommendations carry a lot of subtext.

If you tell me to write 200 more words, your model should be consistent and allow the user to follow its advice. Once the user writes 150 words, the model can't change its mind and recommend to lower the word count.

Guidance also requires clarity: "remove stop words by 50%" is a confusing instruction, but "reduce the length of these 3 sentences" may help users in a more actionable way. A challenge then becomes maintaining performance while using features that are more human understandable.

Essentially, ML writing assistants guide the user through our feature space from an initial point to a better one according to our model. Sometimes, this can involve passing through points that are worse, which can be a frustrating user experience. The product needs to be built with these constraints in mind.

Q: *What are good ways to perform this guidance?*

A: For guidance, precision is much more interesting than recall. If you think of giving advice to a person, recall would be the ability to give advice in all potential relevant domains and some irrelevant ones (of which there are many), while precision would be giving advice in a few promising domains ignoring potential other ones.

When giving advice, the cost of being wrong is very high, so precision is the most useful. Users will also learn from recommendations that your model has previously given and apply them unprompted to future inputs, which makes the precision of these recommendations even more important.

In addition, since we surface different factors, we measure whether users actually take advantage of them. If not, we should understand why not. A practical example is our "active to passive ratio" feature, which was underutilized. We realized that this was because of the recommendation not being actionable enough, so we improved it by highlighting the words themselves that we recommend changing.

Q: *How do you find new ways to guide your users or new features?*

A: Both top-down and bottom-up approaches are valuable.

Top-down hypothesis investigation is domain knowledge-driven and basically consists of feature matching from prior experience. This can come from product or sales teams, for example. A top-down hypothesis may look like "we believe that there is something about the mystery aspect of recruiting emails that helps drive engagement." The challenge in top-down is usually to find a practical way to extract that feature. Only then can we validate whether the feature is predictive.

Bottom-up aims to introspect a classification pipeline to understand what it finds predictive. If we have a general representation of text such as word vectors, tokens, and parts of speech annotations that we then feed to ensembles of models to classify as good or bad text, which features are most predictive of our classification? Domain experts will often be the best equipped to identify these patterns from a model's predictions. The challenge is then to find a way to make these features human understandable.

Q: *How do you decide when a model is good enough?*

A: You shouldn't underestimate how far a small text dataset of relevant language gets you. It turns out that using only a thousand documents in your domain is enough for many use cases. Having an ability to label that small set of data is worthwhile. You can then start by testing your model on out-of-sample data.

You should make it easy to run experiments. An overwhelming majority of the ideas you have about changing your product end up having a net effect that is null, which should allow you to be a little less worried about new features.

Finally, building a bad model is fine and is what you should start with. Fixing the bad models will make your product much more robust to problems and help it evolve faster.

Q: *How do you see how a model is doing once it is in production?*

A: When in production, expose your model's predictions to users clearly and let them override it. Log feature values, predictions, and overwrites so that you can monitor them and analyze them later. If your model produces a score, finding ways to compare this score to usage of your recommendations can be an additional signal. If you are predicting whether an email will be opened, for example, it can be extremely valuable to get access to the ground truth data from your users so you can improve your model.

The ultimate success metric is customer success, which is the most delayed and is influenced by many other factors.

Conclusion

We started by covering concerns with using and storing data. Then, we dove into causes of bias in datasets and tips to identify and reduce them. Next, we looked at the challenges that models face in the wild and how to reduce the risks associated with exposing them to users. Finally, we looked at how to architect systems so that they are designed to be resilient to errors.

These are complex issues, and the field of ML still has much to do to tackle all potential forms of abuse. The first step is for all practitioners to be aware of these concerns and to be mindful of them in their own projects.

We are now ready to deploy models. To start, we will explore the trade-offs between different deployment options in Chapter 9. Then, we will cover methods to mitigate some of the risks associated with deploying models in Chapter 10.

Choose Your Deployment Option

The previous chapters covered the process of going from a product idea to an ML implementation, as well as methods to iterate on this application until you are ready to deploy it.

This chapter covers different deployment options and the trade-offs between each of them. Different deployment approaches are suited to different sets of requirements. When considering which one to choose, you'll want to think of multiple factors such as latency, hardware and network requirements, as well as privacy, cost, and complexity concerns.

The goal of deploying a model is to allow users to interact with it. We will cover common approaches to achieve this goal, as well as tips to decide between approaches when deploying models.

We will start with the simplest way to get started when deploying models and spinning up a web server to serve predictions.

Server-Side Deployment

Server-side deployment consists of setting up a web server that can accept requests from clients, run them through an inference pipeline, and return the results. This solution fits within a web development paradigm, as it treats models as another endpoint in an application. Users have requests that they send to this endpoint, and they expect results.

There are two common workloads for server-side models, streaming and batch. Streaming workflows accept requests as they come and process them immediately. Batch workflows are run less frequently and process a large number of requests all at once. Let's start by looking at streaming workflows.

Streaming Application or API

The streaming approach considers a model as an endpoint that users can send requests to. In this context, users can be end users of an application or an internal service that relies on predictions from a model. For example, a model that predicts website traffic could be used by an internal service that is charged with adjusting the number of servers to match the predicted amount of users.

In a streaming application, the code path for a request goes through a set of steps that are the same as the inference pipeline we covered in "Start with a Simple Pipeline" on page 38. As a reminder, these steps are:

1. Validate the request. Verify values of parameters passed, and optionally check whether the user has the correct permissions for this model to be run.

2. Gather additional data. Query other data sources for any additional needed data we may need, such as information related to a user, for example.

3. Preprocess data.

4. Run the model.

5. Postprocess the results. Verify that the results are within acceptable bounds. Add context to make it understandable to the user, such as explaining the confidence of a model.

6. Return a result.

You can see this sequence of steps illustrated in Figure 9-1.

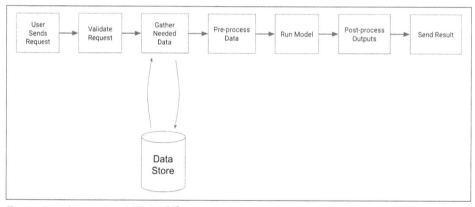

Figure 9-1. Streaming API workflow

The endpoint approach is quick to implement but requires infrastructure to scale linearly with the current number of users, since each user leads to a separate inference call. If traffic increases beyond the capacity of a server to handle requests, they will start to be delayed or even fail. Adapting such a pipeline to traffic patterns thus requires being able to easily launch and shut down new servers, which will require some level of automation.

For a simple demo such as the ML Editor, however, which is only meant to be visited by a few users at a time, a streaming approach is usually a good choice. To deploy the ML Editor, we use a lightweight Python web application such as Flask (*https://oreil.ly/cKLMn*), which makes it easy to set up an API to serve a model with a few lines of code.

You can find the deployment code for the prototype in the book's GitHub repository (*https://github.com/hundredblocks/ml-powered-applications*), but I'll give a high-level overview here. The Flask application consists of two parts, an API that takes in requests and sends them to a model for processing using Flask, and a simple website built in HTML for users to input their text and to display results. Defining such an API does not require much code. Here, you can see two functions that handle the bulk of the work to serve the v3 of the ML Editor:

```python
from flask import Flask, render_template, request

@app.route("/v3", methods=["POST", "GET"])
def v3():
    return handle_text_request(request, "v3.html")

def handle_text_request(request, template_name):
    if request.method == "POST":
        question = request.form.get("question")
        suggestions = get_recommendations_from_input(question)
        payload = {"input": question, "suggestions": suggestions}
        return render_template("results.html", ml_result=payload)
    else:
        return render_template(template_name)
```

The v3 function defines a route, which allows it to determine the HTML to display when a user accesses the /v3 page. It uses the function handle_text_request to decide what to display. When a user first accesses the page, the request type is GET and so the function displays an HTML template. A screenshot of this HTML page is shown in Figure 9-2. If a user clicks the "Get recommendation" button, the request type is POST, so handle_text_request retrieves the question data, passes it to a model, and returns the model output.

Which question would you like to ask?

This is a test question. Is it good?

Get recommendation   Back to main page

Figure 9-2. Simple webpage to use a model

A streaming application is required when strong latency constraints exist. If the information a model needs will be available only at prediction time and the model's prediction is required immediately, you will need a streaming approach. For example, a model that predicts the price for a specific trip in a ride hailing app requires information about the user's location and the current availability of drivers to make a prediction, which is available only at request time. Such a model also needs to output a prediction immediately, since it must be displayed to the user for them to decide whether to use the service.

In some other cases, the information required to compute predictions is available ahead of time. In those cases, it can be easier to process a large number of requests at once rather than processing them as they arrive. This is called *batch prediction*, and we will cover it next.

Batch Predictions

The batch approach considers the inference pipeline as a job that can be run on multiple examples at once. A batch job runs a model on many examples and stores predictions so they can be used when needed. Batch jobs are appropriate when you have access to the features needed for a model before the model's prediction is required.

For example, let's say you'd like to build a model to provide each salesperson on your team with a list of companies that are the most valuable prospects to contact. This is a common ML problem called *lead scoring*. To train such a model, you could use features such as historical email conversations and market trends. Such features are available before a salesperson is deciding which prospect to contact, which is when a prediction is required. This means you could compute a list of prospects in a nightly batch job and have the results ready to be displayed by the morning, when they will be needed.

Similarly, an app that uses ML to prioritize and rank the most important message notifications to read in the morning does not have strong latency requirements. An appropriate workflow for this app would be to process all unread emails in a batch in the morning and save the prioritized list for when the user needs it.

A batch approach requires as many inference runs as a streaming approach, but it can be more resource efficient. Because predictions are done at a predetermined time and the number of predictions is known at the start of a batch, it is easier to allocate and parallelize resources. In addition, a batch approach can be faster at inference time since results have been precomputed and only need to be retrieved. This provides similar gains to caching.

Figure 9-3 shows the two sides of this workflow. At batch time, we compute predictions for all the data points and store the results we produce. At inference time, we retrieve the precomputed results.

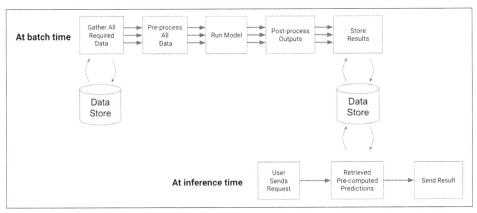

Figure 9-3. Example of batch workflow

It is also possible to use a hybrid approach. Precompute in as many cases as possible and at inference time either retrieve precomputed results or compute them on the spot if they are not available or are outdated. Such an approach produces results as rapidly as possible, since anything that can be computed ahead of time will be. It comes with the cost of having to maintain both a batch pipeline and a streaming pipeline, which significantly increases the complexity of a system.

We've covered two common ways of deploying applications on a server, streaming and batch. Both of these approaches require hosting servers to run inference for customers, which can quickly become costly if a product becomes popular. In addition, such servers represent a central failure point for your application. If the demand for predictions increases suddenly, your servers may not be able to accommodate all of the requests.

Alternatively, you could process requests directly on the devices of the clients making them. Having models run on users' devices reduces inference costs and allows you to maintain a constant level of service regardless of the popularity of your application, since clients are providing the necessary computing resources. This is called *client-side deployment*.

Client-Side Deployment

The goal of deploying models on the client side is to run all computations on the client, eliminating the need for a server to run models. Computers, tablets, modern smartphones, and some connected devices such as smart speakers or doorbells have enough computing power to run models themselves.

This section only covers *trained models* being deployed on device for inference, not training a model on the device. Models are still trained in the same manner and are then sent to the device for inference. The model can make its way to the device by being included in an app, or it can be loaded from a web browser. See Figure 9-4 for an example workflow to package a model in an application.

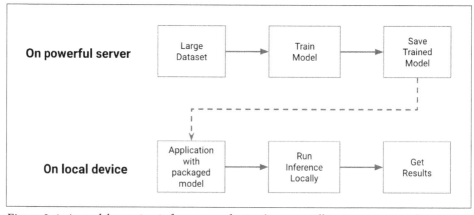

Figure 9-4. A model running inference on device (we can still train on a server)

Pocket-sized devices offer more limited compute power than powerful servers, so this approach limits the complexity of the models that can be used, but having models run on device can offer multiple advantages.

First, this reduces the need to build infrastructure that can run inference for every single user. In addition, running models on devices reduces the quantity of data that needs to be transferred between the device and the server. This reduces network latency and can even allow an application to run with no access to the network.

Finally, if the data required for inference contains sensitive information, having a model run on device removes the need for this data to be transferred to a remote server. Not having sensitive data on servers lowers the risk of an unauthorized third party accessing this data (see "Data Concerns" on page 172 for why this can be a serious risk).

Figure 9-5 compares the workflow for getting a prediction to a user for server-side models and client-side models. At the top, you can see that the longest delay for a server-side workflow is often the time it takes to transfer data to the server. On the bottom, you can see that while client-side models incur next to no latency, they often process examples slower than servers because of hardware constraints.

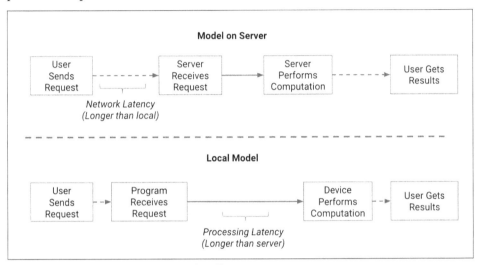

Figure 9-5. Running on a server, or locally

Just like for server-side deployment, there are multiple ways to deploy applications client side. In the following sections, we will cover two methods, deploying models natively and running them through the browser. These approaches are relevant for smartphones and tablets, which have access to an app store and web browser, but not for other connected devices such as microcontrollers, which we will not cover here.

On Device

Processors in laptops and phones are not usually optimized to run ML models and so will execute an inference pipeline slower. For a client-side model to run quickly and without draining too much power, it should be as small as possible.

Reducing model size can be done by using a simpler model, reducing a model's number of parameters or the precision of calculations. In neural networks, for example, weights are often pruned (removing those with values close to zero) and quantized (lowering the precision of weights). You may also want to reduce the number of features your model uses to further increase efficiency. In recent years, libraries such as Tensorflow Lite (*https://oreil.ly/GKYDs*) have started providing useful tools to reduce the size of models and help make them more easily deployable on mobile devices.

Because of these requirements, most models will suffer a slight performance loss by being ported on device. Products that cannot tolerate model performance degradation such as ones that rely on cutting-edge models that are too complex to be run on a device such as a smartphone should be deployed on a server. In general, if the time it would take to run inference on device is larger than the time it would take to transmit data to the server to be processed, you should consider running your model in the cloud.

For other applications such as predictive keyboards on smartphones that offer suggestions to help type faster, the value of having a local model that does not need access to the internet outweighs the accuracy loss. Similarly, a smartphone application built to help hikers identify plants by taking a photo of them should work offline so that it can be used on a hike. Such an application would require a model to be deployed on device, even if it means sacrificing prediction accuracy.

A translation app is another example of an ML-powered product that benefits from functioning locally. Such an app is likely to be used abroad where users may not have network access. Having a translation model that can run locally becomes a requirement, even if it isn't as precise as a more complex one that could run only on a server.

In addition to network concerns, running models in the cloud adds a privacy risk. Sending user data to the cloud and storing it even temporarily increases the odds of an attacker getting access to it. Consider an application as benign as superimposing filters on photos. Many users may not feel comfortable with their photos being transmitted to a server for processing and stored indefinitely. Being able to guarantee to users that their photos never leave the device is an important differentiator in an increasingly privacy conscious world. As we saw in "Data Concerns" on page 172, the best way to avoid putting sensitive data at risk is making sure it never leaves the device or gets stored on your servers.

On the other hand, quantizing pruning and simplifying a model is a time-consuming process. On-device deployment is only worthwhile if the latency, infrastructure, and privacy benefits are valuable enough to invest the engineering effort. For the ML Editor, we will limit ourselves to a web-based streaming API.

Finally, optimizing models specifically so they run on a certain type of device can be time-consuming, as the optimization process may differ between devices. More options exist to run models locally, including ones that leverage commonalities between devices to reduce required engineering work. An exciting area in this domain is ML in the browser.

Browser Side

Most smart devices have access to a browser. These browsers have often been optimized to support fast graphical calculations. This has led to rising interest in libraries that use browsers to have the client perform ML tasks.

The most popular of these frameworks is Tensorflow.js (*https://www.tensorflow.org/js*), which makes it possible to train and run inference in JavaScript in the browser for most differentiable models, even ones that were trained in different languages such as Python.

This allows users to interact with models through the browser without needing to install any additional applications. In addition, since models run in the browser using JavaScript, computations are done on the user's device. Your infrastructure only needs to serve the web page that includes the model weights. Finally, Tensorflow.js supports WebGL, which allows it to leverage GPUs on the clients' device if they are available to make computations faster.

Using a JavaScript framework makes it easier to deploy a model on the client side without requiring as much device-specific work as the previous approach. This approach does come with the drawback of increasing bandwidth costs, since the model will need to be downloaded by clients each time they open the page as opposed to once when they install the application.

As long as the models you use are a few megabytes or smaller and can be downloaded quickly, using JavaScript to run them on the client can be a useful way to lower server costs. If server costs ever became an issue for the ML Editor, deploying the model using a framework like Tensorflow.js would be one of the first methods I would recommend exploring.

So far, we've considered clients purely to deploy models that have already been trained, but we could also decide to train models on clients. In the next part, we will explore when this could be useful.

Federated Learning: A Hybrid Approach

We have mostly covered different ways to deploy models that we have already trained (ideally by following the guidelines in the previous chapters) and that we are now choosing how to deploy. We have looked at different solutions for getting a unique model in front of all our users, but what if we wanted each user to have a different model?

Figure 9-6 shows the difference between a system at the top that has a common trained model for all users and one at the bottom where each user has a slightly different version of the model.

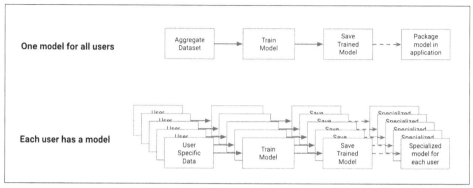

Figure 9-6. One big model or many individual ones

For many applications such as content recommendation, giving writing advice, or healthcare, a model's most important source of information is the data it has about the user. We can leverage this fact by generating user-specific features for a model, or we can decide that each user should have their own model. These models can all share the same architecture, but each user's model will have different parameter values that reflect their individual data.

This idea is at the core of federated learning, an area of deep learning that has been getting increasing attention recently with projects such as OpenMined (*https://www.openmined.org/*). In federated learning, each client has their own model. Each model learns from their user's data and sends aggregated (and potentially anonymized) updates to the server. The server leverages all updates to improve its model and distills this new model back to individual clients.

Each user receives a model that is personalized to their needs, while still benefiting from aggregate information about other users. Federated learning improves privacy for users because their data is never transferred to the server, which only receives aggregated model updates. This stands in contrast to training a model the traditional way by collecting data about each user and storing all of it on a server.

Federated learning is an exciting direction for ML, but it does add an additional layer of complexity. Making sure that each individual model is performing well and that the data transmitted back to the server is properly anonymized is more complicated than training a single model.

Federated learning is already used in practical applications by teams that have the resources to deploy it. For example, as described in this article by A. Hard et al., "Federated Learning for Mobile Keyboard Prediction" (*https://arxiv.org/abs/1811.03604*), Google's GBoard uses federated learning to provide next-word predictions for smartphone users. Because of the diversity of writing styles among users, building a unique model that performs well for all users proved challenging. Training models at the user level allows GBoard to learn about user-specific patterns and to provide better predictions.

We've covered multiple ways to deploy models on servers, on devices, or even on both. You should consider each approach and its trade-offs based on the requirements of your application. As with other chapters in this book, I encourage you to start with a simple approach and move to a more complex one only once you've validated that it is necessary.

Conclusion

There are multiple ways to serve an ML-powered application. You can set up a streaming API to allow a model to process examples as they arrive. You can use a batch workflow that will process multiple data points at once on a regular schedule. Alternatively, you can choose to deploy your models on the client side by either packaging them in an application or serving them through a web browser. Doing so would lower your inference costs and infrastructure needs but make your deployment process more complex.

The right approach depends on your application's needs, such as latency requirements, hardware, network and privacy concerns, and inference costs. For a simple prototype like the ML Editor, start with an endpoint or a simple batch workflow and iterate from there.

Deploying a model comes with more than just exposing it to users, however. In Chapter 10, we will cover methods to build safeguards around models to mitigate errors, engineering tools to make the deployment process more effective, and approaches to validate that models are performing the way they should be.

Build Safeguards for Models

When designing databases or distributed systems, software engineers concern themselves with fault tolerance, the ability for a system to continue working when some of its components fail. In software, the question is not whether a given part of the system will fail, but when. The same principles can be applied to ML. No matter how good a model is, it will fail on some examples, so you should engineer a system that can gracefully handle such failures.

In this chapter, we will cover different ways to help prevent or mitigate failures. First, we'll see how to verify the quality of the data that we receive and produce and use this verification to decide how to display results to users. Then, we will take a look at ways to make a modeling pipeline more robust to be able to serve many users efficiently. After that, we'll take a look at options to leverage user feedback and judge how a model is performing. We'll end the chapter with an interview with Chris Moody about deployment best practices.

Engineer Around Failures

Let's cover some of the most likely ways for an ML pipeline to fail. The observant reader will notice that these failure cases are somewhat similar to the debugging tips we saw in "Debug Wiring: Visualizing and Testing" on page 130. Indeed, exposing a model to users in production comes with a set of challenges that mirrors the ones that come with debugging a model.

Bugs and errors can show up anywhere, but three areas in particular are most important to verify: the inputs to a pipeline, the confidence of a model, and the outputs it produces. Let's address each in order.

Input and Output Checks

Any given model was trained on a specific dataset that exhibited particular characteristics. The training data had a certain number of features, and each of these features was of a certain type. Furthermore, each feature followed a given distribution that the model learned in order to perform accurately.

As we saw in "Freshness and Distribution Shift" on page 28, if production data is different from the data a model was trained on, a model may struggle to perform. To help with this, you should check the inputs to your pipeline.

Check inputs

Some models may still perform well when faced with small differences in data distributions. However, if a model receives data that is very different from its training data or if some features are missing or of an unexpected type, it will struggle to perform.

As we saw previously, ML models are able to run even when given incorrect inputs (as long as these inputs are of the right shape and type). Models will produce outputs, but these outputs may be widely incorrect. Consider the example illustrated in Figure 10-1. A pipeline classifies a sentence into one of two topics by first vectorizing it and applying a classification model on the vectorized representation. If the pipeline receives a string of random characters, it will still transform it into a vector, and the model will make a prediction. This prediction is absurd, but there is no way to know it only by looking at the results of the model.

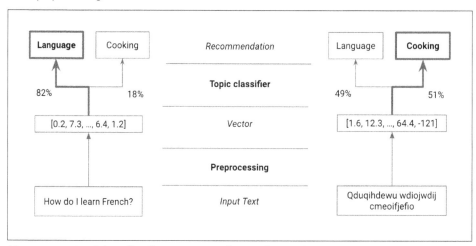

Figure 10-1. Models will still output a prediction for random inputs

To prevent a model from running on incorrect outputs, we need to detect that these inputs are incorrect before passing them to the model.

Checks Versus Tests

In this section, we are speaking of input checks, as opposed to the input tests we saw in "Test Your ML Code" on page 136. The difference is subtle but important. Tests validate that code behaves as expected given a known, predetermined input. Tests are commonly run every time code or models change to validate that a pipeline still works properly. The input checks in this section are part of the pipeline itself and change the control flow of a program based on the quality of inputs. Input checks that fail may result in running a different model or not running a model at all.

The checks cover similar domains to the tests in "Test Your ML Code" on page 136. In order of importance, they will:

1. Verify that all necessary features are present
2. Check every feature type
3. Validate feature values

Verifying feature values in isolation can be hard, as feature distributions can be complex. A simple way to perform such validation is to define a reasonable range of values a feature could take and validate that it falls within that range.

If any of the input checks fail, the model should not run. What you should do depends on the use case. If the data that is missing represents a core piece of information, you should return an error specifying the source of the error. If you estimate that you can still provide a result, you can replace a model call with a heuristic. This is an additional reason to start any ML project by building a heuristic; it provides you with an option to fall back on!

In Figure 10-2, you can see an example of this logic, where the path taken depends on the results of the input checks.

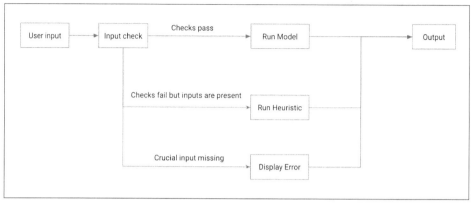

Figure 10-2. Example branching logic for input checks

Following is an example of some control flow logic from the ML Editor that checks for missing features and feature types. Depending on the quality of the input, it either raises an error or runs a heuristic. I've copied the example here, but you can also find it on this book's GitHub repository (*https://github.com/hundredblocks/ml-powered-applications*) with the rest of the ML Editor code.

```
def validate_and_handle_request(question_data):
    missing = find_absent_features(question_data)
    if len(missing) > 0:
        raise ValueError("Missing feature(s) %s" % missing)

    wrong_types = check_feature_types(question_data)
    if len(wrong_types) > 0:
        # If data is wrong but we have the length of the question, run heuristic
        if "text_len" in question_data.keys():
            if isinstance(question_data["text_len"], float):
                return run_heuristic(question_data["text_len"])
        raise ValueError("Incorrect type(s) %s" % wrong_types)

    return run_model(question_data)
```

Verifying model inputs allows you to narrow down failure modes and identify data input issues. Next, you should validate a model's outputs.

Model outputs

Once a model makes a prediction, you should determine whether it should be displayed to the user. If the prediction falls outside of an acceptable range of answers for a model, you should consider not displaying it.

For example, if you are predicting the age of a user from a photo, output values should be between zero to a little over 100 years old (if you are reading this book in the year 3000, feel free to adjust the bounds). If a model outputs a value outside of this range, you should not display it.

In this context, an acceptable outcome is not only defined by an outcome that is plausible. It also depends on your estimation of the kind of outcome that would be *useful to our user*.

For our ML editor, we want to only provide recommendations that are actionable. If a model predicts that everything a user wrote should be entirely deleted, this would consist of a rather useless (and insulting) recommendation. Here is an example snippet validating model outputs and reverting to a heuristic if necessary:

```
def validate_and_correct_output(question_data, model_output):
    # Verify type and range and raise errors accordingly
    try:
        # Raises value error if model output is incorrect
        verify_output_type_and_range(model_output)
    except ValueError:
        # We run a heuristic, but could run a different model here
        run_heuristic(question_data["text_len"])

    # If we did not raise an error, we return our model result
    return model_output
```

When a model fails, you can revert to a heuristic just as we saw earlier or to a simpler model you may have built earlier. Trying an earlier type of model can often be worthwhile because different models may have uncorrelated errors.

I've illustrated this on a toy example in Figure 10-3. On the left, you can see a better-performing model with a more complex decision boundary. On the right, you can see a worse, simpler model. The worse model makes more mistakes, but its mistakes are different from the complex model because of the different shape of its decision boundary. Because of this, the simpler model gets some examples right that the complex model gets wrong. This is the intuition for why using a simple model as a backup is a reasonable idea when a primary model fails.

If you do use a simpler model as a backup, you should also validate its outputs in the same manner and fall back to a heuristic or display an error if they do not pass your checks.

Validating that the outputs of a model are in a reasonable range is a good start, but it isn't sufficient. In the next section, we will cover additional safeguards we can build around a model.

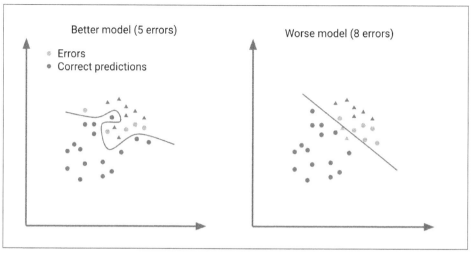

Figure 10-3. A simpler model often makes different errors

Model Failure Fallbacks

We have built safeguards to detect and correct erroneous inputs and outputs. In some cases, however, the input to our model can be correct, and our model's output can be reasonable while being entirely wrong.

To go back to the example of predicting a user's age from a photo, guaranteeing that the age predicted by the model is a plausible human age is a good start, but ideally we'd like to predict the correct age for this specific user.

No model will be right 100 percent of the time, and slight mistakes can often be acceptable, but as much as possible, you should aim to detect when a model is wrong. Doing so allows you to potentially flag a given case as too hard and encourages users to provide an easier input (in the form of a well-lit photo, for example).

There are two main approaches to detecting errors. The simplest one is to track the confidence of a model to estimate whether an output will be accurate. The second one is to build an additional model that is tasked with detecting examples a main model is likely to fail on.

For the first method, classification models can output a probability that can be used as an estimate of the model's confidence in its output. If those probabilities are well calibrated (see "Calibration Curve" on page 114), they can be used to detect instances where a model is uncertain and decide not to display results to a user.

Sometimes, models are wrong despite assigning a high probability to an example. This is where the second approach comes in: using a model to filter out the hardest inputs.

Filtering model

On top of not always being trustworthy, using a model's confidence score comes with another strong drawback. To get this score, the entire inference pipeline needs to be run regardless of whether its predictions will be used. This is especially wasteful when using more complex models that need to be run on a GPU, for example. Ideally, we would like to estimate how well a model will perform on an example without running the model on it.

This is the idea behind filtering models. Since you know some inputs will be hard for a model to handle, you should detect them ahead of time and not bother running a model on them at all. A filtering model is the ML version of input tests. It is a binary classifier that is trained to predict whether a model will perform well on a given example. The core assumption between such a model is that there are trends in the kind of data points that are hard for the main model. If such hard examples have enough in common, the filtering model can learn to separate them from easier inputs.

Here are some types of inputs you may want a filtering model to catch:

- Inputs that are qualitatively different from ones the main model performs well on
- Inputs that the model was trained on but struggled with
- Adversarial inputs that are meant to fool the main model

In Figure 10-4, you can see an updated example of the logic in Figure 10-2, which now includes a filtering model. As you can see, the filtering model is only run if the input checks pass, because you only need to filter out inputs that could have made their way to the "Run Model" box.

To train a filtering model, you simply need to gather a dataset containing two categories of examples; categories that your main model succeeded on and others that it failed on. This can be done using our training data and requires no additional data collection!

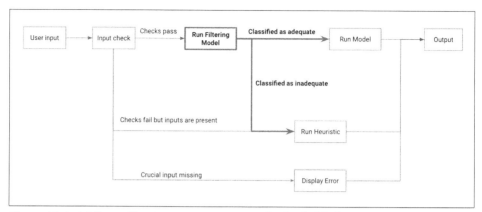

Figure 10-4. Adding a filtering step to our input checks (bolded)

In Figure 10-5, I show how to do this by leveraging a trained model and its result on a dataset, as seen in the chart on the left. Sample some data points that the model predicted correctly and some that the model failed on. You can then train a filtering model to predict which of the data points are ones that the original model failed on.

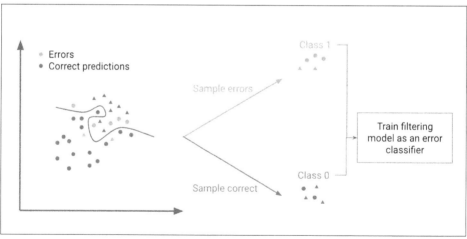

Figure 10-5. Getting training data for a filtering model

Once you have a trained classifier, training a filtering model can be relatively straightforward. Given a test set and a trained classifier, the following function will do just that.

```
def get_filtering_model(classifier, features, labels):
    """
    Get prediction error for a binary classification dataset
    :param classifier: trained classifier
    :param features: input features
    :param labels: true labels
```

```
    """
    predictions = classifier.predict(features)
    # Create labels where errors are 1, and correct guesses are 0
    is_error = [pred != truth for pred, truth in zip(predictions, labels)]

    filtering_model = RandomForestClassifier()
    filtering_model.fit(features, is_error)
    return filtering_model
```

This approach is used by Google for their Smart Reply feature, which suggests a few short responses to an incoming email (see this article by A. Kanan et al., "Smart Reply: Automated Response Suggestion for Email" (*https://oreil.ly/2EQvu*)). They use what they call a triggering model, responsible for deciding whether to run the main model that suggests responses. In their case, only about 11% of emails are suitable for this model. By using a filtering model, they reduce their infrastructure needs by an order of magnitude.

A filtering model generally needs to satisfy two criteria. It should be fast since its whole purpose is to reduce the computational burden, and it should be good at eliminating hard cases.

A filtering model that tries to identify hard cases doesn't need to be able to catch all of them; it simply needs to detect enough to justify the added cost of running it on each inference. Generally, the faster your filtering model is, the less effective it needs to be. Here is why:

Let's say your average inference time using only one model is i.

Your average inference time using a filtering model will be $f + i(1 - b)$ where f is the execution time of your filtering model, and b is the average proportion of examples it filters out (b for block).

To reduce your average inference time by using a filtering model, you thus need to have $f + i(1 - b) < i$, which translates to $\frac{f}{i} < b$.

This means the proportion of cases your model filters out needs to be higher than the ratio between its inference speed and the speed of your larger model.

For example, if your filtering model is 20 times faster than your regular model ($\frac{f}{i} = 5\%$), it would need to block more than 5% of cases ($5\% < b$) to be useful in production.

Of course, you would also need to make sure that the precision of your filtering model is good, meaning that the majority of the inputs it blocks are actually too hard for your main model.

One way to do this would be to regularly let a few examples through that your filtering model would have blocked and examine how your main model does on them. We will cover this in more depth in "Choose What to Monitor" on page 219.

Since the filtering model is different from the inference model and trained specifically to predict hard cases, it can detect these cases more accurately than by relying on the main model's probability output. Using a filtering model thus helps both decreasing the likelihood of poor results and improving resource usage.

For these reasons, adding filtering models to existing input and output checks can significantly increase the robustness of a production pipeline. In the next section, we will tackle more ways to make pipelines robust by discussing how to scale ML applications to more users and how to organize complex training processes.

Engineer for Performance

Maintaining performance when deploying models to production is a significant challenge, especially as a product becomes more popular and new versions of a model get deployed regularly. We will start this section by discussing methods to allow models to process large amounts of inference requests. Then, we will cover features that make it easier to regularly deploy updated model versions. Finally, we will discuss methods to reduce variance in performance between models by making training pipelines more reproducible.

Scale to Multiple Users

Many software workloads are horizontally scalable, meaning that spinning up additional servers is a valid strategy to keep response time reasonable when the number of requests increases. ML is no different in this aspect, as we can simply spin up new servers to run our models and handle the extra capacity.

If you use a deep learning model, you may need a GPU to serve results in an acceptable time. If that is the case and you are expecting to have enough requests to require more than a single GPU-enabled machine, you should run your application logic and your model inference on two different servers.

Because GPU instances are often an order of magnitude more expensive than regular instances for most cloud providers, having one cheaper instance scale out your application and GPU instances tackling only inference will significantly lower your compute costs. When using this strategy, you should keep in mind that you are introducing some communication overhead and make sure that this is not too detrimental to your use case.

In addition to increasing resource allocation, ML lends itself to efficient ways to handle additional traffic, such as caching.

Caching for ML

Caching is the practice of storing results to function calls so that future calls to this function with the same parameters can be run faster by simply retrieving the stored results. Caching is a common practice to speed up engineering pipelines and is very useful for ML.

Caching inference results. A least recently used (LRU) cache is a simple caching approach, which entails keeping track of the most recent inputs to a model and their corresponding outputs. Before running the model on any new input, look up the input in the cache. If a corresponding entry is found, serve the results directly from the cache. Figure 10-6 shows an example of such a workflow. The first row represents the caching step when an input is initially encountered. The second row depicts the retrieval step once the same input is seen again.

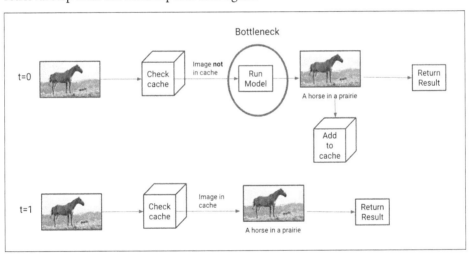

Figure 10-6. Caching for an image captioning model

This sort of caching strategy works well for applications where users will provide the same kind of input. It is not appropriate if each input is unique. If an application takes in photos of paw prints to predict which animal they belong to, it should rarely receive two identical photos, so a LRU cache would not help.

When using caching, you should only cache functions with no side effects. If a run_model function also stores results to a database, for example, using an LRU cache will cause duplicate function calls to not be saved, which may not be the intended behavior.

In Python, the `functools` module proposes a default implementation (*https://oreil.ly/B73Bo*) of an LRU cache that you can use with a simple decorator, as shown here:

```
from functools import lru_cache

@lru_cache(maxsize=128)
def run_model(question_data):
    # Insert any slow model inference below
    pass
```

Caching is most useful when retrieving features, processing them, and running inference is slower than accessing a cache. Depending on your approach to caching (in memory versus on disk, for example) and the complexity of the model you are using, caching will have different degrees of usefulness.

Caching by indexing.   While the caching method described is not appropriate when receiving unique inputs, we can cache other aspects of the pipeline that can be precomputed. This is easiest if a model does not only rely on user inputs.

Let's say we are building a system that allows users to search for content that is related to either a text query or an image they provide. It is unlikely that caching user queries would boost performance by much if we expect queries to vary significantly. Since we are building a search system, however, we have access to a list of potential items in our catalog that we could return. This list is known to us in advance, whether we are an online retailer or a document indexing platform.

This means that we could precompute modeling aspects that depend only on the items in our catalog. If we chose a modeling approach that allows us to do this computation ahead of time, we can make inference significantly faster.

For this reason, a common approach when building a search system is to first embed all indexed documents to a meaningful vector (refer to "Vectorizing" on page 69 for more on vectorization methods). Once embeddings are created, they can be stored in a database. This is illustrated on the top row of Figure 10-7. When a user submits a search query, it is embedded at inference time, and a lookup is performed in the database to find the most similar embeddings and return the products that correspond to these embeddings. You can see this illustrated in the bottom row of Figure 10-7.

This approach significantly speeds up inference since most of the calculations have been done ahead of time. Embeddings have been successfully used in large-scale production pipelines at companies such as Twitter (see this post on Twitter's blog (*https://oreil.ly/3R5hL*)) and Airbnb (see this article by M. Haldar et al., "Applying Deep Learning To Airbnb Search" (*https://arxiv.org/abs/1810.09591*).

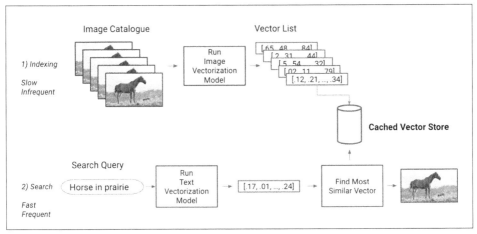

Figure 10-7. A search query with cached embeddings

Caching can improve performance, but it adds a layer of complexity. The size of the cache becomes an additional hyperparameter to tune depending on your application's workload. In addition, any time a model or the underlying data is updated, the cache needs to be cleared in order to prevent it from serving outdated results. More generally, updating a model running in production to a new version often requires care. In the next section, we will cover a few domains that can help make such updates easier.

Model and Data Life Cycle Management

Keeping caches and models up-to-date can be challenging. Many models require regular retraining to maintain their level of performance. While we will cover when to retrain your models in Chapter 11, I'd like to briefly talk about how to deploy updated models to users.

A trained model is usually stored as a binary file containing information about its type and architecture, as well as its learned parameters. Most production applications load a trained model in memory when they start and call it to serve results. A simple way to replace a model with a newer version is to replace the binary file the application loads. This is illustrated in Figure 10-8, where the only aspect of the pipeline that is impacted by a new model is the bolded box.

In practice, however, this process is often much more involved. Ideally, an ML application produces reproducible results, is resilient to model updates, and is flexible enough to handle significant modeling and data processing changes. Guaranteeing this involves a few additional steps that we will cover next.

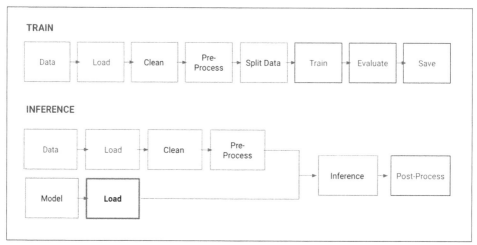

Figure 10-8. Deploying an updated version of the same model can seem like a simple change

Reproducibility

To track down and reproduce errors, you'll need to know which model is running in production. To do so requires keeping an archive of trained models and the datasets they were trained on. Each model/dataset pair should be assigned a unique identifier. This identifier should be logged each time a model is used in production.

In Figure 10-9, I've added these requirements to the load and save boxes to represent the complexity this adds to an ML pipeline.

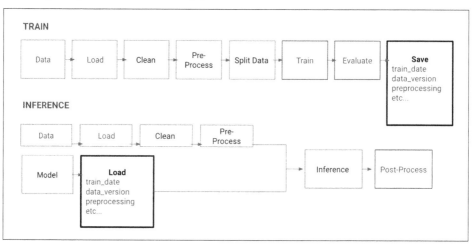

Figure 10-9. Adding crucial metadata when saving and loading

In addition to being able to serve different versions of existing models, a production pipeline should aim to update models without significant downtime.

Resilience

Enabling an application to load a new model once it is updated requires building a process to load a newer model, ideally without disrupting service to your users. This can consist of launching a new server serving the updated model and slowly transition traffic to it, but it quickly becomes more complex for larger systems. If a new model performs poorly, we'd like to be able to roll back to the previous one. Doing both of these tasks properly is challenging and would traditionally be categorized in the realm of DevOps. While we won't cover this domain in depth, we will introduce monitoring in Chapter 11.

Production changes can be more complex than updating a model. They can include large changes to data processing, which should also be deployable.

Pipeline flexibility

We previously saw that the best way to improve a model is often by iterating on data processing and feature generation. This means that new versions of a model will often require additional preprocessing steps or different features.

This kind of change is reflected in more than just the model binary and would often be tied to a new version of your application. For this reason, the application version should also be logged when a model makes a prediction in order to make this prediction reproducible.

Doing so adds another level of complexity to our pipeline, depicted with the added preprocessing and postprocessing boxes in Figure 10-10. These now also need to be reproducible and modifiable.

Deploying and updating models is challenging. When building a serving infrastructure, the most important aspect is to be able to reproduce the results of a model running in production. This means tying each inference call to the model that was run, the dataset that model was trained on, and the version of the data pipeline that served this model.

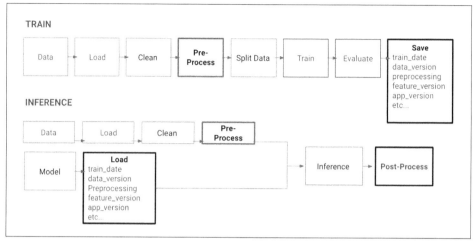

Figure 10-10. Adding model and application version

Data Processing and DAGs

To produce reproducible results as described earlier, a training pipeline should also be reproducible and deterministic. For a given combination of dataset, preprocessing steps, and model, a training pipeline should produce the same trained model on every training run.

Many successive transformation steps are required to building a model, so pipelines will often break at different locations. This makes guaranteeing that each part was run successfully and that they were all run in the right order.

One way to make this challenge easier is by representing our process of going from raw data to trained model as a directed acyclic graph (DAG), with each node representing a processing step and each step representing a dependency between two nodes. This idea is at the core of dataflow programming, a programming paradigm that the popular ML library TensorFlow is based on.

DAGs can be a natural way to visualize preprocessing. In Figure 10-11, each arrow represents a task that depends on another one. The representation allows us to keep each task simple, using the graph structure to express complexity.

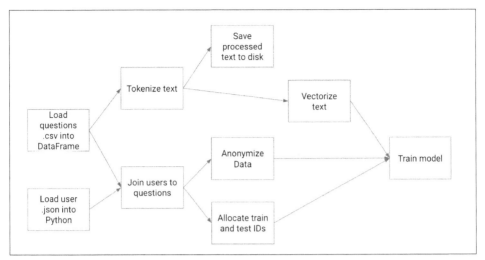

Figure 10-11. An example of a DAG for our application

Once we have a DAG, we can then guarantee that we follow the same set of operations for each model that we produce. There are multiple solutions to define DAGs for ML, including active opensource projects such as Apache Airflow (*https://oreil.ly/8ztqj*) or Spotify's Luigi (*https://oreil.ly/jQFj8*). Both packages allow you to define DAGs and provide a set of dashboards to allow you to monitor the progress of your DAGs and any associated logs.

When first building an ML pipeline, using a DAG can be unnecessarily cumbersome, but once a model becomes a core part of a production system, reproducibility requirements make DAGs very compelling. Once models are being regularly retrained and deployed, any tool that helps systematize, debug, and version a pipeline will become a crucial time-saver.

To conclude this chapter, I will cover an additional and direct way to guarantee that a model is performing well—asking users.

Ask for Feedback

This chapter covered systems that can help ensure we give every user an accurate result in a timely manner. To guarantee the quality of results, we covered tactics to detect whether a model's predictions are inaccurate. Why don't we ask users?

You can gather feedback from users both by explicitly asking for feedback and by measuring implicit signals. You can ask for explicit feedback when displaying a model's prediction, by accompanying it with a way for users to judge and correct a prediction. This can be as simple as a dialog asking "was this prediction useful?" or something more subtle.

The budgeting application Mint, for example, categorizes each transaction on an account automatically (categories include *Travel*, *Food*, etc.). As depicted in Figure 10-12, each category is shown in the UI as a field the user can edit and correct if needed. Such systems allow valuable feedback to be collected to continuously improve models in a way that is less intrusive than a satisfaction survey, for example.

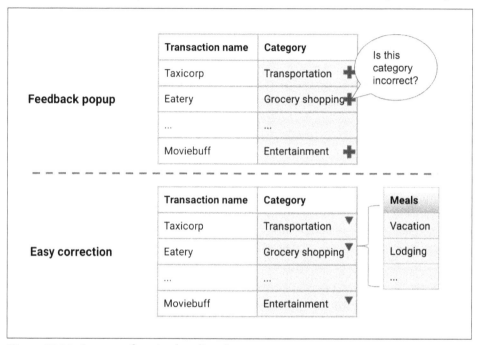

Figure 10-12. Let users fix mistakes directly

Users cannot provide feedback for each prediction a model makes, so gathering implicit feedback is an important way to judge ML performance. Gathering such feedback consists of looking at actions users perform to infer whether a model provided useful results.

Implicit signals are useful but harder to interpret. You shouldn't hope to find an implicit signal that always correlates with model quality, only one that does so in aggregate. For example, in a recommendation system, if a user clicks on a recommended item, you can reasonably assume that the recommendation was valid. This will not be true in all cases (people click on the wrong things sometimes!), but as long as it is true more often than not, it is a reasonable implicit signal.

By collecting this information, as shown in Figure 10-13, you can then estimate how often users found results useful. The collection of such implicit signals is useful but comes with the added risk of collecting and storing this data and potentially introducing negative feedback loops as we discussed in Chapter 8.

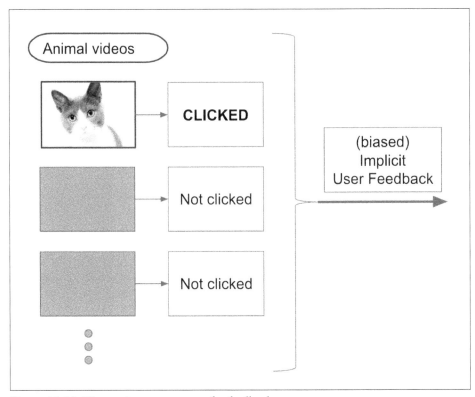

Figure 10-13. User actions as a source for feedback

Building implicit feedback mechanisms in your product can be a valuable way to gather additional data. Many actions can be considered a mix of implicit and explicit feedback.

Let's say we added a "Ask the question on Stack Overflow" button to the recommendations of our ML editor. By analyzing which predictions led to users clicking this button, we could measure the proportion of recommendations that were good enough to be posted as questions. By adding this button, we aren't directly asking users whether the suggestion is good, but we allow them to act on it, thus giving us a "weak label" (see "Data types" on page 13 for a reminder on weakly labeled data) of question quality.

In addition to being a good source of training data, implicit and explicit user feedback can be the first way to notice a degradation in performance in an ML product. While ideally errors should be caught before being displayed to users, monitoring such feedback helps detect and fix bugs quicker. We will cover this in more detail in Chapter 11.

Strategies for deploying and updating models vary tremendously depending on the size of a team and their experience with ML. Some of the solutions in this chapter are excessively complex for a prototype such as the ML Editor. On the other hand, some teams that have invested a significant amount of resources into ML have built complex systems that allow them to simplify their deployment process and guarantee a high level of quality to users. Next, I'll share an interview with Chris Moody, who leads Stitch Fix's AI Instruments team and will take us through their philosophy when it comes to deploying ML models.

Chris Moody: Empowering Data Scientists to Deploy Models

Chris Moody came from a physics background from Caltech and UCSC and is now leading Stitch Fix's AI Instruments team. He has an avid interest in NLP and has dabbled in deep learning, variational methods, and Gaussian processes. He's contributed to the Chainer (*http://chainer.org/*) deep learning library, contributed to the super fast Barnes–Hut version of t-SNE to scikit-learn (*https://oreil.ly/t3Q0k*), and written (one of the few!) sparse tensor factorization libraries in Python (*https://oreil.ly/tS_qD*). He also built his own NLP model, lda2vec (*https://oreil.ly/t7XFr*).

Q: *What part of the model life cycle do data scientists work on at Stitch Fix?*

A: At Stitch Fix, data scientists own the entire modeling pipeline. This pipeline is broad and includes things such as ideation, prototyping, design and debugging, ETL, and model training in languages and frameworks such as scikit-learn, pytorch, and R. In addition, data scientists are in charge of setting up systems to measure metrics and building "sanity checks" for their models. Finally, data scientists run the A/B test, monitor errors and logs, and redeploy updated model versions as needed based on what they observe. To be able to do this, they leverage the work done by the platform and engineering team.

Q: *What does the platform team do to make data science work easier?*

A: The goal of engineers on the platform team is to find the right abstractions for modeling. This means they need to understand how a data scientist works. Engineers don't build individual data pipelines for data scientists working on a given project. They build solutions that enable data scientists to do so themselves. More generally, they build tools to empower data scientists to own the entire workflow. This empowers engineers to spend more time making the platform better and less time building one-off solutions.

Q: *How do you judge the performance of models once they are deployed?*

A: A big part of Stitch Fix's strength is in making humans and algorithms work together. For example, Stitch Fix spends a lot of time thinking about the right way to present information to their stylists. Fundamentally, if you have an API that exposes your model on one end and a user such as a stylist or merchandise buyer on the other hand, how should you design interactions between them?

At first glance, you could be tempted to build a frontend to simply present the results of your algorithm to users. Unfortunately, this can lead users to feel like they have no control over the algorithm and the overall system and can lead to frustration when it isn't performing well. Instead, you should think about this interaction as a feedback loop, allowing users to correct and adjust results. Doing so lets users train algorithms and have a much larger impact on the entire process by being able to give feedback. In addition, this allows you to gather labeled data to judge the performance of your models.

To do this well, data scientists should ask themselves how they can expose a model to a user in order to both make their job easier and empower them to make the model better. This means that since data scientists know best what kind of feedback would be the most useful for their models, it is integral for them to own the process end-to-end up to this point. They can catch any errors because they can see the entire feedback loop.

Q: *How do you monitor and debug models?*

A: When your engineering team builds great tooling, monitoring and debugging get much easier. Stitch Fix has built an internal tool that takes in a modeling pipeline and creates a Docker container, validates arguments and return types, exposes the inference pipeline as an API, deploys it on our infrastructure, and builds a dashboard on top of it. This tooling allows data scientists to directly fix any errors that happen during or after deployment. Because data scientists are now in charge of troubleshooting models, we have also found that this setup incentivizes simple and robust models that tend to break more rarely. Ownership of the entire pipeline leads individuals to optimize for impact and reliability, rather than model complexity.

Q: *How do you deploy new model versions?*

A: In addition, data scientists run experiments by using a custom-built A/B testing service that allows them to define granular parameters. They then analyze test results, and if they are deemed conclusive by the team, they deploy the new version themselves.

When it comes to deployment, we use a system similar to canary development where we start by deploying the new version to one instance and progressively update instances while monitoring performance. Data scientists have access to a dashboard that shows the number of instances under each version and continuous performance metrics as the deployment progresses.

Conclusion

In this chapter, we've covered ways to make our responses more resilient by detecting potential failures of our model proactively and finding ways to mitigate them. This has included both deterministic validation strategies and the use of filtering models. We also covered a few of the challenges that come with keeping a production model up-to-date. Then, we discussed some of the ways that we can estimate how well a model is performing. Finally, we took a look at a practical example of a company that deploys ML frequently and at large scale, and the processes they have built to do so.

In Chapter 11, we will cover additional methods to keep an eye on the performance of models and leverage a variety of metrics to diagnose the health of an ML-powered application.

## CHAPTER 11

Monitor and Update Models

Once a model is deployed, its performance should be monitored just like any other software system. As they did in "Test Your ML Code" on page 136, regular software best practices apply. And just like in "Test Your ML Code" on page 136, there are additional things to consider when dealing with ML models.

In this chapter, we will describe key aspects to keep in mind when monitoring ML models. More specifically, we will answer three questions:

1. Why should we monitor our models?
2. How do we monitor our models?
3. What actions should our monitoring drive?

Let's start by covering how monitoring models can help decide when to deploy a new version or surface problems in production.

Monitoring Saves Lives

The goal of monitoring is to track the health of a system. For models, this means monitoring their performance and the quality of their predictions.

If a change in user habits suddenly causes a model to produce subpar results, a good monitoring system will allow you to notice and react as soon as possible. Let's cover some key issues that monitoring can help us catch.

Monitoring to Inform Refresh Rate

We saw in "Freshness and Distribution Shift" on page 28 that most models need to be regularly updated to maintain a given level of performance. Monitoring can be used to detect when a model is not fresh anymore and needs to be retrained.

For example, let's say that we use the implicit feedback that we get from our users (whether they click on recommendations, for example) to estimate the accuracy of a model. If we continuously monitor the accuracy of the model, we can train a new model as soon as accuracy drops below a defined threshold. Figure 11-1 shows a timeline of this process, with retraining events happening when accuracy dips below a threshold.

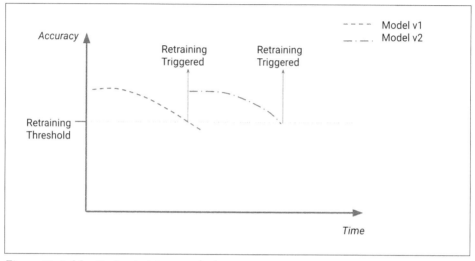

Figure 11-1. Monitoring to trigger redeploy

Before redeploying an updated model, we would need to verify that the new model is better. We will cover how to do this later in this section, "CI/CD for ML" on page 223. First, let's tackle other aspects to monitor, such as potential abuse.

Monitor to Detect Abuse

In some cases such as when building abuse prevention or fraud detection systems, a fraction of users are actively working to defeat models. In these cases, monitoring becomes a key way to detect attacks and estimate their success rate.

A monitoring system can use anomaly detection to detect attacks. When tracking every attempt to log in to a bank's online portal, for example, a monitoring system could raise an alert if the number of login attempts suddenly increased tenfold, which could be a sign of an attack.

This monitoring could raise an alert based on a threshold value being crossed, as you can see in Figure 11-2, or include more nuanced metrics such as the rate of increase of login attempts. Depending on the complexity of attacks, it may be valuable to build a model to detect such anomalies with more nuance than a simple threshold could.

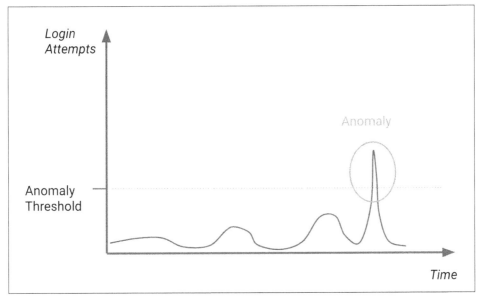

Figure 11-2. An obvious anomaly on a monitoring dashboard. You could build an additional ML model to automatically detect it.

In addition to monitoring freshness and detecting anomalies, which other metrics should we monitor?

Choose What to Monitor

Software applications commonly monitor metrics such as the average time it takes to process a request, the proportion of requests that fail to be processed, and the amount of available resources. These are useful to track in any production service and allow for proactive remediation before too many users are impacted.

Next, we will cover more metrics to monitor to detect when a model's performance is starting to decline.

Performance Metrics

A model can become stale if the distribution of data starts to change. You can see this illustrated in Figure 11-3.

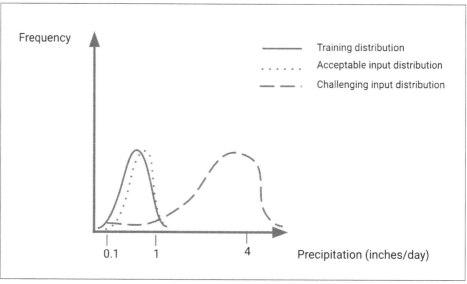

Figure 11-3. Example of drift in a feature's distribution

When it comes to distribution shifts, both the input and the output distribution of data can change. Consider the example of a model that tries to guess which movie a user will watch next. Given the same user history as an input, the model's prediction should change based on new entries in a catalog of available movies.

- *Tracking changes in the input distribution* (also called feature drift) is easier than tracking the output distribution, since it can be challenging to access the ideal value of outputs to satisfy users.

- *Monitoring the input distribution* can be as simple as monitoring summary statistics such as the mean and variance of key features and raising an alert if these statistics drift away from the values in the training data by more than a given threshold.

- *Monitoring distribution shifts* can be more challenging. A first approach is to monitor the distribution of model outputs. Similarly to inputs, a significant change in the distribution of outputs may be a sign that model performance has degraded. The distribution of the results users would have liked to see, however, can be harder to estimate.

One of the reasons for why estimating ground truth can be hard is that a model's actions can often prevent us from observing it. To see why that may be the case, consider the illustration of a credit card fraud detection model in Figure 11-4. The distribution of the data that the model will receive is on the left side. As the model makes predictions on the data, application code acts on these predictions by blocking any transaction predicted as fraudulent.

Once a transaction is blocked, we are thus unable to observe what would have happened if we had let it through. This means that we are not be able to know whether the blocked transaction was actually fraudulent or not. We are only able to observe and label the transactions we let through. Because of having acted on a model's predictions, we are only able to observe a skewed distribution of nonblocked transactions, represented on the right side.

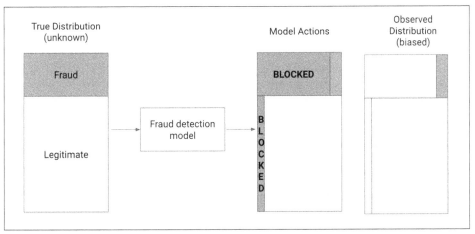

Figure 11-4. Taking action based on a model's predictions can bias the observed distribution of data

Only having access to a skewed sample of the true distribution makes it impossible to correctly evaluate a model's performance. This is the focus of *counterfactual evaluation*, which aims to evaluate what would have happened if we hadn't actioned a model. To perform such evaluation in practice, you can withhold running a model on a small subset of examples (see the article by Lihong Li et al., "Counterfactual Estimation and Optimization of Click Metrics for Search Engines" (*https://arxiv.org/abs/1403.1891*)). Not acting on a random subset of examples will then allow us to observe an unbiased distribution of fraudulent transactions. By comparing model predictions to true outcomes for the random data, we can begin to estimate a model's precision and recall.

This approach provides a way to evaluate models but comes at the cost of letting a proportion of fraudulent transactions go through. In many cases, this trade-off can be favorable since it allows for model benchmarking and comparisons. In some cases, such as in medical domains where outputting a random prediction is not acceptable, this approach should not be used.

In "CI/CD for ML" on page 223, we'll cover other strategies to compare models and decide which ones to deploy, but first, let's cover the other key types of metrics to track.

Business Metrics

As we've seen throughout this book, the most important metrics are the ones related to product and business goals. They are the yardstick against which we can judge our model's performance. If all of the other metrics are in the green and the rest of the production system is performing well but users don't click on search results or use recommendations, then a product is failing by definition.

For this reason, product metrics should be closely monitored. For systems such as search or recommendation systems, this monitoring could track the CTR, the ratio at which people that have seen a model's recommendation clicked on it.

Some applications may benefit from modifications to the product to more easily track product success, similarly to the feedback examples we saw in "Ask for Feedback" on page 211. We discussed adding a share button, but we could track feedback at a more granular level. If we can have users click on recommendations in order to implement them, we can track whether each recommendation was used and use this data to train a new version of the model. Figure 11-5 shows an illustrated comparison between the aggregate approach on the left side and the granular one on the right.

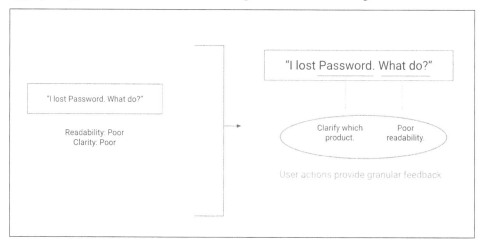

Figure 11-5. Proposing word-level suggestions gives us more opportunities to collect user feedback

Since I do not expect the ML Editor prototype to be used frequently enough for the method described to provide a large enough dataset, we will abstain from building it here. If we were building a product we were intending to maintain, collecting such data would allow us to get precise feedback about which recommendations the user found the most useful.

Now that we have discussed reasons and methods to monitor models, let's cover ways to address any issues detected by monitoring.

CI/CD for ML

CI/CD stands for continuous integration (CI) and continuous delivery (CD). Roughly speaking, CI is the process of letting multiple developers regularly merge their code back into a central codebase, while CD focuses on improving the speed at which new versions of software can be released. Adopting CI/CD practices allows individuals and organizations to quickly iterate and improve on an application, whether they are releasing new features or fixing existing bugs.

CI/CD for ML thus aims to make it easier to deploy new models or update existing ones. Releasing updates quickly is easy; the challenge comes in guaranteeing their quality.

When it comes to ML, we saw that having a test suite is not enough to guarantee that a new model improves upon a previous one. Training a new model and testing that it performs well on held-out data is a good first step, but ultimately, as we saw earlier, there is no substitute for live performance to judge the quality of a model.

Before deploying a model to users, teams will often deploy them in what Schelter et al., in their paper, "On Challenges in Machine Learning Model Management" (*https://oreil.ly/zbBjq*), refer to as *shadow mode*. This refers to the process of deploying a new model in parallel to an existing one. When running inference, both models' predictions are computed and stored, but the application only uses the prediction of the existing model.

By logging the new predicted value and comparing it both to the old version and to ground truth when it is available, engineers can estimate a new model's performance in a production environment without changing the user experience. This approach also allows to test the infrastructure required to run inference for a new model that may be more complex than the existing one. The only thing shadow mode doesn't provide is the ability to observe the user's response to the new model. The only way to do that is to actually deploy it.

Once a model has been tested, it is a candidate for deployment. Deploying a new model comes with the risk of exposing users to a degradation of performance. Mitigating that risk requires some care and is the focus of the field of experimentation.

Figure 11-6 shows a visualization of each of the three approaches we covered here, from the safest one of evaluating a mode on a test set to the most informative and dangerous one of deploying a model live in production. Notice that while shadow mode does require engineering effort in order to be able to run two models for each inference step, it allows for the evaluation of a model to be almost as safe as using a test set and provides almost as much information as running it in production.

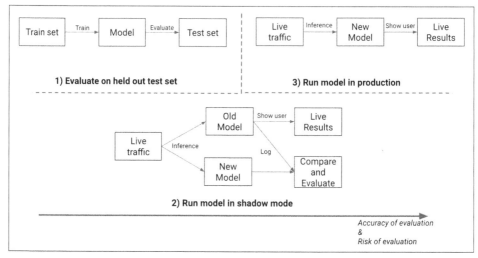

Figure 11-6. Ways to evaluate a model, from safest and least accurate to riskiest and most accurate

Since deploying models in production can be a risky process, engineering teams have developed methods to deploy changes incrementally, starting by showing new results to only a subset of users. We will cover this next.

A/B Testing and Experimentation

In ML, the goal of experimentation is to maximize chances of using the best model, while minimizing the cost of trying out suboptimal models. There are many experimentation approaches, the most popular being A/B testing.

The principle behind A/B testing is simple: expose a sample of users to a new model, and the rest to another. This is commonly done by having a larger "control" group being served the current model and a smaller "treatment" group being served a new version that we want to test. Once we have run an experiment for a sufficient amount of time, we compare the results for both groups and choose the better model.

In Figure 11-7, you can see how to randomly sample users from a total population to allocate them to a test set. At inference time, the model used for a given user is determined by their allocated group.

The idea behind A/B testing is simple, but experimental design concerns such as choosing the control and the treatment group, deciding which amount of time is sufficient, and evaluating which model performs better are all challenging issues.

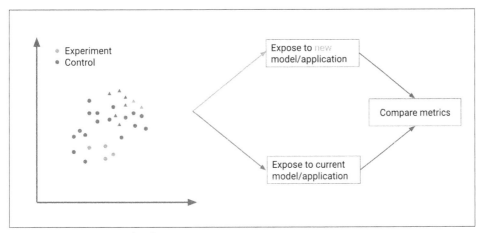

Figure 11-7. An example of an A/B test

In addition, A/B testing requires the building of additional infrastructure to support the ability to serve different models to different users. Let's cover each of these challenges in more detail.

Choosing groups and duration

Deciding which users should be served which model comes with a few requirements. Users in both groups should be as similar as possible so that any observed difference in outcome can be attributed to our model and not to a difference in cohorts. If all users in group A are power users and group B contains only occasional users, the results of an experiments will not be conclusive.

In addition, the treatment group B should be large enough to draw a statistically meaningful conclusion, but as small as possible to limit exposure to a potentially worse model. The duration of the test presents a similar trade-off: too short and we risk not having enough information, too long and we risk losing users.

These two constraints are challenging enough, but consider for a minute the case of large companies with hundreds of data scientists who run dozens of A/B tests in parallel. Multiple A/B tests may be testing the same aspect of the pipeline at the same time, making it harder to determine the effect of an individual test accurately. When companies get to this scale, this leads them to building experimentation platforms to handle the complexity. See Airbnb's ERF, as described in Jonathan Parks's article, "Scaling Airbnb's Experimentation Platform" (*https://oreil.ly/VFcxu*); Uber's XP as described in A. Deb et al.'s post, "Under the Hood of Uber's Experimentation Platform" (*https://eng.uber.com/xp/*); or the GitHub repo for Intuit's open source Wasabi (*https://oreil.ly/txQJ2*).

Estimating the better variant

Most A/B tests choose a metric they would like to compare between groups such as CTR. Unfortunately, estimating which version performed better is more complex than selecting the group with the highest CTR.

Since we expect there to be natural fluctuations in any metric results, we first need to determine whether results are statistically significant. Since we are estimating a difference between two populations, the most common tests that are used are two-sample hypothesis tests.

For an experiment to be conclusive, it needs to be run on a sufficient amount of data. The exact quantity depends on the value of the variable we are measuring and the scale of the change we are aiming to detect. For a practical example, see Evan Miller's sample size calculator (*https://oreil.ly/g4Bs3*).

It is also important to decide on the size of each group and the length of the experiment before running it. If you instead continuously test for significance while an A/B test is ongoing and declare the test successful as soon as you see a significant result, you will be committing a repeated significance testing error. This kind of error consists of severely overestimating the significance of an experiment by opportunistically looking for significance (once again, Evan Miller has a great explanation here (*https://oreil.ly/Ybhmu*)).

While most experiments focus on comparing the value of a single metric, it is important to also consider other impacts. If the average CTR increases but the number of users who stop using the product doubles, we probably should not consider a model to be better.

Similarly, results of A/B tests should take into account results for different segments of users. If the average CTR increases but the CTR for a given segment plummets, it may be better to not deploy the new model.

Implementing an experiment requires the ability to assign users to a group, track each user's assignment, and present different results based on it. This necessitates building additional infrastructure, which we cover next.

Building the infrastructure

Experiments also come with infrastructure requirements. The simplest way to run an A/B test is to store each user's associated group with the rest of user-related information, such as in a database.

The application can then rely on branching logic that decides which model to run depending on the given field's value. This simple approach works well for systems where users are logged in but becomes significantly harder if a model is accessible to logged-out users.

This is because experiments usually assume that each group is independent and exposed to only one variant. When serving models to logged out users, it becomes harder to guarantee that a given user was always served the same variant across each session. If most users are exposed to multiple variants, this could invalidate the results of an experiment.

Other information to identify users such as browser cookies and IP addresses can be used to identify users. Once again, however, such approaches require building new infrastructure, which may be hard for small, resource-constrained teams.

Other Approaches

A/B testing is a popular experimentation method, but other approaches exist that try to address some of A/B testing's limitations.

Multiarmed bandits are a more flexible approach that can test variants continually and on more than two alternatives. They dynamically update which model to serve based on how well each option is performing. I've illustrated how multiarmed bandits work in Figure 11-8. Bandits continuously keep a tally of how each alternative is performing based on the success of each request they route. Most requests are simply routed to the current best alternative, as shown on the left. A small subset of requests gets routed to a random alternative, as you can see on the right. This allows bandits to update their estimate of which model is the best and detect if a model that is currently not being served is starting to perform better.

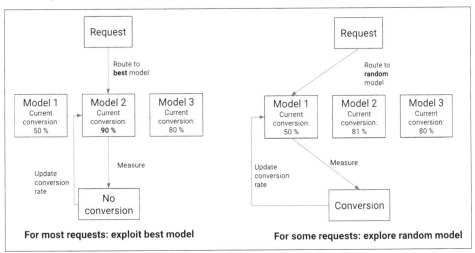

Figure 11-8. Multiarmed bandits in practice

Contextual multiarmed bandits take this process even further, by learning which model is a better option for each particular user. For more information, I recommend this overview (*https://oreil.ly/K5Jpx*) by the Stitch Fix team.

 While this section covered the usage of experimentation to validate models, companies increasingly use experimentation methods to validate any significant change they make to their applications. This allows them to continuously evaluate which functionality users are finding useful and how new features are performing.

Because experimentation is such a hard and error-prone process, multiple startups have started offering "optimization services" allowing customers to integrate their applications with a hosted experimentation platform to decide which variants perform best. For organizations without a dedicated experimentation team, such solutions may be the easiest way to test new model versions.

Conclusion

Overall, deploying and monitoring models is still a relatively new practice. It is a crucial way to verify that models are producing value but often requires significant efforts both in terms of infrastructure work and careful product design.

As the field has started to mature, experimentation platforms such as Optimizely (*https://www.optimizely.com/*) have emerged to make some of this work easier. Ideally, this should empower builders of ML applications to make them continuously better, for everyone.

Looking back at all the systems described in this book, only a small subset aims to train models. The majority of work involved with building ML products consists of data and engineering work. Despite this fact, most of the data scientists I have mentored found it easier to find resources covering modeling techniques and thus felt unprepared to tackle work outside of this realm. This book is my attempt at helping bridge that gap.

Building an ML application requires a broad set of skills in diverse domains such as statistics, software engineering, and product management. Each part of the process is complex enough to warrant multiple books being written about it. The goal of this book is to provide you with a broad set of tools to help you build such applications and let you decide which topics to explore more deeply by following the recommendations outlined in "Additional Resources" on page x, for example.

With that in mind, I hope this book gave you tools to more confidently tackle the majority of the work involved with building ML-powered products. We've covered every part of the ML product life cycle, starting by translating a product goal to an

ML approach, then finding and curating data and iterating on models, before validating their performance and deploying them.

Whether you've read this book cover to cover or dove into specific sections that were most relevant to your work, you should now have the required knowledge to start building your own ML-powered applications. If this book has helped you to build something or if you have any questions or comments about its content, please reach out to me by emailing *mlpoweredapplications@gmail.com*. I look forward to hearing from you and seeing your ML work.

Index

metrics for binary classification, 111
Minimum Viable Product (MVP), 43
ML writing assistants, 180
ML-powered applications
    building initial prototype, 43-91
        first end-to-end pipeline, 45-54
        initial dataset, 55-91
    deployment and monitoring, 169-229
        building model safeguards, 195-216
        deployment options, 183-193
        deployment planning, 171-182
        monitoring and updating models,
            217-229
    determining what is possible, 4, 20-22
    identifying the right ML approach, 1-41
        creating a plan, 23-41
        from product goal to ML framing, 3-22
    iterating on models, 46, 93-167
        core parts of process, 46
        debugging, 127-151
        training and evaluation, 95-125
        using classifiers for writing recommen-
            dations, 153-167
ML–powered applications
    build challenges, ix
    build process overview, xii-xiv
ML–powered editors, xiii (see also case study)
model disclaimers, 177
model metrics, 25
models
    debugging (see debugging)
    evaluating
        calibration curves, 114
        confusion matrices, 110
        contrasting data and predictions, 109
        error analysis, 116
        feature importance, 121-125
        looking beyond accuracy, 109
        ROC curves, 111
        top-k method, 116-121
    identifying failure modes and resolutions,
        52, 101, 195-204
    key to building successful, 109
    levels of increasing complexity, 23
    performance metrics, 25-28
        generating additional model metrics, 27
        making modeling tasks easier, 26
        model precision, 28
        reasonable expectations for, 27

selecting, 3-5, 95-109
    based on data patterns, 98
    benefits of prototypes for, 51
    data driven assumptions, 82
    determining deployability, 97
    estimating what is possible, 4
    flowchart for, 99
    quick to implement, 96
    scoring models based on simplicity, 97
    understandable models, 96
taxonomy of
    autoregressive, 17
    catalog organization, 11
    classification and regression, 7
    end-to-end, 16
    generative, 12
    knowledge extraction from unstructured
        data, 8
    labeled versus unlabeled data, 6, 14
    list of approaches, 6
    sequence-to-sequence, 16
    structured versus unstructured data, 8
    supervised versus unsupervised, 6, 28
training
    data leakage, 102
    eliminating undesirable bias in, 175-180
    judging performance, 106-109
    relative proportions of data, 102
    split datasets, 99
    test datasets, 101, 174
    validation datasets, 100
Moody, Chris, 214
movie recommendations, 11
multi-layer neural networks, 98
Munro, Robert, 89

N

naive Bayes classifiers, 98
natural language processing, 74, 89
neural networks, 144
neural style transfer, 12
nonlinear models, 98

O

object detection, 9, 121
offline metrics, 25
one-hot encoding, 69
open source code, 32, 35
optimization problems, 144

X

About the Author

Emmanuel Ameisen has been building ML-powered products for years. He is currently working on ML engineering at Stripe (*https://www.stripe.com*). Previously, he was head of AI at Insight Data Science (*https://www.insightdata.ai*), where he led more than 150 ML projects. Before, Emmanuel was a data scientist at Zipcar (*https://www.zipcar.com/*), where he worked on on-demand prediction and building frameworks and services to help deploy ML models in production. He has a background at the intersection of ML and business, with an M.S. in AI from Université Paris-Sud, an M.S. in Engineering from CentraleSupélec, and an M.S. in Management from ESCP Europe.

Colophon

The animal on the cover of *Building Machine Learning Powered Applications* is the poplar admiral butterfly (*Limenitis populi*). This butterfly is a large but increasingly rare butterfly of North Africa, northern Asia, the Middle East, and Europe.

Poplar admirals have a three-inch wingspan. Its wings are white-spotted dark brown above with margins of slate and orange, and undersides marked in orange.

In late August, butterflies lay their eggs on the leaves of poplar trees (mostly trembling aspen, *Populus tremula*), as the caterpillars eat only these leaves. Caterpillars have horn-like appendages, and molt through shades of green and brown as they grow, for camouflage. They begin growing in late summer, but in the fall start spinning silk for a protective cocoon where they overwinter. In spring, they re-emerge as the first poplar leaves bud and immediately begin feeding, to complete their final transition: in late May, they attach themselves with silk to a leaf and grow a hard surface skin in which they pupate, emerging as butterflies in June and July.

Unlike most butterflies, poplar admirals do not visit flowers for nectar, instead using their probing proboscis to draw food and nutrients from carrion, animal droppings, tree sap, and the salts in mud (and at times the salts in human sweat). They seem attracted to smells of decomposition.

Poplar admiral numbers are declining as deciduous forests are cleared for development, though its current IUCN Red List is "Least Concern." Many of the animals on O'Reilly covers are endangered; all of them are important to the world.

The color illustration on the cover is by Jose Marzan Jr., based on a black-and-white engraving from the *Meyers Kleines Lexicon*. The cover fonts are Gilroy Semibold and Guardian Sans. The text font is Adobe Minion Pro; the heading font is Adobe Myriad Condensed; and the code font is Dalton Maag's Ubuntu Mono.

Milton Keynes UK
Ingram Content Group UK Ltd.
UKHW050046230924
448644UK00004B/17